# INVESTING

~~in~~ with ~~for~~

# AFRICA

Brett Johnson

Investing with Africa

Context, Considerations, Call to Action

This edition published in 2026 by Indaba Publishing,
a division of The Institute for Innovation, Integration & Impact, Inc.



ISBN 978-1-947599-50-5 (e-book)
ISBN 978-1-947599-51-2 (Paperback)

http://brettjohnson.biz/resources



Contact information.

Link to Amazon author page

For more resources, case studies and details behind Zones and more, visit http://investingwithafrica.com

## How to interact with "Investing with Africa"

There are several parts to Investing with Africa:

1. The Flyover or executive summary for those inclined to broad themes without too much detail.
2. The main book which builds on topics covered in the Flyover and others the Flyover misses.
3. Surveys that build the data behind the book where you can offer your own expertise
    a. Where you invest
    b. Your assessment of the various investment zones, by country
4. A website, http://investingwithafrica.com that contains details that would otherwise bog down the main book.
    a. The Zone Matrix for four zones shared in the book
    b. Links to the surveys
    c. Case studies
    d. Resource lists
    e. Reference materials
    f. Glossary

As you read the Flyover you may ask "what about" and hopefully there are landing places in the main book from which you can take your ideas further. The Africa investment landscape changes daily. The Zone Matrix and corresponding investment journeys will be enriched by the participation of many. I invite you to add your contributions.

Investing with Africa may not be easy, but it can be rewarding. I trust you will be equipped with the frameworks for grounded investing and inspired to capture the African winds under your wings.

# Disclaimer

*Investing with Africa* is a work of research, reflection, and principles-based thinking. It is written to inform, to challenge assumptions, and to propose a framework for how capital can be deployed on the African continent in a manner consistent with sound investment principles and values-driven intent.

This book does not constitute investment advice. Nothing contained in these pages should be construed as a recommendation, solicitation, or offer to buy or sell any security, fund, financial instrument, or investment product of any kind. The author is not a licensed investment adviser, broker-dealer, or financial planner, and nothing in this book creates or implies such a relationship between the author and the reader.

Investment in African markets — whether through direct investment, private equity, venture capital, listed securities, debt instruments, impact funds, or any other vehicle — involves substantial risk, including the possible loss of principal. Past performance of any market, sector, fund, or investment described or referenced in this book is not indicative of future results. All investments carry risk; investments in emerging and frontier markets carry additional risks, including but not limited to currency fluctuation, political instability, regulatory uncertainty, limited liquidity, and incomplete or unreliable market data.

The case studies, examples, statistics, and market observations referenced in this book are included for illustrative and educational purposes only. They do not represent a complete or current picture of any market, company, fund, or investment opportunity, and should not be relied upon as the basis for any investment decision. Market conditions change. Information that was accurate at the time of writing may no longer reflect current circumstances.

Readers are strongly encouraged to conduct their own independent due diligence and to seek advice from qualified legal, financial, tax, and regulatory professionals before making any investment decision. The appropriate investment strategy for any individual or institution will depend on factors specific to that person or entity — including risk tolerance, investment horizon, liquidity needs, tax situation, and applicable regulatory requirements — none of which this book can assess or address on the reader's behalf.

Any reference to specific countries, regions, sectors, asset classes, funds, or organizations in this book is for contextual and illustrative purposes only and does not constitute an endorsement, recommendation, or guarantee of performance. The author has endeavored to ensure the accuracy of information presented, but makes no warranty, express or implied, as to its completeness, accuracy, or fitness for any particular purpose.

The views expressed in this book are those of the author alone and do not represent the views of any organization, institution, fund, or entity with which the author is or has been affiliated.

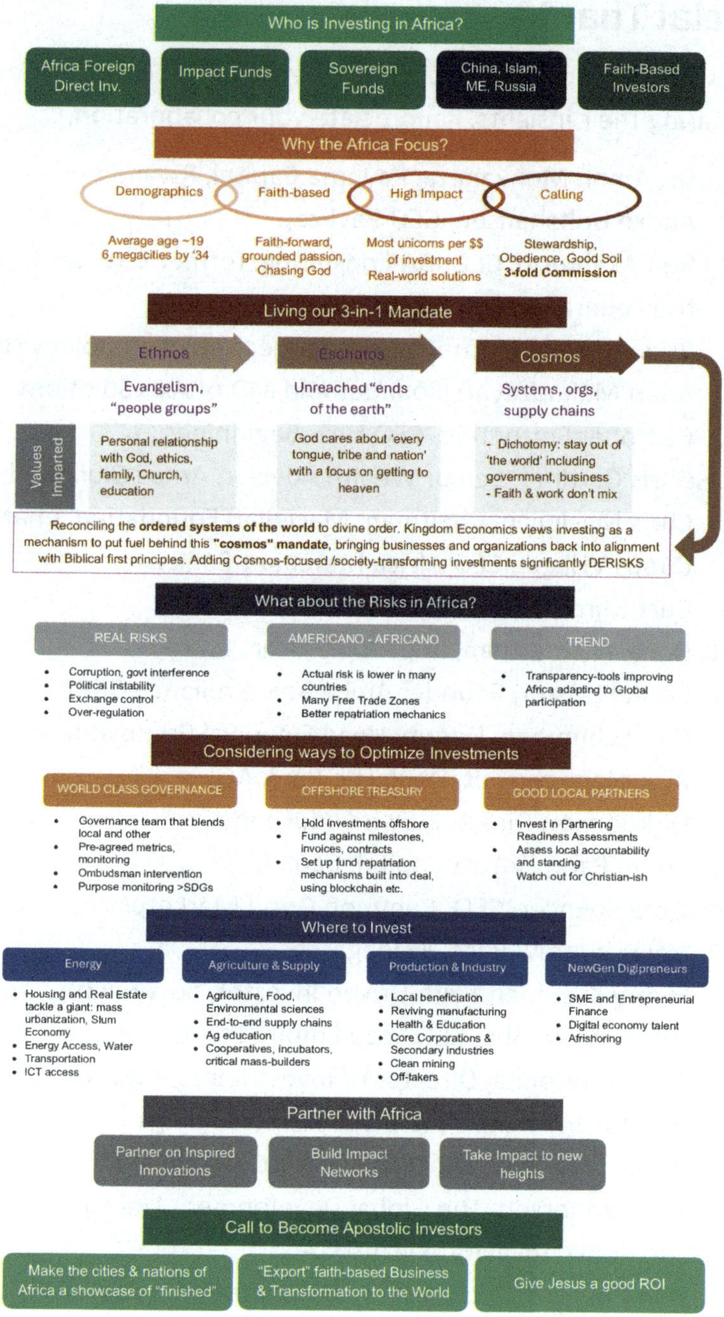
Who is Investing in Africa?
Africa Foreign Direct Inv.
Impact Funds
Sovereign Funds
China, Islam, ME, Russia
Faith-Based Investors
Why the Africa Focus?
Demographics
Faith-based
High Impact
Calling
Average age ~19
6 megacities by '34
Faith-forward, grounded passion, Chasing God
Most unicorns per $$ of investment
Real-world solutions
Stewardship, Obedience, Good Soil
3-fold Commission
Living our 3-in-1 Mandate
Ethnos
Eschatos
Cosmos
Evangelism, "people groups"
Unreached "ends of the earth"
Systems, orgs, supply chains
Values Imparted
Personal relationship with God, ethics, family, Church, education
God cares about 'every tongue, tribe and nation' with a focus on getting to heaven
- Dichotomy: stay out of 'the world' including government, business
- Faith & work don't mix
Reconciling the ordered systems of the world to divine order. Kingdom Economics views investing as a mechanism to put fuel behind this "cosmos" mandate, bringing businesses and organizations back into alignment with Biblical first principles. Adding Cosmos-focused /society-transforming investments significantly DERISKS
What about the Risks in Africa?
REAL RISKS
• Corruption, govt interference
• Political instability
• Exchange control
• Over-regulation
AMERICANO - AFRICANO
• Actual risk is lower in many countries
• Many Free Trade Zones
• Better repatriation mechanics
TREND
• Transparency-tools improving
• Africa adapting to Global participation
Considering ways to Optimize Investments
WORLD CLASS GOVERNANCE
• Governance team that blends local and other
• Pre-agreed metrics, monitoring
• Ombudsman intervention
• Purpose monitoring >SDGs
OFFSHORE TREASURY
• Hold investments offshore
• Fund against milestones, invoices, contracts
• Set up fund repatriation mechanisms built into deal, using blockchain etc.
GOOD LOCAL PARTNERS
• Invest in Partnering Readiness Assessments
• Assess local accountability and standing
• Watch out for Christian-ish
Where to Invest
Energy
• Housing and Real Estate tackle a giant: mass urbanization, Slum Economy
• Energy Access, Water
• Transportation
• ICT access
Agriculture & Supply
• Agriculture, Food, Environmental sciences
• End-to-end supply chains
• Ag education
• Cooperatives, incubators, critical mass-builders
Production & Industry
• Local beneficiation
• Reviving manufacturing
• Health & Education
• Core Corporations & Secondary industries
• Clean mining
• Off-takers
NewGen Digipreneurs
• SME and Entrepreneurial Finance
• Digital economy talent
• Afrishoring
Partner with Africa
Partner on Inspired Innovations
Build Impact Networks
Take Impact to new heights
Call to Become Apostolic Investors
Make the cities & nations of Africa a showcase of "finished"
"Export" faith-based Business & Transformation to the World
Give Jesus a good ROI

## Special Thanks

Thanks to the following people for reviewing this book at various stages and sharing their insights. I appreciate your collaboration.

1. Dr. Amon Munyaneza, Kavuma Capital, Rwanda
2. Andre Holtshausen, CEO PayProp
3. Ben Akabueze, CEO IBA Consulting, former Director General for the Federal Budget Office, Nigeria
4. Brian Mckenzie, Co-Founder Kentegra Biotechnology Holdings
5. Brian Mukudzavhu, Founder and MD of Axis Solutions Africa
6. Campher Serfontein, CEO New Beginnings
7. Chris Gardner, Senior Wealth Advisor, Arkos Global Advisors
8. Chris Maclellan, Chairman, Maclellan Foundation, Chattanooga
9. Cobus Visagie, CEO Africa Merchant Bank
10. Curt Laird, reFrontier, Kenya
11. Dana Wichterman, Impact investor
12. Daniel Hoster, Founder Alpha Value Alliance GmbH
13. Dirk Schumann, Deputy Head Financial Crime and Compliance Risk Management, Deutsche Bank AG
14. Dirk Jonker, Director, Swiss eduGlobe
15. Ethan Park, Extract Capital, Canada
16. Greg Spencer, CEO, Common Good Marketplace
17. Haja (Jeremy) Raso, Madagascar
18. Henry Kaestner, Faith Driven Investor, Sovereign's Capital
19. Henry Molombe, CEO Sozo Empire Ltd, Cameroon
20. James Noronha, Director of Investments, AgGrandize Global
21. Johann Snyman, SAAD Investment Holdings
22. Johan Du Preez, SAAD Investment Holdings
23. John Anderson, The Global Development Universe
24. Jon Kontz, Investor, Kigali/USA
25. Ken Churchill, A2B Ventures, Generational Capital Partners
26. Matthew Rohrs, CEO Sinapis
27. Mike Harsanyi, Seedbridge Capital, Europe
28. Nader Iskander, Founder & Chairman EME International, Egypt

29. Nissi Ekpott, Investor
30. Norman Noland, Africa Growth and Private Equity (AGAPE)
31. Dr. Okey Enelamah, Founder, Africa Capital Alliance, former Min. Trade & Investments
32. Paul Venter, 52Africa
33. Peter Cunningham, CEO, Hamara
34. Peter Flynn, CEO Libryo
35. Pieter Faure, Mergon Foundation
36. Rachel McDonough, Wealth Advisor & Consultant, Wealth Squared
37. Richard Lackey, Chairman, World Food Bank Group
38. Sid Mofya, Founder MOTIF54
39. Dr. Stephan Pretorius, CEO AGES (Pty) Ltd.
40. Wes Lyons, General Partner, Eagle Venture Fund
41. Zach Wazara, Founder and CEO of Spiritage Group
42. Zienzi Dillon (Musamirapamwe), Founder, Carmel Global Capital

# Endorsements

*Brett Johnson lives Africa and the West. He sees the world in models, evaluated from a Kingdom perspective. I appreciate his important contribution to the nexus of capital and culture. In the decades ahead, Africa will flourish or suffer. The near future calls on global stewards of capital and the peoples of Africa to act in ways that allow societies, people, and portfolios to flourish. – Ken Churchill, A2B Ventures, Generational Capital Partners*

I absolutely applaud the content; it is full of "solid gold" insights and information. A must-read for people who are interested in financial investment, the future of the world, business, or living a faith based, purposeful life. I wish more people would contemplate your message. – *Mike Harsanyi, Seedbridge Capital*

*In this Book, Brett challenges us to move beyond the normal approach to financing in Africa, to partner with Africa in building systems that generate both prosperity and purpose. He sets in place a great balance between an apostolic call to action and a blueprint to sustain long-term impact. I recommend this book to the purpose-driven investor who desires to create wealth by harnessing opportunities in Africa and, at the same time, leave a lasting legacy. – Nissi Ekpott, Investor*

This book pushes you to rethink what you are actually doing with your money. Most people view investing as a way to grow wealth. This challenges that. It reframes capital as something entrusted to us—meant to be used with intention, not just accumulated. The idea of investing with rather than in or for is simple, but it sticks. It shifts the focus from transactions to partnership, from extraction to stewardship. I appreciate the reminder that money doesn't sit on the sidelines: it is always doing something—either reinforcing broken systems or helping build something better.

This is not a how-to manual. It's a perspective shift. And it's a helpful one. It forces a better question: What is my money actually building? – *Chris Gardner, Wealth Manager, Arkos Global Advisors*

*Investing with Africa is a powerful combination of theology, practical context, and the wisdom that comes only through lived experience. Brett Johnson has created a priceless resource for anyone interested in directing investment capital toward this high potential, and often misunderstood, continent. I grew up in Kenya and have invested with multiple Africa-focused asset managers and I still learned an enormous amount from this excellent resource. I highly recommend it to Western investors who want to expand their perspective, expose their hidden biases, and approach African investment with both head and heart. – Rachel McDonough, CFP®, CKA® Founder - Wealthfluence, LLC, Founder & President - Wealth Squared*

Brett makes a very compelling case for how and why to invest in and **with** Africa. – *Chris Maclellan, Chairman, Maclellan Foundation, Chattanooga*

*Few resources are as timely and relevant as Investing with Africa. It offers a powerful blueprint for investment, wealth creation, and sustainable impact, positioning Africa as a strategic partner in shaping the future of global prosperity. – Henry Molombe, CEO CEO Sozo Empire Ltd, Cameroon*

# Who will read a book on Investing with Africa?

- **Foundations and Trusts** Africa's scale of need and depth of opportunity offers foundations and trusts a rare chance to deploy patient, catalytic capital that builds lasting systems — not just funds projects.
- **Family Offices** With multi-generational wealth comes a multi-generational question: *what is our money actually building?* — and Africa is one of the most compelling places on earth to answer it well.
- **Private Equity Firms** Africa's demographic dividend, under-institutionalized markets, and rising entrepreneurial class represent a PE opportunity that early movers will own and latecomers will wish they hadn't missed.
- **Impact Investors** Africa is where impact investing either proves its thesis or reveals its limits — the continent's real-world problems demand the integrated approach of financial return *and* societal transformation that this flyover frames.
- **Donor Advised Funds** DAFs sit at the intersection of generosity and strategy; this flyover helps donors see how capital deployed *with* Africa — rather than *for* Africa — multiplies both the blessing and the return.
- **High Net Worth Individuals** Sophisticated wealth requires sophisticated thinking about where the world is going — and Africa's billion-plus young population, faith-friendly culture, and untapped markets make it one of the most important investment conversations of the next decade.
- **Individual Investors and Investor Networks** You don't need a nine-figure portfolio to invest with Africa — you need a framework, and this short flyover gives you one.
- **Africans Investing Across Africa** The most grounded capital on the continent is African capital — and this flyover offers a framework for deploying it across borders with the discernment, relational trust, and long-term vision that outside investors simply cannot replicate.
- **Industry** Businesses with the potential to scale beyond their own country of origin by tapping into Africa's growing market, either through organic growth or acquisition.

# Flyover of Investing with Africa

This helicopter view of Investing with Africa is intended to be brief: if you find yourself agreeing/disagreeing with the synopsis, you will find corroboration in the book itself. Africa is no longer just a safari destination; it is an exciting investment territory. The risks must be seen clearly, the rewards framed in African-time, and the impacts weighed strategically. Rose-tinted lenses soon become dusty in Africa. Know why, where and how you are investing. Wrap your arms around this land mass that easily subsumes the US, China, India, Japan and much of Europe then ask yourself, “Why invest in Africa, or even for Africa, when you can invest with Africa?”

## Part A – Framing the Situation

A.1 Our Investment **motivation** determines how we invest.

| Invest in Africa | Invest for Africa | Invest with Africa |
|---|---|---|
| • Returns<br>• Place, assets, minerals<br>• Extractive<br>• Asset dividend | • Flourishing<br>• Patient capital<br>• Population dividend | • Collaboration<br>• Transformation<br>• Mobilization<br>• Kingdom dividend |

Are you, in your heart of hearts, looking for an Asset, Population or Kingdom Dividend? And do these have to be mutually exclusive?

A.2 The **type of investor** you are and want to be influences your focus.

- **Planners**: apply financial basics, faithfulness, predictability
- **Pilgrims**: stepped out of the boat, adventurous, once-off deals, edge cases, "by faith"
- **Planters**: compounding growth, multiple income streams, noble-case investing/charity, work within the system
- **Platform-reformers**: see the flaws in current systems, work to change rules, adjust fundamentals, make new systems, return to biblical roots of faith-based finance.

The mapping between traditional investor categories and the four archetypes is not a clean one-to-one exercise, and that tension is actually the point. Traditional categories — limited partners, family offices, institutional investors, trusts — are defined by structure and role. My four archetypes are defined by posture and motivation. The same family office can show up as a Planner, a Planter, or a Platform-reformer depending entirely on what they believe capital is for. The table that follows captures that nuance as a matrix, but the more important question is the one you need to answer before you open it: which archetype are you, and which one do you want to become?

There are enough opportunities from PPPs, to corporate M&A-style deals to on-the-ground social entrepreneurs that will interest all types of investors. Know who you are and let Africa help you grow to become who you want to be.

Overlooking the African Diaspora would be a huge mistake. In the main body of the book I unpack this thought. Forty million people living in London and Lagos-expat communities in Houston, Paris, Dubai, Toronto, and Sydney send $104 billion home every single year — roughly twice the level of all official development assistance combined, and neck and neck with the entire continent's foreign direct investment flows. It is almost entirely invisible in the investment conversation.

**INVESTOR TYPE MAPPING · Traditional Categories × Brett Johnson's Four Investor Archetypes**

*Fit ratings: ●●● Primary fit ●●○ Strong secondary ●○○ Possible ○○○ Rare / unlikely*

| TRADITIONAL INVESTOR TYPE | PLANNERS<br>Financial basics<br>Faithfulness<br>Predictability | PILGRIMS<br>Adventurous<br>Once-off deals<br>Edge cases / "by faith" | PLANTERS<br>Compounding growth<br>Multiple income streams<br>Noble-case investing | PLATFORM-REFORMERS<br>Change the rules<br>New systems<br>Faith-based finance roots |
|---|---|---|---|---|
| Limited Partners (LPs) | ●●● Primary | ●○○ Possible | ●●○ Strong secondary | ●○○ Possible |
| General Partners (GPs) | ●●○ Strong secondary | ●●○ Strong secondary | ●●● Primary | ●●○ Strong secondary |
| Private Equity Firms | ●●● Primary | ●○○ Possible | ●●○ Strong secondary | ●○○ Possible |
| High Net Worth Individuals (HNWIs) | ●●○ Strong secondary | ●●● Primary | ●●○ Strong secondary | ●●○ Strong secondary |
| Family Offices | ●●○ Strong secondary | ●●○ Strong secondary | ●●● Primary | ●●○ Strong secondary |
| Institutional Investors (pension funds, endowments, sovereign wealth funds) | ●●● Primary | ○○○ Rare | ●●○ Strong secondary | ●○○ Possible |
| Trusts & Foundations (European; faith-aligned) | ●○○ Possible | ●●○ Strong secondary | ●●○ Strong secondary | ●●● Primary |
| African Diaspora (remittance-to-investment) | ●●○ Strong secondary | ●●○ Strong secondary | ●●● Primary | ●●○ Strong secondary |

*"The African diaspora earns approximately $667 billion annually abroad, yet currently sends only about 15% back home." — United Nations*

European faith-based trusts and foundations could be the most natural Platform-reformers in the entire traditional investor universe — structurally freer than institutional investors, longer-horizons than most PE, and mission-aligned in a way that makes systemic change their actual mandate rather than a side effect. Will North American faith-forward funders find the will to aggregate resources and have the heft that enables them to become Platform Reformers?

A.3 Africa is a huge continent comprising 54 countries. The USA, China, India and much of Europe fits size-wise into Africa. It is the second largest continent covering about one-fifth of the total land surface of Earth. Maps seldom do justice to its true size. Cairo to Cape Town is about 6,200 miles which is roughly twice the flying time between the East and West Coasts in the USA... assuming you can get a direct flight in Africa, which is unlikely. These maps give a rough idea of how various land masses fit into Africa.

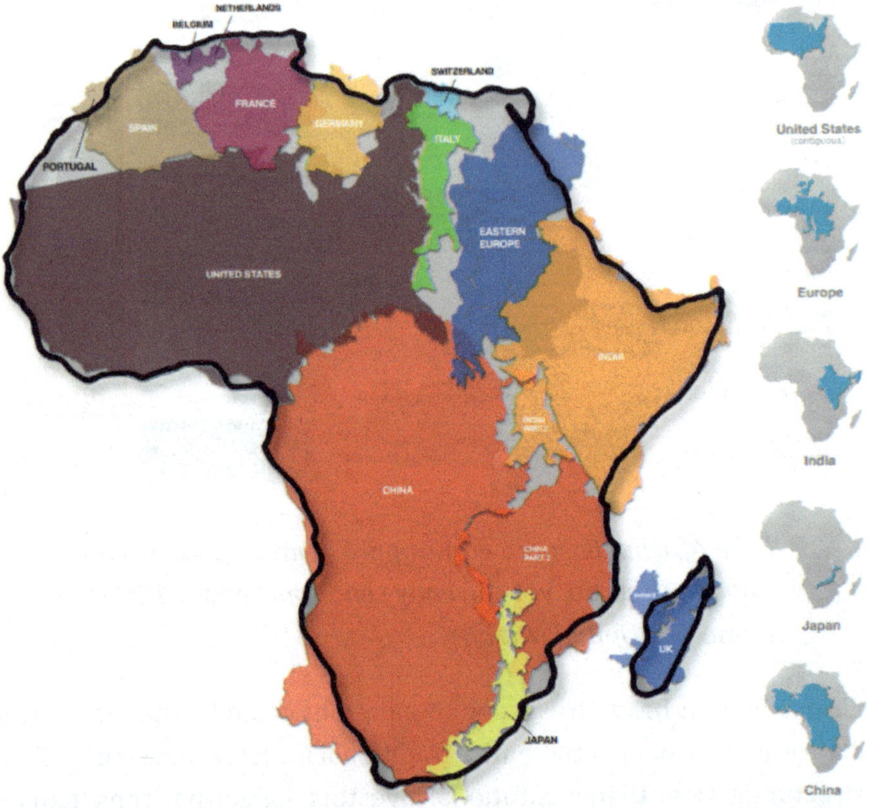


A.4 Africa has established **economic zones**, but they are not working well. Despite talks of trans-continental collaboration, there are infrastructure and other impediments. Economic unevenness is the norm. If investments in infrastructure do not strengthen cross-regional collaboration will Africa realize its full potential?

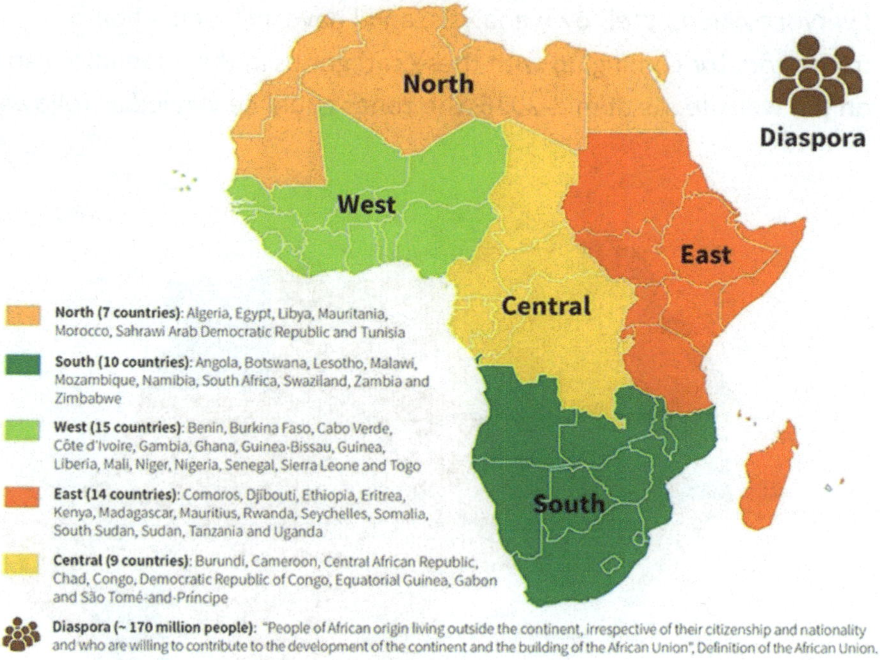


Image credit: SWAC/OECD

A.5 When deciding to invest in Africa, **consider four investment zones** that are influenced by *Trust* and *Diversity*. The tremendous diversity in Africa can be an asset or a liability, and there are different levels of trust inherent in the societies of Africa. These should factor into investment decisions.

| | Low Trust | High Trust |
|---|---|---|
| High Ethnic Diversity | FRICTION | RESILIENCE |
| Modern Ethnic Diversity | TRANSITION | OPPORTUNITY |

Diversity in Africa is not a risk: unrecognized and unmanaged diversity is a risk. How should investors evaluate diversity?

A.6 The Zones and Actors can be mapped across Africa. Africa cannot be understood through static categories. Its realities are relational, dynamic, and often sub-national—requiring discernment, not just data.

Everyone can do their own analysis, and I have included a board framework for coming up with these categories in the appendices and on the website. As of mid-2026, the zones could be viewed as follows.

Where do you see the four zones trending five, ten, and fifteen years from now? And what role might faith play in triggering the trends?

## Part B – The Advantage of Faith communities

Faith-driven investors could consider Four Actors in investment scenarios. This section, part B of the Flyover, explains how faith-based communities have the opportunity to change the trust environment. Unlike some western nations, Government is always an assumed actor in Africa, but could the faith factor be what tips Africa toward its destiny?

| Actor | Primary Function | Core Asset |
| --- | --- | --- |
| Churches | Build trust & identity | Relational capital |
| NGOs | Build (upliftment) systems & capacity | Technical and Human capital |
| Kingdom Businesses | Create sustainable value, scale employment | Economic capital with purpose |
| Investors | Scale what works, businesses | Financial capital, storehouses |

B.1 Faith-related communities can shift the needle on Trust levels and offset the Low Trust in Friction and Transition zones. The huge rise in interest in Africa is a plus and gives investors of faith a potential advantage.

B.2 This potential faith-factor advantage will not materialize. unless we have three things:

1. Investments in all 3-strands of the gospel:
    a. **ethnos**, peoples, people groups (Matthew 28:19-20) – the world
    b. **eschatos**, the ends of the earth (Acts 1:8)
    c. **cosmos**, the ordered systems of the world (Mark 16:15 and many other references such as Matthew 24:14, 26:13 and John 3:16... 'For God so loved the world/cosmos!')
2. A holistic and systematic view of societal transformation across all 10 spheres or sectors
3. Investing in platforms, systems, ecosystems.

How can we nudge our investing from "deals" towards "platforms"?

B.3 The devastating effects of our neglect of both our first commission (to work in collaboration with the Godhead) and the *cosmos* aspect of the Great Commission are apparent throughout Africa. Africa is the most Christianized continent on the planet but many of its core systems have been untouched by the Gospel. This is partly because of our dichotomized thinking which has allowed us to focus on people groups or *ethnos* and the ends of the earth or *eschatos*. We have under-appreciated the instruction to reconcile the *cosmos* to Christ. Societal transformation only happens when we address the ordered systems of society to bring alignment with eternal truths. This is our "ministry of reconciliation."

B.4 Transforming society has four key elements, and it begins with seeing with our faith eye the Glory of God seen visible in Africa.

- Fixing, Repairing, Relaying Foundations
- Stewarding and Rebuilding Assets
- Repurposing the 10 Spheres of Society
- Restoring Glory

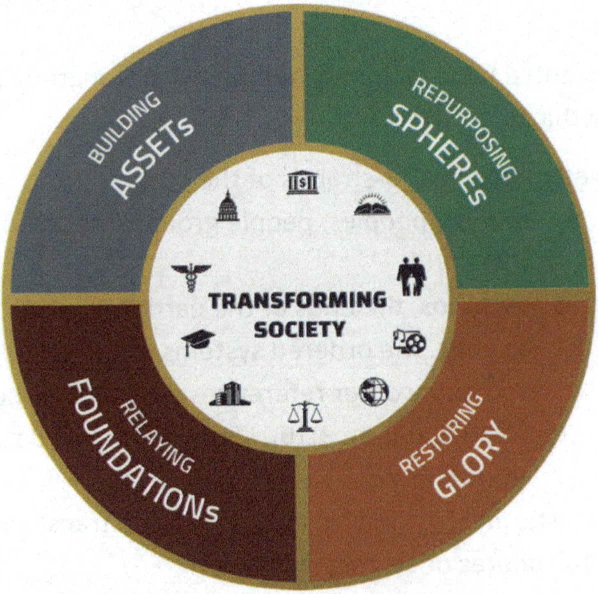


In Promised Land Economics focus fuels imagination, which feeds faith that supports investing. How can we focus on the Restored Glory to ensure our investment thinking is heaven-to-earth inspired?

B.5 Investment portfolios should be built around the **network** of entities required to restore glory in towns, cities, and nations. To ensure sustainability, we must identify everything that can be accomplished through for-profit businesses and only direct those efforts to churches and NGOs that cannot be handled by a business.

B.6 Restricted investing in point solutions without addressing ecosystems increases risk. The relational and functional networking of faith-based marketplace communities can enhance trust, advance opportunities, and mitigate risk.

## Part C – Alignment is key to investment strategies

The book unpacks four broad areas where there are investment opportunities. There are other studies by McKinsey et al that have a more granulated view. The four major categories for investment are:

- Core infrastructure and energy, often avoided – why we need fund collaboration
- Agriculture and Supply Chains – with a diligence to overcome weakest links
- Production and Industry with some exploration of how to get light industry into rural areas
- NewGen Digipreneurs, participants in the Gig Economy who can work anywhere from Africa.

Getting back to alignment: we need to align our Investment Opportunities with the Investment Zones and the 3-Strands of the Great Commission, considering the Type of Investor we aspire to be... business as usual, or agents for positive change.

| Investment opportunities | Investment Zones | Three strands of the Great Commission | Type of investor we aspire to be |
|---|---|---|---|
| • Core infrastructure and energy<br>• Agriculture and supply chains.<br>• Production and industry<br>• NewGen<br>• DigiPreneurs |  | 1. Ethnos<br>2. Cosmos<br>3. Eschatos | • Planners<br>• Pilgrims<br>• Planters<br>• Platform-reformers |

We may invest in people groups or ethnos because of a heart connection. We may invest in eschatos or the ends of the earth because of conviction and compassion. Both are good. Investing in the systems of society that must be ordered consistent with or reconciled to biblical principles is an additional key. This is Cosmos Level Investing. Cosmos investing is key to restoring dignity. It is critical to invest WITH Africa, not just invest IN Africa or FOR Africa. When scripture says, "God was in Christ reconciling *the world* to himself," it is not talking about people only — kosmos means not just people, but everything that makes up the world: its systems, its economies, its created order. Reconciliation in this sense is not just personal. It is structural.

## Part D – Risk Paradigm

D.1 Investing with Africa needs a new risk paradigm. We must shift from "Americano" to "Africano." Overlaying a Western mindset onto African risk analysis can lead to missed opportunities for investors and investees

| Americano says… | Africano says… |
|---|---|
| You don't have any outside investors; who believes in you? | I don't have any debt; I have proven it myself |
| This has no appeal in the international market. | I serve the African market, and it is big enough to get good returns |

| Americano says... | Africano says... |
|---|---|
| How quickly can you exit? | I am here to stay; I want to grow, not exit |
| Could this be a unicorn? | We have enough real animals in Africa to not depend on fake ones. |
| Your team needs the Big 3: CEO, CPO, CMO | We have a set of competencies in a plural leadership structure with shared power |
| Do these three key leaders have a track record? Have they raised capital and exited before? | I have potential leaders who will do well when given the opportunity. I have a faith-based trust network to support them. |
| How can you scale quickly? | How can I build permanently? |
| You need an independent board. | I need good governance including a network of relationships, connections |
| Investors are the key stakeholder and must be taken care of first. | I have a complex community that benefits if I do well, and this included investors |

D.2 We must embrace mechanisms that optimize investments and mitigate risk.

- World-class governance including a common lexicon around "kingdom business" —but be aware that the jargon of Kingdom Business creates its own risks. The words can sound the same but mean different things to different people.
- Offshore treasury or other currency repatriation hedges. This also creates an opportunity for the pooling of funds to address societal transformation.
- Excellent local “eyes wide open” partnerships, particularly in low-trust zones.

**Considering ways to Optimize Investments**

**WORLD CLASS GOVERNANCE**

- Governance team that blends local and other
- Pre-agreed metrics, monitoring
- Ombudsman intervention
- Purpose monitoring >SDGs

**OFFSHORE TREASURY**

- Hold investments offshore
- Fund against milestones, invoices, contracts
- Set up fund repatriation mechanisms built into deal, using blockchain etc.

**GOOD LOCAL PARTNERS**

- Invest in Partnering Readiness Assessments
- Assess local accountability and standing
- Watch out for Christian-ish

D.3 Recognize where faith-based communities change the complexion of traditional risk analysis.

How do we add a weighting categorization for faith-based communities that changes the risk analysis for faith-driven investments?

D.4 Consider funds of funds to tackle the societal transformation efforts that might be beyond the scope of an individual investor group. "Make disciples of all nations" requires capital. As you will read in the book, other nations and groups are out-investing evangelical Christians by a huge margin.

D.5 At least consider that our view of the world and our operating premise might be different from other investor groups. At a 2026 Up Movement conference in Zambia, Peter Cunningham presented this summary of how Islamic, Eastern and Western investors view Africa and aspire to community, economic, or governance control.

**Comparison of Worldviews and Operating systems**

| ISLAMIC | EASTERN | WESTERN |
|---|---|---|
| "Africa needs guiding" | "Africa is an opportunity" | "Africa needs fixing" |
| Operating Model: | Operating Model: | Operating Model: |
| Legitimacy → Services → Institutions → Leaders → Rules → Narrative | Capital → Infrastructure → Operations → Dependency → Influence | Funding → Programs → Conditions → Reforms → Reporting |
| — Faith, law, finance & education integrated | — $180B+ loans across the continent | — $42B in annual aid |
| — 369M Muslims → 670M by 2050 | — 1,300+ bilateral agreements | — IMF, World Bank, foundations & NGOs |
| — Zakat, waqf & embedded giving systems | — Roads, rail, ports & telecom systems | — Aid conditionality & policy influence |
| — Education pipelines & imam networks | — Multi-decade strategic planning | — Health, education & humanitarian programs |
| COMMUNITY CONTROL | ECONOMY CONTROL | GOVERNANCE CONTROL |

Are these modes of control counter-biblical? How does our worldview influence our investment analysis, and how should our thinking on Africa progress?

## Part E – Why is Africa in focus?

Africa is at a crossroads and could become a basket case with societal issues impacting the whole planet. We have already seen a flood of refugees from North Africa into Europe, to name just one example. Africa could also be the next "good soil" location where demographics, an openness to faith and a potential for massive impact fuse together. The way that investors from within Africa and outside of Africa team up to approach this opportunity may well decide its future.

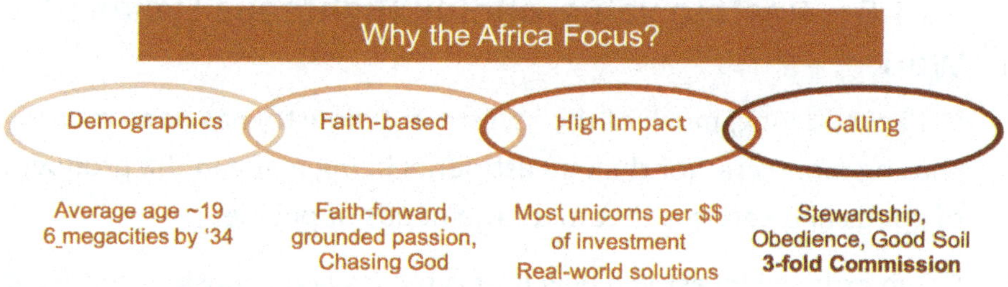


## Part F – A call to Invest with Africa

F.1 Partner on Inspired Innovations: add financial capital to redemptive innovation capital. I have a separate book dedicated to Inspired Innovation™ that showcases many good examples that are truly Out of Africa.

F.2 Build impact networks with our Africa-based brothers and sisters. Invest in ecosystems and platforms, not just individual "deals." This shows commitment and longevity, builds trust, and reduces risk.

F.3 Become Apostolic Investors: Do not just send your capital to Africa, come to Africa. New Testament apostles spurred believers on towards city-to-city investing and nation-to-nation generosity. The goal of investing in Africa is not just to improve life for Africans, but to see

African cities and nations become a showcase of God's glory and goodness, creativity and productivity.

F.4 We should not stop until Africa is exporting faith-based business and transformation to other nations in the world. Many Africans have no problem integrating their work and their faith. They are not debating whether scripture should influence the whole of their lives. As the blending of work and spirituality increases, there is the potential for Africa to export faith-based entrepreneurs to the rest of the world.

F.5 Jesus Christ is entitled to a good return on investment: How will we invest in such a way that he receives a good return on the thousands of years of investment he has made in Africa?

## Part G – Restore value-adding Righteous Cycles of Work

G.1 For too long, much of the investment industry has been money chasing money rather than investments being made in the production of goods and services that meet the needs of people.

G.2 In order to invest in a way that is biblically responsible, we need to consider how to cover the full spectrum of the Societal Value Chain.

G.3 We also need to re-capture the concept of Storehouses. This, then, is where the sophisticated investment capabilities from those outside of Africa can add real value.

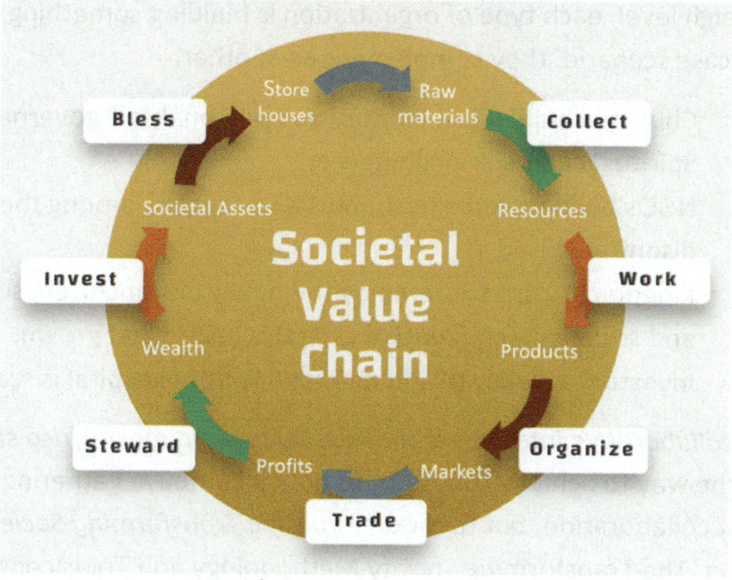


## Investing Strategies by Zone

The seeds that will evidence restored glory in Africa already lie in Africa's soil. Where should we start and in what direction should we move? This depends on the type of organization we are investing in. At a high level, the table below posits a possible (generalized) path for the different actors, ignoring Governments for the moment:

| | Start here | Expand here | Scale here | Partner here |
|---|---|---|---|---|
| Investors | Start here | Expand here | | Partner here |
| Churches | Start here | Expand here | | |
| NGOs | Start here | Expand here | | |
| Kingdom Business | Start here | Platform | Scale | Embed |

Transition
Opportunity
Friction
Resilience

At a high level, each type of organization is building something. In a best-case scenario, they complement each other.

- Churches build trust, identity and personal self-governance. Spiritual capital is incubated.
- NGOs build systems to support and capacity among the disenfranchised
- Kingdom Businesses employ the newly enfranchised, sustain and scale impact. Spiritual capital is tested and grown.
- Investors accelerate and multiply. Spiritual capital is scaled.

*This collaborative interplay is the missing layer in most Africa strategies* and the way to achieve this is not to hold a kumbaya gathering to talk about collaboration, but to tackle a *specific Transforming Society project.* The Transforming Society Methodology and Tools considers all role players by looking at the network of competencies required to transform society wherever they might be, whether in kingdom businesses, investors, NGOs, or churches.

Unpacking what this might look like for a "kingdom business" we could think about four steps of deployment. Note the intentionality to move the business and investors from a beginning place to becoming societal transformers.

| **Step 1** | **Step 2** | **Step 3** | **Step 4** |
|---|---|---|---|
| START IN | SCALE IN | EMBED IN | PLATFORM IN |
| **Build:**<br>• Culture<br>• Integrity<br>• Employment<br>• Trust | **Build:**<br>• Growth<br>• Efficiency<br>• Investor confidence<br>• Regional reach | **Bring:**<br>• Jobs<br>• Stability<br>• Cross-tribal collaboration<br>• Long-term trust | **Create:**<br>• National transformation<br>• Replicable models<br>• Training pipelines<br>• Multi-sector integration |

| Transitional | Opportunity | Friction | Resilience |
|---|---|---|---|

## Beware of the Potholes – or Own & Fix them

A word of caution: Africa has potholes. You may look at a map and think, "This is a one-hour journey—why is the Google map saying four hours?" Then you encounter the first pothole. This book has potholes. A friend commented that he is reading four or five books in one book and that a separate book on Risk or Repurposing NGOs, by way of example, might be needed. If you are looking for more detail on Promised Land economics, a comparison of Jewish, Islamic, and Christian finance, and how capital plays a role in societal transformation, or even 50 Principles of Faith-Based Financing, I have covered these topics in other books.

If a chapter seems like a pothole—not very deep, and not very clear—this may inspire others to dig deeper or, perhaps, gather for an indaba around a fire somewhere in Africa.

## Investors have an Historic Opportunity

We have questions before us as investors. How, then, shall we invest?

(a) **Afrihelping:** Perpetuate aid, helplessness. The aid economy (or NGO Industrial Complex) has been substantially degraded in recent years. This is clearly not an answer for Africa.

(b) **Afrisourcing**: Extract resources, be they minerals or people, and perpetuate asset colonization. We sometimes think the answer is pulling Africans out of Africa or helping them develop apps that can be sold in the international market. We can do better.

(c) **Afrishoring:** Raise up pockets of DigiPreneurs or educated people who can do great work at lower costs? I appreciate the businesses that provide an opportunity for Africans to stay in Africa while earning well in the gig economy, but this is for the relative few.

(d) Or will we partner with Africa to capitalize, commission, and export faith-based, truly kingdom business-led transformation? My belief, of course, is that this is where the real work will take place.

And if we choose the path of practically walking out our biblical mandate with all three strands, how then shall we Invest with Africa? I trust this Flyover will be a useful primer in stimulating the right questions. And I hope many will go on to read the full ***Investing with Africa: Context, Considerations, Call to Action.***

# Table of Contents

# 0. Introduction

My father was born on a farm in Sea Point, a now densely populated suburb of Cape Town on the Atlantic seaboard. I grew up in South Africa and traveled a little to surrounding countries including Botswana, Zimbabwe (Rhodesia), Eswatini (Swaziland) and Namibia. None of this prepared me for Nigeria. Landing in Lagos in July of 2008 was a jolt. Lagos seemed to be like the Wild West and New York of Africa all rolled into one. The traffic was 3rd World, the business suits were Wall Street, the people I met were smart with a hustle that was essential just to survive. Business, church, and political leaders had a natural optimism and a belief that "tomorrow could be better." Our first night there we attended an all-night prayer meeting with a million people. A few days later, I preached at a local church, and the impression I shared was that faith-based entrepreneurs could become Nigeria's best export in the future. This was a long time before Nigeria had its first unicorn or the investment marketplace began to flourish. But I could see it then with the eye of faith, and today I see it even more: The story of Africa is not about what the West, the East, or any other group can do for Africa. It is about the impact Africa could have on every other continent on the planet.

In US business, people talk about a BHAG: a big hairy audacious goal. The Redeemed Christian Church of God (RCCG) in Nigeria has a goal of having a church within five minutes' walk or drive of every person on the planet. Is that not a BHAG?

On the cautionary side, as I traveled between Silicon Valley and South Africa in the early 2000s, I worried that unless there was an infusion of faith-based entrepreneurship in South Africa, it could end up like Zimbabwe. Many countries of Africa are at a crossroads. Some hang in the balance. And much of what happens in the future will depend upon how we engage in Africa, with Africa, for the sake of the Kingdom of God.

## Why "Investing with Africa"?

Is there a difference between investing *in* Africa, investing *for* Africa and investing *with* Africa? It's a small word change, but "for→in→with" can tweak my heart posture. At the end of this book I will advocate investing *with* Africa for the advancement of God's kingdom, but before we get there, let's talk through investing in and for Africa.

## Africa is not a Country

Readers of this book will, of course, know that Africa is not a country and it helps to remember the size of Africa. The maps below from visualcapitalist.com help give some understanding of the scale of Africa. The sheer size and number of countries creates some complexity. You can comfortably fit the USA, China, India and chunks of Europe into Africa. We will try to unpack some of this and create guide rails for potential investors but bear in mind that some generalizing will be inevitable.

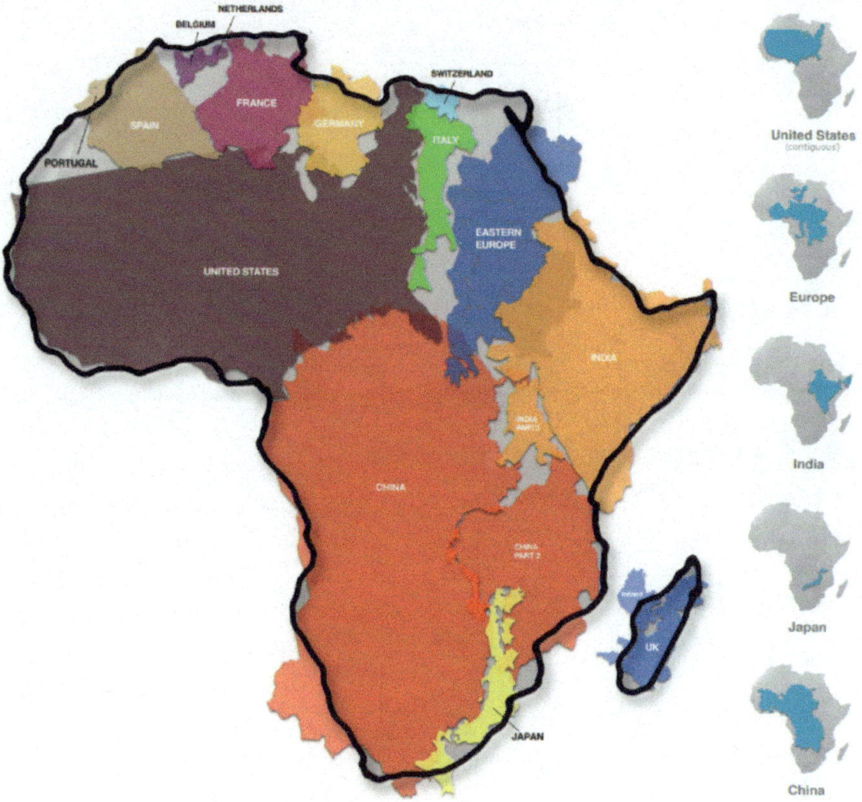
NETHERLANDS
BELGIUM
FRANCE
SWITZERLAND
SPAIN
GERMANY
ITALY
PORTUGAL
EASTERN EUROPE
UNITED STATES
INDIA
CHINA
UK
JAPAN
United States
(contiguous)
Europe
India
Japan
China

# 1. Who is Investing in Africa?

Before we dig into who is investing in Africa, let's get a sense of the scale of investments in Africa at a high level across the traditional asset categories. Overall traditional foreign investment in Africa is heavily FDI-led, somewhere below $100 billion.

## Africa is investing in Africa

It might be too soon to call it a movement, but I do see a groundswell of Africans investing in Africa. This comes at the right time, since capital coming from outside the continent is partly essential, partly welcomed, and partly suspect. Major infrastructure projects — transportation, power grids, ports — still depend heavily on international capital. Younger entrepreneurs welcome the know-how of Western investors, particularly if it comes with access to international markets. But those who are somewhat suspicious of outside capital have a point: capital always carries an agenda.

African capital is more grounded, one might say, than Western private equity and venture capital. The "roll the dice, throw money at it and hope for a unicorn" thinking of some Western investors does not fly well in a continent where people are rooted to place, community, and history. This creates a particular opening for faith-based investors — because those who venture into Africa are, almost by definition, a subset who have stepped outside their local culture and are thinking seriously about doing business for good in another part of the world.

They have something in common with the African entrepreneur trying to break out of cycles of limited opportunity.

So how much is Africa actually investing in Africa? The short answer: more than it used to, less than it should. Total foreign investment into Africa runs at roughly $100 billion annually. Of that, intra-African investment — Africans investing in Africa — accounts for somewhere between 10 and 20 percent of new projects, and a rising share of accumulated capital, particularly in sub-Saharan Africa. The big infrastructure plays are still funded from outside. But the growing share — the companies expanding across borders, the banks opening regional offices, the retailers moving into new markets — that is increasingly African. According to the New African Financial Architecture for Development (NAFAD), Africa has approximately US$4 trillion in medium- and long-term savings that could potentially be mobilized for development financing.

You can see it on the ground. Travel to Lagos and you will find Shoprite, a mid-market South African grocery chain, offering its wares. South African banks — Standard Bank, FirstRand, ABSA — operate across more than twenty countries. The Kenyan, Nigerian, Moroccan, and Egyptian private sectors are expanding. This is not charity. It is commerce following opportunity.

The macro picture matters here, not as a data dump, but as a signal. Intra-African investment in sub-Saharan Africa represented around 21 percent of total accumulated foreign investment in the region between 2020 and 2023 — up from 15 percent the decade before. For context, that's roughly double Latin America's equivalent figure, and four times the Middle East's. The trend line is moving in the right direction, even if the absolute numbers still lag. The African Continental Free Trade Area (AfCFTA) is accelerating this — reducing barriers, encouraging cross-border expansion, and creating the conditions for regional integration that colonial-era infrastructure was specifically designed to prevent.

Why does this matter to a faith-based investor coming from outside the continent? Because it tells you where Africans themselves are placing their bets. God often invests collaboratively where his people — his junior partners, as I sometimes think of us — deem things to be investable. Isolated capital invests *in* Africa for gain, or *for* Africa with a hint of charity. The optimum is to invest *with* Africa: learning from those who have the dirt of Africa between their toes, the sounds of Africa in their ears, the breeze of Africa in their hair. The direction of intra-African capital is one of your best maps.

## Islamic Finance is a real thing in Africa

A good friend was on a flight from Zimbabwe to Tanzania recently and sat next to a fellow traveler. When my friend inquired about the man's business, he said he was working on a small project to build a mosque every two to three kilometers on the edge of Lake Malawi. The strategy was that locals would come to the mosque for assistance and then "when 10% of the country is Muslim, we will declare it a Muslim nation." The total cost of the project was a mere $60 million. This is a strategic use of capital. Is this an isolated story? Saudi Arabia, Qatar, Turkey, Iran, and a network of private Islamic charities have been systematically funding mosques, Islamic centers, and education institutions across Africa for decades — collectively in the hundreds of millions of dollars annually, with Africa as a primary focus. The coordination behind these efforts is more strategic than most Western observers realize, and it is accelerating.

This is separate from Islamic finance and investments in Africa broadly, which are in the tens of billions of USD. Islamic finance in Africa is projected to be a $5 trillion opportunity by 2030, with demand coming from countries like Nigeria, Kenya, and Senegal. If you want a deeper dive into the comparison of Islamic, Jewish and Christian financing, please read *Repurposing Capital* or its companion extract, *50 Principles of Faith-Based Financing,* which distills the core financial principles in a more accessible format.[1]

---

[1] https://www.brettjohnson.biz/resources

## China is also investing

China's investments in Africa encompass three main types:

1. Foreign direct investment (FDI) with equity stakes by Chinese firms
2. Loans mostly for infrastructure and engineering and
3. Construction projects under the Belt and Road Initiative (BRI)

FDI flows for new annual equity investments reached over $3 billion in 2024 after peaking at $5 billion in 2008. FDI stock for accumulated equity sits at around $50 billion. Loans make up about $180 billion. BRI engagement was a record $61.2 billion in 2025. (There is a resource on the website looking at China's investments in ports.)

## Catholics seem more coordinated than other Christians

While I have heard estimates of a large Catholic fund dedicated to Africa, I have not found research to back this up. Some optimistic estimates indicate that the value of the Catholic Church's assets in Africa is around $70 billion. Given their total asset holding worldwide, this might be on the high side. What I have heard is that the Catholic Church is urging its members to figure out how to get a return on assets in Africa. I also was told they have set up a $70 million fund to specifically invest in transformative initiatives in Africa through businesses that will provide a return.

## The Investor the Frameworks Forgot: The African Diaspora

Every list of who is investing in Africa has the same cast of characters. FDI. Private equity. Venture capital. Development finance institutions. Islamic finance. Chinese state capital. They are all real. They all matter. But every one of those lists is missing someone — someone who has been investing in Africa longer than any fund, with more skin in the game than any boardroom, and with a motivation structure that none of our existing frameworks can fully contain.

Meet the African diaspora.

They are forty million strong, live in expat communities in London, Houston, Paris, Dubai, Toronto, and Sydney. They send $104 billion home every single year — roughly twice the level of all official development assistance combined, and neck and neck with the entire continent's foreign direct investment flows. Diaspora Dollars are almost entirely invisible in the investment conversation.

> *"The African diaspora earns approximately $667 billion annually abroad, yet currently sends only about 15% back home." — United Nations*

Let that land. Fifteen percent. That is what remittances represent. The other 85% is sitting in Western financial systems, building wealth in the U.S., UK, and Gulf markets — financing other people's economies. The mobilization opportunity is staggering. And it is largely untapped.

## Who They Are and Where They Live

The contemporary investing diaspora — the cohort that matters most for the conversation in this book — is the post-1945 economic migration wave. These are professionals, entrepreneurs, and tradespeople who left Africa in search of opportunity and education, built careers abroad, and now hold capital that could flow back home.

Their geographic concentrations tell you a lot about which African nations are most engaged:

- United States: the largest single hub, drawing heavily from Nigeria, Ghana, Ethiopia, Kenya, and South Africa. Nigerian-Americans alone account for over $19 billion in annual remittances — 35% of all Sub-Saharan Africa's total.

- United Kingdom: approximately 2.5 million people of African descent, strongly Nigerian, Ghanaian, Zimbabwean, and South African, concentrated in London, Birmingham, and Manchester.
- France: the dominant European hub — over half of the EU's 9.6 million Sub-Saharan African diaspora lives in France, overwhelmingly West and Central African.
- Gulf States (UAE, Saudi Arabia, Qatar): a major and often-overlooked corridor for North and East Africans, particularly Ethiopians, Egyptians, Kenyans, and Ugandans.
- Australia and Canada: growing secondary destinations, with South African-born communities significant in both.

The South African diaspora deserves its own mention: highly professional, capital-bearing, and clustered in the UK, Australia, UAE, and the U.S. — a diaspora with significant investable assets and a complex relationship to home.

## The Numbers Are Not Small

The top remittance-receiving countries in 2024 make a compelling case for why the diaspora belongs in any serious analysis of African investment:

- Egypt: $22.7 billion — Africa's largest recipient, boosted by exchange rate liberalization and diaspora savings instruments.
- Nigeria: $19.8 billion — representing 35% of all Sub-Saharan African remittance inflows.
- Morocco: over $12 billion, primarily from France, Spain, and Italy.
- Kenya: $4.4 billion in 2024, up 18% year-over-year — now outpacing coffee and tourism as a foreign exchange earner.
- Ghana: officially $6.65 billion, with informal channels pushing the real figure toward $11.5 billion — nearly one-third of Ghana's foreign exchange earnings, more than cocoa or gold.

These are not feel-good family transfers. These are macroeconomic forces. In many countries, the diaspora is already the de facto development finance institution — faster, more trusted, and more targeted than anything the World Bank has ever designed.

The cost problem is real and worth naming: it currently costs 8.9% to send money to Southern Africa and 9.9% to East Africa. That toll is an injustice and a business opportunity simultaneously. The SDG target is 3% by 2030. Africa is nowhere near it. Anyone building the infrastructure to close that gap will unlock serious capital flows.

## Beyond Remittances: The Evolving Investor

Here is the story that is still being written. The African diaspora is transitioning from sender to investor. The maturation arc goes something like this: first you send money to Mom. Then you buy a piece of land back home. Then you start asking whether you could put capital to work rather than just park it. Then you find that the infrastructure to do so has been largely absent — and that someone is now building it.

What does diaspora investment look like beyond wire transfers?

- Real estate: the most intuitive entry point. Diaspora communities across the US, UK, and Gulf are buying property back home, often as retirement planning, family housing, or Airbnb income. Platforms like Borderless are formalizing this — a collective formed in 2024 is already pooling capital into Kenyan real estate, with due diligence and compliance built into the rails.
- Startup and angel investing: the Nigerian, Ghanaian, and Kenyan professional diaspora is increasingly the first check into African tech companies. In Algeria, measurable increases in diaspora angel investing into local early-stage startups were recorded in 2024.
- Capital markets: West Africa's BRVM regional exchange delivered over 53% returns year-to-date in 2025, compared to the S&P 500's roughly 10%. Platforms like Daba Finance are opening African stocks, bonds, and money market funds to diaspora investors from anywhere in the world.

- Diaspora bonds: governments have experimented (Ethiopia, Nigeria, Kenya). Results have been modest — Nigeria's diaspora bond raised less than 2% of the country's annual remittance flow. Trust and governance infrastructure need to mature before this instrument scales.
- Informal syndicates and chamas (Kenya) or stokvels (Southern Africa): the most underreported channel. Savings and investment clubs among diaspora communities — especially East African and West African women's groups — pool capital and invest collectively in home-country assets.

One analyst has estimated that if just 10% of diaspora transfers into Francophone West Africa were redirected into capital markets, it would generate $300 million in annual returns to diaspora investors. The returns are there. The rails are being built.

## Why Diaspora is a Distinct Investor Category

The diaspora investor is not a PE fund manager deploying capital from a mandate, nor a Western development finance institution pursuing concessional lending targets. Not a first-time impact investor dabbling in emerging markets because ESG is fashionable. They occupy genuinely different motivational and relational territory.

Five things make them categorically distinct:

- Skin in the game that is not metaphorical. They have family at the receiving end. This produces high motivation, deep local knowledge — and specific distortions, like over-concentration in home countries and emotional over-weighting of certain sectors.
- Local knowledge, distant capital. They understand the culture, often speak the language, have networks on the ground. But they operate across time zones, regulatory jurisdictions, and a persistent trust gap between formal financial systems and home-country realities.

- The remittance-to-investment pipeline. Most diaspora investors started as remitters. “Sending money back home” is the on-ramp. The transition to investor is the maturation story of the entire category — and it is happening in real time.
- Trust as the primary bottleneck. Many diaspora investors have been burned. Informal deals have gone wrong. Relatives disappeared with capital. Transparency was promised, opacity persisted. Building formal, auditable, trustworthy investment infrastructure is the critical unlock — not just marketing.
- Home is not a destination. For most other investor categories in this book, Africa is a destination they chose. For the diaspora, Africa is home. That changes everything about risk tolerance, time horizon, and what “return” even means. A Yoruba woman in London investing in a Lagos real estate project is not making a geographic bet — she is making a statement about who she is.

## Africans Leading Capital

The most compelling proof that the "invest with Africa" posture is not aspirational but operational is found not in the unicorn founders but in the fund managers — Africans in the GP seat, setting the terms, making the calls, with Western and international capital as the co-investor rather than the principal.

Okey Enelamah co-founded African Capital Alliance in Lagos in 1997 — when Nigeria had a military head of state and was not a country international investors were pouring into. His investment thesis was simple and countercultural: with deregulation, the private sector could do very well in Nigeria and the rest of Africa. The MTN Nigeria deal proved it — $400 million deployed, forty-four times returned. ACA now manages over $1.2 billion in assets and has become a Harvard Business School case study, not as an exotic emerging market story but as a model of disciplined, Africa-led private equity. Enelamah later served as Nigeria's Minister of Industry, Trade and Investment.

Wale Adeosun founded Kuramo Capital in 2010 with a specific mandate: deploy capital to African fund managers that global institutional investors were systematically overlooking. Before Kuramo, there were very few investors anchoring African GPs. Since then, Kuramo has catalyzed $3.5 billion into African businesses, backed over 200 companies across 30 countries, and anchored more than fifteen funds. Adeosun was named LP of the Decade at the Private Equity Africa Awards. The model is the inverse of the traditional Western capital dynamic — an African firm bringing institutional discipline to the GP seat and inviting global capital to co-invest behind it.

Helios Investment Partners has been bridging international capital with African talent and enterprise since 2004, managing funds now totaling approximately $3 billion. Its most recent fund drew a $75 million commitment from the European Investment Bank — a European institution co-investing behind an African-led GP.

These are not exceptional cases that prove the rule of Western-led Africa investing. They are the rule beginning to change. The faith-based investor who arrives in Africa asking, "where can I put my capital?" has already framed the question incorrectly. The better question is: which African-led fund managers, with what track record, in what sectors, am I best positioned to co-invest behind?

## Transformational Western Capital is much needed

Before I go further, I need to be precise about what I mean by "transformation" — because the word is doing very different work depending on who is using it. When I talk about transformation, I have in mind the approach, the frameworks, and the outcomes I've laid out in *Transforming Society*. That is a different animal from what the Western worldview typically means by the term. To understand the difference, it helps to put all three major investor groups in the same room.

Peter Cunningham presented it cleanly at a gathering in Zambia in 2026. Islamic investors operate from the conviction that "Africa needs guiding." Their model moves from legitimacy to services to institutions to leaders — and they are patient about it. They integrate faith, law, finance, and education into a single strategy. Zero-interest financing. Mosque networks doubling as community infrastructure. Education pipelines producing the next generation of Muslim leaders. When they reach critical mass, they declare the outcome. It is comprehensive, it is coordinated, and it is working. [2]

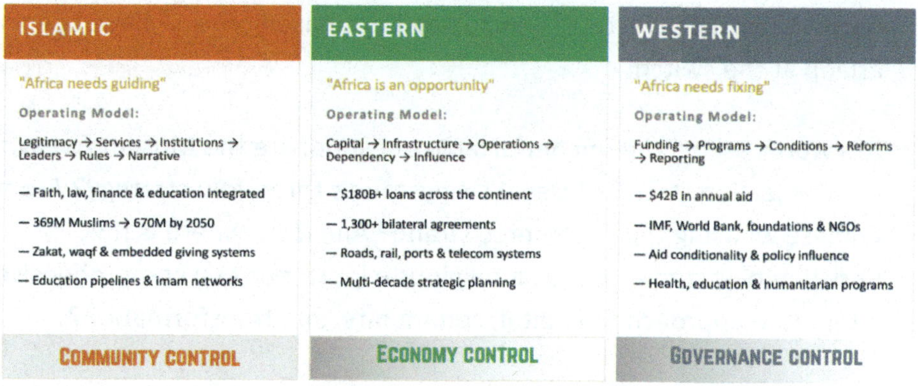


Eastern investors — China, Japan, Korea, India, Turkey — operate from the conviction that "Africa is an opportunity." Their model is capital to infrastructure to operations to dependency to influence. Over $180 billion in loans. More than 1,300 bilateral agreements. Roads, rail, ports, and telecommunications systems built on terms that lock economic participants into Eastern commercial frameworks for decades. They are not cherry-picking deals that will look good in a portfolio. They are building a continent-wide operating system — and they are writing the code.

Western investors, by and large, operate from the conviction that "Africa needs fixing." Funding, programs, conditions, reforms, reporting. $42 billion in annual aid flowing through the IMF, World Bank,

---

[2] Presentation by Peter Cunningham at the Up Forum in Zambia, 2026

foundations, and NGOs. Aid conditionality as policy influence. The posture is moralistic — we will give you capital if you adopt our governance values — and it has produced dependency, not transformation.

Many years ago, I sat with my friend Graham Power and Dawie Spangenberg, who was heading up the Global Day of Prayer at the time. I asked them what the greatest challenge was that they saw in Africa. Dawie didn't hesitate: "The Muslims are buying up the place." In relative terms, Western investors — including faith-based ones — have been asleep at the switch.

It is worth asking the uncomfortable question: are the Muslims weaving the Civilization strand of David Livingstone's three-fold strategy? Are the Chinese weaving the Commerce strand? And if so, where is the Christianity strand — not as a religious export, but as a comprehensive, integrated approach to capital, community, and transformation?

At the individual fund level, traditional faith-based investing has largely focused on ethical exclusion — negative screening, avoiding harm. More recently I have seen Western investors with a faith-forward approach, closer to impact investing, often accepting concessionary returns as the price of conscience. Henry Kaestner is out to prove that you can get a full market return by backing faith-based leaders in Africa — and I believe he is right. But even that is not yet the full picture.

Capital always carries an agenda. The question is whose agenda, and toward what end.

In *Repurposing Capital* I make the point that finance has become unhinged from the original tenets God laid out in Scripture. Western capitalism has also departed from its own roots and been supplanted by greed. That is not a wholesale indictment of capitalism — risk-taking and wealth creation are entirely consistent with Deuteronomy 8:18, where God himself says it is he who gives the ability to produce wealth, as confirmation of his covenant. Capitalism, properly understood, is not premised on greed. Self-interest is tempered by meeting genuine needs. Returns are best generated by deploying capital where it serves rather than extracts.

The problem is that many non-Western nations — rightly or wrongly — equate Western capitalism with Christianity, and by capitalism they mean the god of greed, not the theory in its purer form. That conflation is one reason radical Islam can frame an attack on the World Trade Center as an attack on a value system. They are not entirely wrong about the value system they are opposing. They are entirely wrong about the solution.

Which brings us back to Africa. The "Africa needs fixing" posture is insufficient — not merely morally, but practically. It does not address systemic breakdowns. It treats symptoms. It creates dependency. Investment is not morally neutral: capital either reinforces broken systems or participates in their healing.

What Africa needs — and what faith-based investors are uniquely positioned to provide — is something more than negative screening, more than impact with concessionary returns, and more than infrastructure loans with strings attached. It is transformational capital: patient, purposeful, comprehensively deployed.

In our Repurposing Business (rēp) program at The Institute, the goal has never been to get God into a business. It has been to get the business into God's business. When capital in all its forms — intellectual, relational, spiritual, financial — is invested with that intent, the measure of success is not X percent more profitable. It is eternal ROI.

I believe that since God is just, every nation already has the capital it needs to prosper and to bless other nations. Africa's natural resources are well documented. Less appreciated are its human capital and its spiritual capital — the depth of faith, the relational density, the hunger for genuine transformation that runs through communities across the continent. When those assets are fused with the financial capital, organizational expertise, and centuries of institutional knowledge that outside investors bring, something different becomes possible.

Not Africa fixed. Africa flourishing. Its full portfolio of assets under God's mandate to partner in His purposes.

# 2. Why Africa

## The Demographic Dividend

Africa has 11 of the 20 fastest-growing economies on the planet. Only 0.5 percent of global private equity and venture capital goes there. If that gap does not make you sit up, read it again.

The continent has the youngest population on earth — a demographic dividend that is not a projection but an inevitability. Within the next nine years, Africa will have six cities with populations above ten million. Cairo is already approaching twenty million. Lagos is a City-State heading toward thirty. That is not a development story. That is a market story — and it is one of the largest consumer stories on earth, still largely unwritten.

Across sectors, African entrepreneurs are building locally rooted solutions with a resilience that Silicon Valley would struggle to replicate. Critical gaps in infrastructure, healthcare, education, and governance are not liabilities — they are entry points for investors who know what they are doing. Africa also holds critical minerals that the West needs, and increasingly, Western investors are requiring that mining be done transparently and ethically. That requirement creates opportunity for investors who can deliver it.

None of this is charity. All of it is strategic.

## A Faith-friendly Field

There is something else going on in Africa that does not appear in the McKinsey reports or the development finance institution briefings, and it may be the most important variable of all.

Africa is the most Christianized continent on the planet. In 1900 there were approximately ten million Christians on the continent. Today there are an estimated 734 million — nearly seventy percent of all Christian growth worldwide is now occurring in Africa alone. Major economies are reporting literacy rates above 90 percent, with record graduation rates. The current wave of technology allows solutions to be scaled in ways that were impossible a decade ago. And underneath all of it, there is a spiritual openness — a readiness to integrate faith with work, calling with commerce — that most Western markets lost somewhere in the late twentieth century.

Henry Kaestner frames it correctly: Africa is not a region to be approached through aid paradigms. It is a frontier for strategic, faith-aligned investment where capital can drive systemic change while generating competitive returns. The faith factor is not a risk to be managed. For the investor who understands it, it is a driver of returns.

## Real-world Problems

There is another answer to "Why Africa." One of the reasons I love working in Africa is this: innovations emanating from Africa usually solve real problems, not "First World Problems" like booking the best table at a restaurant or mixing your own organic anti-aging skincare routine. Real problems. Water. Power. Food. Money. Health. Mobility.

I was born in Africa and have worked with hundreds of businesses and thousands of business leaders across the continent. Many are routinely and passionately creating solutions to big problems.

The last chapter of this book will suggest a further reason for investing in Africa — one that has less to do with what can be done *for* Africa and more to do with what Africa might do for the rest of us. That argument can wait. For now, the point is simpler: Africa is producing entrepreneurs who are passionate about solving problems that actually matter. That is not a bad place to put capital.

## Not for Charity

"Because it is Africa" is not a good enough reason to invest. Investors who risk capital in Africa should not be required to throw their logical brain out the window named passion. It is not a question of either financial returns or societal impact. God is the God of AND, so we must exercise fiscal prudence and responsibility and expect that dollars invested bring about societal change.

## Not to advance Western Culture

Kingdom of God people embrace kingdom culture above their national culture, and this is true for both the culture of our sending country and of the country to which we are sent. The Kingdom of God trumps the USA, the UK, the EU, and Africa. At the end of the day, we invest for the advancement of the kingdom of God, not because Africa is a current hot topic.

We must remember that economies existed in many countries before colonial powers arrived. Trade took place, mining was not uncommon, agriculture and animal husbandry existed. Dr. Ruben Richards writes about the economy of the Cape of Good Hope that existed in advance of the Dutch arriving to form a permanent settlement in 1652.[3] Richards argues that long before European arrival, the Cape was not an empty or economically primitive space, but a functioning, sophisticated society with its own established economy rooted in the Khoi and San peoples'

---

[3] Bastaards Or Humans: Origins, identity, culture and challenges, Volume 1, Ruben Richards, Indaba Publishing, 2017

systems of trade, livestock wealth, and social order. He posits that these communities were materially prosperous—measured especially in cattle holdings—and were actively engaged in local and international exchange networks, with leaders who could negotiate across cultures and languages. Far from subsistence survival, this pre-existing economy operated with structure, mobility, and accumulated wealth, challenging the colonial narrative that the Cape required "development." Instead, Richards presents colonization as the disruption and eventual displacement of an already viable and dignified economic system.

> *"While Europe was experiencing the Dark Ages, Africa was in a period of enlightenment with knowledge of iron technology as well as literacy. The Timbuktu Library project driven by former President Mbeki and the new understanding and appreciation of the Mapungubwe Kingdom of 900AD in the Northern part of South Africa, bring fresh perspectives to the sophistication that existed in African society," says Richards.*
>
> *To Richards, celebrating Africa day and African history is necessary to consciously remind Africans of the wealth and sophistication embedded in the African past. "Otherwise," he reckons, "subsequent generations will believe the lie that Africa was always a dark continent and must therefore be thankful of European based enlightenment."*[4]

---

[4] https://www.thejournalist.org.za/books/baastards-or-humans-the-unfolding-truth

## Not to bring Christianity to Africa

Let's settle something before we go further. Africa did not receive Christianity. Africa helped form it.

The faith reached Alexandria in the first century — within decades of Christ. By the third and fourth centuries, North Africa was not a mission field, it was a theological engine. Augustine of Hippo. Tertullian. The Desert Fathers, whose monasticism would shape spiritual practice across the world for centuries. Ethiopia was a Christian nation before most of Europe had heard the gospel. The Coptic Church in Egypt has been continuous for two thousand years.

The widespread presence of Christianity in sub-Saharan Africa is more recent, and yes, it intersects with the era of European missions and colonization. That history is real and worth being honest about. But the conclusion some draw from it — that Christianity is a Western import that arrived with colonial power — is historically wrong. Christianity was African before it was European. Africans were its theologians, its martyrs, its monastic pioneers.

Today, Africa is the most vibrant center of global Christianity on the planet. The faith has been thoroughly indigenized — expressed through local languages, local leadership, local cultural forms. Nearly seventy percent of all Christian growth worldwide is now occurring on the continent. The story is not one of importation. It is one of deep roots, long interruption, and remarkable, unstoppable renewal.

Which means the faith-based investor arriving in Africa is not bringing something new. They are joining something ancient. As a friend in Nigeria put it: "If we can just get Sunday into Monday" — that is the opportunity. Not Christianity to Africa. Christianity *through* Africa, into the marketplace, into the systems, into the world.

That is a different posture. And it changes everything about how you invest.

## Fixing Foundations

Truth often comes wrapped in paradoxes. While investing in Africa is not about bringing Western capitalism to a continent, all investing is spiritual work that should fix foundations.

> *Your people shall rebuild the ancient ruins; the foundations from ages past you shall raise up; "Repairer of the breach," they shall call you, "Restorer of ruined dwellings." Isaiah 58:12 NABRE*

In *Transforming Society* I lay out four movements in the work of societal restoration: fixing and relaying foundations, stewarding and rebuilding assets, repurposing the spheres of society, and restoring glory. They are interlocking components.. You cannot restore glory on a cracked foundation. Tending the fruit without examining the root is not enough — and in Africa, the roots go deep, in both directions.

Dr. Alistair Petrie puts it plainly: "When unholiness goes either undetected or ignored, alternative strongholds invariably become a reality." Before you build, you need to know what you are building on.

When we go into a city or nation to make an investment, we begin by looking for the existing evidence of the glory of God in that place. We use our imagination — godly imagination — to picture what it would look like if the glory of God was fully restored in that industry, that city, that nation. We are looking for glory, not digging for dirt. But we also need to understand what has happened historically that may be counter to God's heart and ways. Both are true at the same time. That tension is the rebuilding work.

Let me give you a practical example of what this looks like on the ground — not in Africa, but in West Texas, because the principle travels.

I was visiting a company run by followers of Jesus — a successful real estate business that purchased land, designed homes, built communities. They were generous people who had built something that was making a real difference in their city. They sponsored employees on mission trips and were genuinely a model of a business contributing to the flourishing of their town. When I sat down with their CFO — who was also, tellingly, their Chief Spiritual Officer — I asked about their business processes. He walked me through them with evident pride.

Then I said: "Apart from writing a Bible verse on the lumber as you frame up the house and handing the customer a Bible at the end, your business process is no different from that of the pagan builder down the road."

The room went quiet. So I started asking questions.

Do you ask God whether he wants you to acquire a particular piece of land in the first place? If he gives you the green light, do you inquire what *purpose* he has for that land? Do you alter the design of the development to fit what the Father is showing you — the layout, the ethos, the branding? What would it look like if Jesus was on the design team? And do you address the four things the Old Testament identifies as defiling a land — bloodshed, broken covenants, sexual immorality, idolatry?

That evening over dinner the conversation involved the entire executive team. The next morning the president arrived to breakfast a little late. He had been up early, meeting with his design team to ask one question: what would it look like if Jesus was on our design team?

That is foundations work. It is not a prayer meeting tacked onto a board meeting. It is a different starting point altogether.

When you invest in Africa, your due diligence needs to get back to the historical foundations of the place — whether they are righteous, where they are broken, and what needs to happen before you start building. This includes a serious, unhurried consideration of the First Nations: who was there before, what covenants were made or broken, what has been carried in the soil. It is the kind of due diligence that does not appear in Best Practices 101. It should.

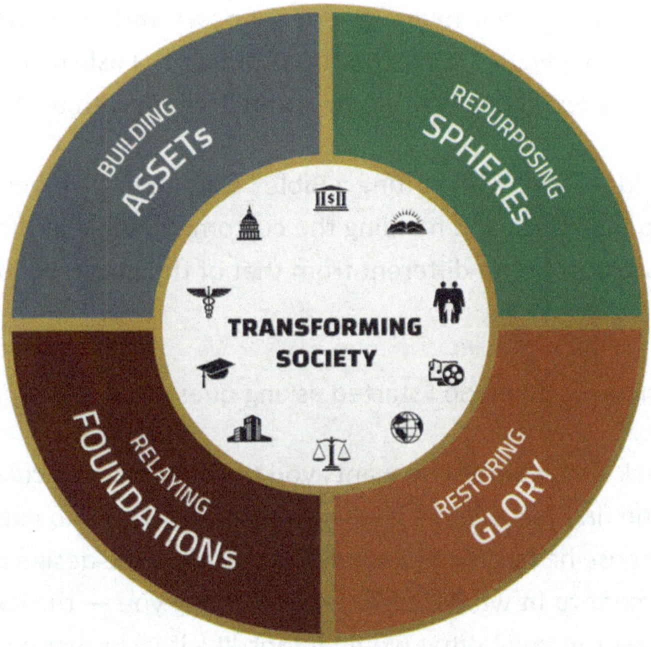

# 3. Theological Foundation: Revisiting our 3-Fold Mandate

Scripture assumes that followers of Jesus will be people who go and get the job done. But where should we go? Is it just the chosen few that become missionaries and travel to another nation? To whom are we going? One of the reasons we have not reached "finished" in two thousand years is that we have forgotten our first commission. The second reason is that we have ignored a critical part of the Great Commission: the mandate given by Jesus Christ has been misconstrued for centuries as focusing on people or ethnic groups.

## Our First Commission

> *Our first commission was to work with God, fill the earth, and bring his design, order and intentions to his planet. His last commission was to make disciples of all nations.*[5]

I was staying at the Victoria Falls Hotel while doing some work for a client and took a stroll one morning to see the falls. As I stepped out of the hotel grounds, a friendly local, dressed in an official uniform, offered to walk alongside me. "Sometimes there are animals that come out of the bush," he said. As we walked together, I noticed the National

[5] Bizcipleship, by Brett Johnson, Indaba Publishing

Motto on his insignia: *Unity, Freedom, Work*. I asked him, "Tell me about work." "We Zimbabweans love to work."

Western Christians, and I would say most Christians around the world, have disconnected our first commission from the Great Commission. Work and witness experienced a great divorce. Too many people have worked in business and given money to those who go to fulfill the Great Commission. If we direct capital investments properly, we will be defeating this demonic dualism, not reinforcing it. To do so, however, we must recapture the triple-braided marching orders given by Jesus.

## Our 3-in-1 Commission is not Preached Fully

Here is something that has bothered me for years. We have preached Matthew 28 to death, hopefully for life — and rightly so. Go and make disciples of all the ethnos, the nations, the peoples, every tribe and tongue. Good text. Clear mandate. The whole church-planting movement is built on it, and it has changed the world. Then we have Acts 1:8 — you will be my witnesses to the eschatos of the earth, the outermost parts, the ends. Also excellent and also world-changing. It gave us frontier mission, unreached peoples group thinking, the whole geography of the Great Commission.

But there is a third text. And we have been strangely quiet about it.

> *Go into all the world and proclaim the gospel to every creature. Mark 16:15*

Here the word *world* is *kosmos*. And if you have ever wondered why the church has historically been better at planting churches than transforming economies — better at saving souls than restoring systems — I think part of the answer is sitting right there in the untranslated Greek. We have been running on two-thirds of the commission.

### What Does Kosmos Actually Mean?

*Kosmos* appears approximately 186 times in the New Testament. That is not a marginal term. It is a load-bearing word, and it carries a range of meaning that most English translations flatten into the single word *world* — which tells us almost nothing.

Strong's Concordance identifies four distinct senses. First, the entire created universe — heaven and earth together, the sum of all that is. Second, the inhabited earth and its people — the human family, which is usually what John means when he says God so loved the world. Third — and this is the sense that makes people uncomfortable — an organized system of human society operating in active rebellion against God: its values, its power structures, its seductions, its financial architectures. And fourth, from the root of the word itself, the idea of order and adornment. Beautiful arrangement. Harmonious design. (The same root gives us cosmetics, incidentally, which tells you something about how the Greeks thought about beauty and order as the same thing.)

Four meanings. One word. And Jesus uses it to describe where we are supposed to go, our commission, our calling. Think about that for a moment.

## The Pattern Is the Point

The *kosmos* commission is not just broader than *ethnos* or *eschatos*. It is structurally different. Because in John 17:18, Jesus does not just say *go to the world*. He says:

> *As you sent me into the **world**, so I have sent them into the **world**. John 17:18*

*Kosmos* in both cases. The Father sent the Son into the *kosmos*. The Son sends us into the *kosmos*. Same word. Same structure. Which means the template for our mission is the incarnation itself.

The incarnation was not a conceptual flyby with a papal wave. It was demonstrated by Jesus himself.

Jesus did not hover above the economic system of first-century Israel dispensing spiritual wisdom from a safe altitude. He worked in it. He told stories about it — about absentee landlords and day laborers and unjust stewards and shrewd managers and merchants who sold everything for one pearl. He operated in a society where Rome set the terms of trade, where the Temple controlled the currency exchange (at usurious rates, as it turned out), where taxation was a form of organized extortion, where land ownership determined social status. He went into that system — not to validate it, not to be captured by it, but to demonstrate what the Kingdom looks like operating inside it with a view to reforming it.

This is the model. Not extraction. Not observation. Presence. You might say kosmos is the place where principles and people and processes and products and planning — all of the key elements of an operating model — intersect.

Which is exactly what *Investing with Africa* requires — and exactly what most Western capital has historically failed to deliver. This might seem like a harsh indictment, but stay with me for a moment, because if we grasp this, it will unlock new doors.

## Three Meanings That Should Keep Investors Awake at Night

Of the four senses of *kosmos*, three speak directly to anyone who is serious about deploying capital on this continent.

**First: the human family.** John 3:16 — the verse that ends up on stadium banners and eye-black — tells us God loved the *kosmos* enough to give his Son for it. Paul unpacks the investment thesis in 2 Corinthians 5:19: God was in Christ reconciling the *kosmos* to himself, and has entrusted to us the "ministry of reconciliation." Not the ministry of extraction. Not the ministry of risk-adjusted returns. Reconciliation. Capital that flows toward Africa in the spirit of that mandate carries a different intention. It does not just ask "What can I make here?" but "Who and what can be made whole here?"

**Second: the system.** 1st John 5:19 says the whole *kosmos* lies in the power of the evil one. John 12:31 names a ruler of this world. I know that language makes some boardrooms uncomfortable. Good. It should. Because the financial architectures that have historically operated in Africa — colonial extraction, structural adjustment programs designed elsewhere, debt instruments that transferred wealth out of the continent for generations — these are not aberrations. They are *kosmos* in its third sense: organized, systemic, structured in ways that work against human flourishing. The faith-based investor does not pretend this history does not exist. They go in with eyes open, knowing they are entering contested territory, and they structure their deals accordingly.

**Third: the created order.** Romans 1:20 tells us the invisible things of God have been clearly seen since the creation of the *kosmos* in the things that are made. Africa is a continent of staggering created abundance — mineral, agricultural, biological, cultural, human. Abraham, Paul tells us in Romans 4:13, was promised that his offspring would be heir of the *kosmos*. Not a spiritual metaphor. The actual earth. Investment in Africa that is rooted in this theology is investment in the stewardship of creation — which is, as we remember, the oldest mandate in the book. Genesis 1:28 came long before Matthew 28.

In It, Not of It — But Actually In It

Jesus does something interesting in John 17 that I have not heard many sermons about — and almost no investment presentations. In the span of four verses, he holds three distinct postures in tension simultaneously. He prays that his disciples would not be taken out of the world (verse 15). He affirms that they are not of the world (verse 16). And he declares that they are sent into the world (verse 18).

Not taken out, not of... sent in.

This is the posture that distinguishes the faith-based investor from every other kind. The purely secular investor goes in unreflectively — often becoming “of the world” in the process, shaped by its incentive structures, complicit in its distortions, measuring only what the system tells them to measure. The religious investor — and I have met many — stays out. They deploy capital only in safe ecclesiastical channels. (Or, what is more likely is that they keep their money safely isolated in their home country and then hand it over to somebody who invests in the Indexes.) This never engages the contested systems where the kosmos commission actually applies. (This is sometimes called stewardship. It is actually avoidance.)

The investor who has internalized Mark 16:15 goes in deliberately. They carry a different set of values into the room. They ask different questions at the deal table. They define return differently. They have a longer time horizon than the next quarter — because their eschatology is longer than the next quarter. They are not in Africa to execute a transaction. They are in Africa because the *kosmos* commission propelled them there.

What does reconciliation actually mean in practice? I spent fourteen years as a Chartered Accountant at Price Waterhouse. Long before that, I was doing the books for my parents' businesses and a key part of that work was bank reconciliations. In those days the banks tended to have a more accurate narrative of the facts than the companies did, so my job was to align the books with the bank statement. We still need bank reconciliations today, but this time it is the banks — and every other financial institution — that need to be reconciled to eternal truth.

That is a useful picture of what the ministry of reconciliation looks like in the marketplace. You are holding the world system in one hand and the King's system in the other and pulling them closer together. Not abandoning one for the other. Not pretending the gap does not exist. Closing it — deliberately, patiently, deal by deal, company by company, city by city.

This is what distinguishes the faith-based investor from the fatalist who accepts the system as it is, and from the isolationist who refuses to engage it at all. The integrationist — the investor operating under the kosmos commission — stays in contact with what is less than optimal in the hope, and with the intention, of improving it. The theological and financial architecture underlying that integrationist posture — including a comparison of how Christian, Islamic, and Jewish traditions have approached capital — is laid out in detail in 50 Principles of Faith-Based Financing, a companion volume to this book.

## The Ending We Are Investing Toward

There is a final *kosmos* text that almost never makes it into investment prospectuses, and I think it should be required reading for every faith-based investor in Africa. Revelation 11:15:

> *The kingdom of the world has become the kingdom of our Lord and of his Christ, and he shall reign forever and ever.*

The unredeemed *kosmos* does not evaporate. It does not get abandoned. It gets *transformed*. The whole created order — the human family, the systems of society, the economies, the land — becomes the Kingdom. This is the eschatological destination toward which the *kosmos* commission points.

Which means we are not changing lightbulbs in a burning house. We are not investing in a continent God plans to write off. We are participating in a long-arc project of reclamation — the bringing of the kosmos, piece by piece, company by company, harvest by harvest, into alignment with its intended future.

Abraham was promised the kosmos as inheritance. The saints will judge the kosmos (1 Corinthians 6:2). The kingdom of the kosmos will become the Kingdom of God. These are not consolation prizes. They are the shape of what is coming. And that shape is what we are investing toward.

## A Different Commission. A Different Investor

*Ethnos* sends us to peoples. *Eschatos* sends us to the ends of the earth. *Kosmos* sends us into the totality — created order, human family, the systems of finance and trade and governance and culture — with the full weight of a mandate that is nothing less than the reclamation of all things.

Africa is not a charity case. It is not a development project. It is not an emerging market waiting to be absorbed into a financial system somebody else designed.

Africa is part of the *kosmos* that "God so loved." It is part of the *kosmos* being reconciled to himself. It is an integral part of the *kosmos* that the Kingdom is coming to claim.

When we invest with Africa, we are not merely deploying capital, we are operating under the *kosmos* commission. This is a different reason to invest, and it produces a different kind of investor.[6]

## Core Convictions

In my earlier book, Kingdom Economics, I unpack the difference between the economic systems of Egypt, the Desert, and the Promised Land. Here I will share just five core convictions:

1. **Stewardship over ownership** – Wealth is entrusted, not possessed. At the same time, there is a biblical principle that says that, while everything I own belongs to God, between me and my neighbors there are property rights and there is legal ownership as a basis for economic growth.
2. **Service over extraction** – Markets exist to serve human flourishing, and markets exist within the context of a healthy Societal Value Chain.
3. **Restoration over maximization** – The goal of capital is shalom: right relationships across society. Capital always carries an agenda and, when used with clear and noble intentions, is a tremendous force for good in society. One productive purpose of capital is to fuel real work, work that is also worship.

---

[6] Note on the Greek: All references to kosmos draw on Strong's Concordance entry G2889. The distribution of the 186 NT occurrences across the four semantic categories is the author's own analysis based on contextual reading, not a claim made by Strong's itself. See the Appendices for more in-depth coverage on this topic. I have used kosmos and cosmos interchangeably.

4. **All three facets of the Great Commission** – not just ethnos and eschatos, but the often overlooked kosmos, where systems, supply chains, organizations, and financial architectures live and breathe. Kingdom investing operates under the full commission, not just the parts that feel familiar.
5. **Recognizing all forms of Capital** – not giving financial or relational or political or spiritual capital, to name some, unfair sway over an investment and its returns.

Risk includes not only financial volatility, but the long-term erosion of social, environmental, and societal systems. Biblical investments reverse such erosion. When it comes to restoration, we can obviously start with individuals and restoring them in their identity and purpose. This includes teaching them to work the way God designed them to work.[7]

We must move, however, to households which includes family structures and businesses with their wide reach. Should we not then consider how we deploy Household to Household expansion to see the restoration of villages, towns, cities, and nations?

## Societal Value Chain

The work involved in getting assets from raw material to a city's storehouse is worth tracing, because understanding where Africa sits in that chain — and where it has been systematically excluded — changes how you think about investing there.

Raw materials are identified. There were no packaged goods in the garden. Once identified, raw materials are gathered to reach critical mass before they become Resources — one ounce of gold does not constitute a refinery. Resources then get transformed into Products through work, sometimes with Inspired Innovation and the George Washington Carver question: "Mr. Creator, why did you make the

---

[7] Work like God in 31 ways, by Brett Johnson. Indaba Publishing 2020

peanut?" A bunch of grapes is not a finished good to a winemaker — a great deal of work lies between the vineyard and the bottle. Products need Markets, and markets give rise to Trade, and trade leads to Profit. But money can be wasted, so for Wealth Creation to actually happen there must be Stewardship — the recognition that what has been built is not just for "I, myself and me" but for something larger. Stewarded wealth creates Societal Assets. And when a city or nation generates so much wealth that it can bless other cities and nations, it has finally arrived at the promise of Genesis 12: "I will bless you, and you will be a blessing to all nations."

That entire cycle should, from a biblical perspective, happen within a nation.[8]

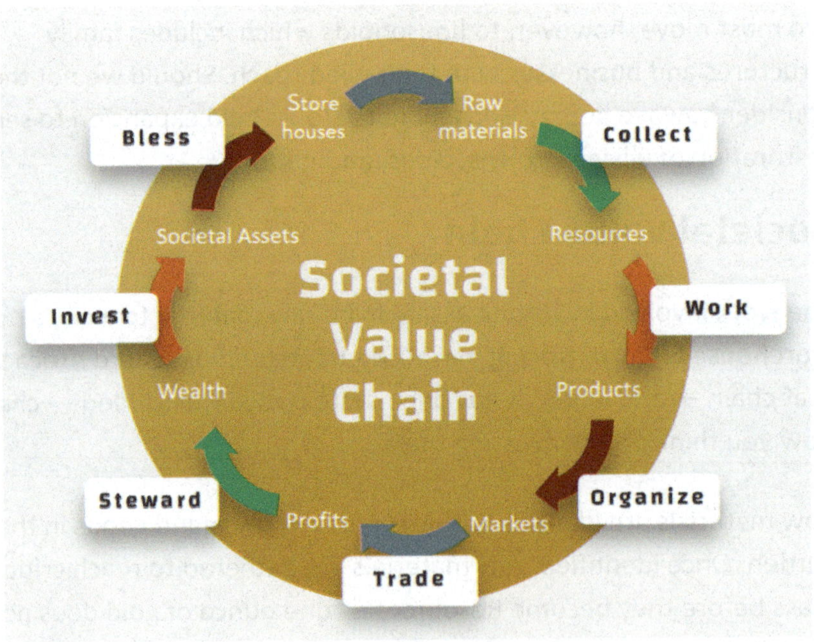


What has happened in Africa is that raw materials have been extracted, removed from Africa, and the products and markets have happened in

[8] Transforming Society, by Brett Johnson – pages 114-115

other nations. How much of the British Empire was financed by the gold and diamonds that came out of South Africa? Is it right that African countries still export crude oil and do not have their own refineries? Until Botswana upset the colonial apple cart, the international diamond market-making was far away from where the diamonds were mined.

We must remember that there were no jewelry stores in the Garden of Eden. It took effort to extract the gold, melt it, create a mold for the ring, pour the molten gold into the mold, etc. There were no supermarkets in the Garden of Eden, no furniture stores. For Africa to be uplifted, the value of work must be elevated to the biblical intent of co-laboring with the Creator. Many parts of Africa import finished goods based on raw materials that came from the soil. Sons and daughters understand the principle of raw materials; slaves get addicted to finished goods.

## Thinking Systemically

Western investment practices have logically divided investments into asset classes, each with its own rules and expected returns. Those countries in Africa that have more established capital markets have followed this same line of thinking, especially where they invite co-investment from outside of their nation. The demands on African investors are higher because risk-adjusted returns can sometimes double the expectations from Africa-based investments. "Why invest in real estate in Lagos at 20% when I can get a 10% return in Detroit without the associated hassle?"

I am arguing that to change the nature of and impact of capital in Africa, we should seriously consider investing in ways that are more systemic and less in traditional asset classes. I also advocate that when making investments, we must be more relational and less mechanical. We partner with local investors who understand the governance, regulatory environment, and leadership challenges of their situation as friends and brothers and sisters in Christ. Indigenous investment groups of many persuasions are critical allies for those bringing capital from other continents to Africa. The ministry of Jesus has fused people from across nations from the outset– he wasn't just some Jewish man speaking only to Jewish people. Jesus was the kid with the Egyptian accent whose opening salvos were heard by Jordanians, Syrians, Romans, and Jews. Why should a multi-national work not have multi-national capital?

# 4. Transforming Society: Cosmos & The 10-Sphere Investment Framework

Societies flourish or fracture across interconnected spheres. Investment that targets only one sphere in isolation often underperforms both socially and financially. In my book, *Transforming Society: A framework for fixing a broken world,* I make the case for a healthy society having ten distinct spheres or sectors: family, media, NGOs, judiciary, business, education, healthcare, government, capital, and religion. Others have different groupings of these spheres of influence, and in my case, I separate out Capital from Business, Law/an independent judiciary from Government, and the NGO industrial complex since it has a large influence on policies, incentives, and outcomes. If a nation is to be discipled then each sphere of society needs to be repurposed.

Transformational investing intentionally strengthens multiple spheres simultaneously especially where there is a clear framework for bringing about societal transformation. In Africa, one needs to identify a whole supply chain and invest in different segments to make sure there are not critical breakages. One does well to look at the network of interconnected organizations which work together to bring about flourishing or shalom in a city.

In Bulawayo, as an example, we are working on a "city on the edge of a city" where for four core businesses—ag business, green building, finance and housing—will spin off a hundred secondary businesses so that a web of mutually beneficial endeavors contributes to the good of whole. (See Appendices)

## Don't stay in your lane

> *"Not in my wheelhouse..." "I am just staying in my lane..."*
> *"Not my circus, not my monkeys..."*

We give statements like these a status close to the 10 Commandments, but is their sentiment biblical? And how does it align with the practitioners who have transformed nations? Was William Carey, considered to be the father of modern missions, staying in one lane? Were the Moravians before him only investing in one industry?

We have looked at the 10 Spheres of Society: unless all 10 are reconciled to God's heart and ways. towns, cities and nations may have cool stories, but they will not be truly transformed. I have a friend who made an investment in a Latin American country: Capital was her sphere of focus. When the bank assets were frozen and her clients' funds were stuck she had to go, meet with leaders from many spheres, engage in prayer, hire lawyers, send press releases, challenge corruption… soon she was touching nearly all 10 spheres. We think focus—God thinks cross-sphere influence.

Sometimes we do get impact through focus. Boiling the ocean seldom works. Investments in emerging markets do best when we take care of the whole, however, and do not cuddle with cliques. Ezra failed at getting the temple rebuilt until Nehemiah took care of the city wall—then the temple building could be finished. Invest in city walls otherwise your investments in smaller niches (SMEs, churches, missions organizations and NGOs) are less likely to be sustainable.

## But does the Gospel call for…

There are three inadequate responses to the biblical mandate to make disciples. The Defeatists say the job cannot be done and things will get worse before Jesus returns, so there is no point in trying. The Evangelist said that if we can just get enough people saved, we will reach a tipping point where things get better.

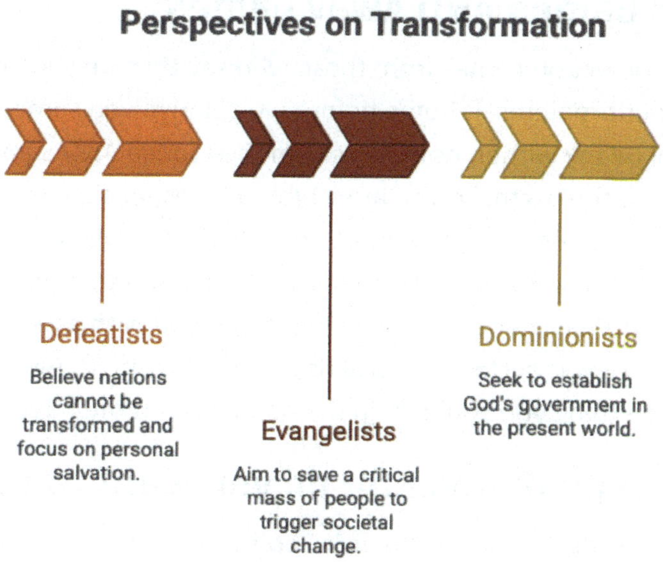

The Dominionist says we can have a Christian president and dedicate the nation to God. The problem with the dominionist position is not the ambition — it is the method and the motivation. We are not called to seize the systems of the world but to demonstrate, within them, what they look like when ordered by a different King. The goal is not control. It is realigning to Christ. This is salt work, light work.

None of these three bad approaches demands of us that we roll up our sleeves, put on our thinking caps, and really figure out what it looks like for the glory of God to be restored (in each of the spheres of society and in every business or organization that forms part of such sector). In fact, when we use the language of the glory of God, and discipleship, and transformation without getting in the trenches and reconciling systems, enterprises, and entities to the principles laid out by the King of the Universe we confuse people. Sunday does not touch Monday. Often it is easier for us to live with our secular-sacred dichotomy intact than to hold the spheres of the world in one hand and the Kingdom of God in the other and play a reconciling role in bringing them together. To mask our spiritual disconnect we shrink from larger and deeper investments and advocate allocating capital narrowly.

## Home Games AND Away Games

Another objection comes from those who say that we should first take care of our problems at home before we get involved somewhere else. "You will be my witnesses in Jerusalem AND Judea AND Samaria AND the ends of the earth." If you are a biblically responsible investor, a kingdom capitalist, then you must not substitute AND with OR, or THEN. When Jesus called you, he recruited you to a team that plays home games and away games. When he endowed you with assets in many forms, there was certainly a local deployment in mind, AND Jesus had in mind something you could do in the nations, with the nations.

## What Type of Investor do you want to be?

Imagine having 15 minutes to pick God's brain about money: what would you ask? Or, if this is too much of a stretch, what if an earnest young person asked you to tell them the key principles of faith-based financing in the same 15 minutes: what would you say? I have given this some thought and, in my view, *it depends more on who you are than who Jesus is*. Is this a relativistic statement? Why would I say this? Surely God's truth is truth and applies evenly to all?

I covered **50 Principles of Faith-based Financing** in Repurposing Capital and in a separate short book. Readers might expect to gain wisdom from it for their financial present and future. I then began to wonder how I could boil these 50 principles into the Top 7 or 10 tips that could change a reader's view of money and perhaps their financial habits. The book breaks the principles into categories:

1. Sources of funds
2. Uses & Nature of finance
3. Stewardship & Spending
4. Generosity & Giving
5. Investing
6. Remedial action (where there has been financial wrongdoing)

Principles are principles, but there is not a "one size fits all" answer. I have observed different categories of Christ-followers when it comes to the matter of money and concluded there are four groups. Each has a particular lens through which they view finances and will take away different things from what I say. Let me explain these groups a little more:

- Planners
- Pilgrims
- Planters
- Platform-reformers

**Planners** are those who follow the basic principles of working hard, spending less than they earn, giving to charity, saving a little, and having something set aside for a rainy day. Theirs is a predictable life, and one that relies on faithful application of basic principles. Working professionals who are planners prefer steady jobs over risky endeavors.

**Pilgrims** are the "water walkers" who have stepped out of the boat of predictable income and decided to trust God for unusual provision for their adventures. Some call this "living by faith," but this is a misnomer in that faith is required for all four groups. Pilgrims are different from Planners, but not better. Pilgrims in the marketplace are often involved in entrepreneurship or "deal making" that may bring in once-off income.

**Planters** are those who work the system of compound interest, stock market investing and property accumulation to generate either capital for reinvesting, or alternative (often passive) income streams. The extra capital they create is invested in noble causes such as giving to charity or investing in "kingdom" businesses. They aim to leave a financially-fueled legacy. At a base level, however, they accept the reality of financial systems as they are, taking the good with the bad, and aim to use them for noble purposes.

**Platform-reformers** are a relative handful of people who see the errors of what they call "the world's system" (which they see as being based on debt, excessive interest, fiat* currencies and greed) and aim to reform the system as a whole. [*Paper *money* or coins of little or no intrinsic value in themselves and not convertible into gold or silver but made legal tender by *fiat* (order) of the government.] These people are intent on returning to a more biblical system, not just maximizing returns from the current system.

Finances are the ledger of our values, the evidence of our priorities and the measure of our practicality. Far from being separate from faith, finances are a window into how we view the world. Since worldview is a set of presuppositions held in faith concerning how life works, it inevitably incorporates both faith and finances.

How does this tie into our four groups? Each group asks different questions about money because they focus on different outcomes, seeking solutions that help them live in their chosen reality. Groupies gravitate towards books that reinforce their position. Planners, for example, read Dave Ramsey and Ron Blue while Pilgrims read Loren

Cunningham's *Daring to live on the Edge.* Planters read Robert Kiyosaki's *Rich Dad, Poor Dad* or Sunday Adelaja's *Money won't make you rich*. Platform-reformers read lesser-known works such as Uli Kortsch's *The Next Money Crash* or, perhaps, *Repurposing Capital* and *Kingdom Economics*, which, full disclosure, I wrote.

Relatively few approach scripture asking questions that help them transition from one group to another. Fewer still dare to live life spanning all four camps. Why is this? Perhaps we lack information. We might be afraid of the unknown. A key reason I have observed: we do not like a fight. For all the talk of spiritual warfare and being in God's army and plundering hell to populate heaven, we are comfortable in our category. Planners want to stay Planners; Pilgrims don't want to become Planters; Planters do not want to be Platform-reformers. We are prone to accept what works without giving thought to how things should work. The convenient truth is that there are scriptures to support every group, and you can choose to stay at any level. But you cannot avoid a fight. Planners fight disorder, debt, and the comparison trap. Pilgrims fight the pull back to the predictable — the voice that says the boat was safer than the water. Planters fight the pride of life: the quiet conviction that what they have accumulated is theirs to enjoy rather than deploy. Platform-reformers fight the fear of facing giants that may not fall in their lifetime. Different battles. The same enemy stands behind all of them.

Behind each battle is a force Jesus called Mammon which, by definition, is greed deified. The magnetic pull of mammon seeks to stick people to their current reality, squeezing the courage out of them when they venture to break a barrier and go to a new arena. This is true personally, but also at an organizational and a national level. Changing systems involves a fight and we need to choose our battles based on what we believe is our calling, our level of faith (if faith has levels) and the mandate for our lives. When you look back on your life, what will you have given your life to? Where do you want to end up? For which battles will you enlist? Decide this before you venture into investing in Africa.

> *"Your people will come as volunteers that day; they will be a sight to see: on that day, you will lead your army, noble in their holiness. As the new day dawns and dew settles on the grass, your young volunteers will make their way to you." Psalm 110:3*

This dialogue in heaven, a promise of Father God to Jesus Christ, is profound. When transferred from the kingdom of darkness into the kingdom of light we became soldiers in an army, not just citizens of a future-coming kingdom. Kingdom economics is a now thing that demands bold action. Know your grouping and pick a fight. Tackle personal debt, curtail greedy expenditure, become a hilarious giver, store seed for planting and plant well. Then pick a fight with a system, not just a personal inconvenience (like not allocating enough money for your wants). Let Jonathan and his armor bearer be a model.

> *Jonathan said, "Come on, then; we will cross over toward them and let them see us. If they say to us, 'Wait there until we come to you,' we will stay where we are and not go up to them. But if they say, 'Come up to us,' we will climb up, because that will be our sign that the Lord has given them into our hands."*
>
> *So both of them showed themselves to the Philistine outpost. "Look!" said the Philistines. "The Hebrews are crawling out of the holes they were hiding in." The men of the outpost shouted to Jonathan and his armor-bearer, "Come up to us and we'll teach you a lesson." So Jonathan said to his armor-bearer, "Climb up after me; the Lord has given them into the hand of Israel."*

Note how Jonathan took the odds-against-them situation as an indication of God's leading: "But if they say, 'Come up to us'..." We too often see financial opposition as in indicator that we should quit the fight and stay home.

There is, perhaps, a fifth category: **Plunderers**. These are people who use economic systems, specifically banking and finance, to plunder people, corporations and nations. They make onerous loans, promise exorbitant returns, hold onto what is not rightfully theirs, and enslave others either through the promise of wealth or the reality of debt. It is the job of Platform-reformers to take on the Plunderers, even though the odds do not look good.

Back to the 15 minute interview with Jesus. Before I start asking God for financial tips, riches or prosperity, I might want to ask myself, "What group am I in today? What is my current battle, and how am I doing? Is the Lord calling me into a new financial fight? Am I willing to go there?"

## Traditional Investor Categories

The mapping between traditional investor categories and the four archetypes is not a clean one-to-one exercise, and that tension is actually the point. Traditional categories — limited partners, family offices, institutional investors, trusts — are defined by structure and role. My four archetypes are defined by posture and motivation. The same family office can show up as a Planner, a Planter, or a Platform-reformer depending entirely on what they believe capital is for. The spreadsheet that follows captures this nuance as a matrix, but the more important question is the one you need to answer before you open it: which archetype are you, and which one do you want to become?

## Mapping the Diaspora to Our Four Types

The African diaspora maps across all four of our categories — which is what makes it both interesting and explains why it was missing from the original framework. It does not sit neatly in any single lane.

- You will find diaspora Planners: the Nigerian nurse in Manchester who sends a fixed monthly amount home, invests in a property in Lagos, and plans to retire there. Steady, predictable, faithful application of financial basics — just with a transatlantic dimension.

- You will find diaspora Pilgrims: the Ghanaian entrepreneur in Toronto who invests in three different startups back home on faith, conviction, and a network of WhatsApp connections. Once-off deals, edge cases, water-walking capital.
- You will find diaspora Planters: the South African professional in Sydney quietly compounding returns through JSE-listed stocks and African private credit funds, building generational wealth that bridges two continents. Working the system. Leaving a legacy.
- And you will find diaspora Platform-reformers: the Joe Kinvis building Borderless, the Boum IIIs building Daba Finance, the fintech founders in Nairobi and Lagos who are re-architecting the rails through which diaspora capital flows. These are people who looked at a broken system — 8.9% transfer fees, opacity, exclusion — and decided to replace it rather than use it.

The case for naming the diaspora as a fifth category is not that they are a fundamentally different type of investor in motivation. It is that their starting position is categorically different from every other investor in this book. For the diaspora, Africa is not a portfolio allocation — it is a birthright.

Every other investor in this book chose Africa. The diaspora did not choose it — Africa chose them. That is a different kind of investment.

| African Diaspora Remittance Flows vs Other Capital (2024, USD Billions) | | |
|---|---|---|
| **Capital Source** | **Amount ($B)** | **Notes** |
| Official Dev. Assistance (ODA) | 52 | All bilateral/multilateral aid to Africa |
| FDI (ex-Egypt mega-project) | 62 | Adjusted 2024 FDI; one Egypt project = $35B |
| Total FDI (incl. Egypt) | 97 | Record 2024 FDI, skewed by single project |
| **Diaspora Remittances** | **104** | **World Bank 2024; ~2x ODA** |
| **Diaspora Earnings (total)** | **667** | **UN estimate; only 15% currently sent home** |

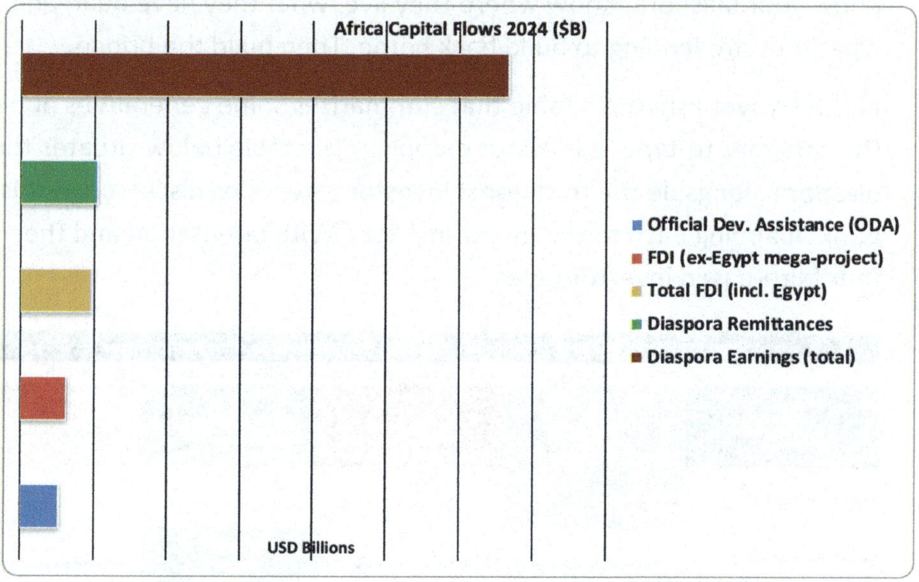


## What This Means for Faith-Based Investors

There is a particular conversation to be had here with the African Christian professional diaspora concentrated in Nigerian, Ghanaian, Zimbabwean, and South African communities across the US and UK. This cohort is already predisposed toward kingdom thinking about money. They have grown up with tithing, generosity and the idea that wealth has a purpose beyond accumulation. Many of them are already Planters in their personal finances.

What they often lack is a credible, trustworthy vehicle to channel that disposition back into Africa. The church has been a conduit for charitable flows but rarely for investment capital. The faith-based investment infrastructure that could engage this community — transparent, governed well, aligned with kingdom purposes — remains largely unbuilt.

That is an invitation, not a criticism. The diaspora is not waiting to be discovered. They are already moving. The question is whether faith-based investors, funds, and platform-builders will show up as partners — or whether that $667 billion annual earnings pool will continue financing other people's economies while Africa waits.

Know your diaspora. Know where they live, what they have built, and what they are longing to build back home. Then build the bridge.

In the Flyover I shared a table that summarizes some generalities about the category-to-type of investor mapping. The table below situates the diaspora alongside the traditional investor categories discussed in this book, mapping each to the Invest In / For / With orientation and the four faith-based investor types.

**INVESTOR TYPE MAPPING · Traditional Categories × Brett Johnson's Four Investor Archetypes**

*Fit ratings: ●●● Primary fit ●●○ Strong secondary ●○○ Possible ○○○ Rare / unlikely*

| TRADITIONAL INVESTOR TYPE | PLANNERS<br>Financial basics<br>Faithfulness<br>Predictability | PILGRIMS<br>Adventurous<br>Once-off deals<br>Edge cases / "by faith" | PLANTERS<br>Compounding growth<br>Multiple income streams<br>Noble-case investing | PLATFORM-REFORMERS<br>Change the rules<br>New systems<br>Faith-based finance roots |
|---|---|---|---|---|
| Limited Partners (LPs) | ●●● Primary | ●○○ Possible | ●●○ Strong secondary | ●○○ Possible |
| General Partners (GPs) | ●●○ Strong secondary | ●●○ Strong secondary | ●●● Primary | ●●○ Strong secondary |
| Private Equity Firms | ●●● Primary | ●○○ Possible | ●●○ Strong secondary | ●○○ Possible |
| High Net Worth Individuals (HNWIs) | ●●○ Strong secondary | ●●● Primary | ●●○ Strong secondary | ●●○ Strong secondary |
| Family Offices | ●●○ Strong secondary | ●●○ Strong secondary | ●●● Primary | ●●○ Strong secondary |
| Institutional Investors (pension funds, endowments, sovereign wealth funds) | ●●● Primary | ○○○ Rare | ●●○ Strong secondary | ●○○ Possible |
| Trusts & Foundations (European; faith-aligned) | ●○○ Possible | ●●○ Strong secondary | ●●○ Strong secondary | ●●● Primary |
| African Diaspora (remittance-to-investment) | ●●○ Strong secondary | ●●○ Strong secondary | ●●● Primary | ●●○ Strong secondary |

The diaspora is the only investor category that can authentically occupy all four types simultaneously — and the only one for whom "investing with Africa" is not a strategic posture but a lived reality.

Investors have to be focused. I get this. But the work that needs to be done to complete the Great Commission will require different types of investors partnering together — different deal structures, different incentives, different time horizons, all pointed at the same purpose. This requires an orchestrator: someone or some entity that can see the possible players, assemble the right combination of Planners, Planters, Pilgrims, and Platform-reformers for each situation, and hold the coalition together long enough for the compounding to begin. That orchestrator role is one of the least filled and most needed roles in faith-based investing in Africa today.

# 5. Faith-Based Africa Investment Thesis

Here is what I believe, stated plainly: Africa represents one of the most significant strategic opportunities for faith-based investors in the world today. Not because it needs rescuing. Not because the returns are concessionary and the conscience gets a workout. But because the gospel mandate — all three strands of it — points directly at this continent, and because capital deployed in alignment with that mandate can generate competitive financial returns *and* participate in something with an eternal dimension.

That is the thesis. Let me unpack what sits underneath it.

Capital is a tool of discipleship, stewardship, and service. It is not primarily a tool of wealth accumulation — though wealth creation is entirely consistent with the biblical mandate. The business world, when well ordered, contributes disciplines that ripple through the whole of society. A business is not just an economic unit. It is a household — *oikos* in Greek, which is also the root word for economics. Household management. When a business leader grasps that framing, the bottom line stops being the only line that matters.

Sustainable returns flow from properly ordered systems. This is not idealism — it is a practical observation from two decades of working with businesses across Africa and beyond. When you invest in a business that is part of a broken system, the system eventually pulls the business down with it. When you invest in a business that is actively repairing the system around it, you have something that compounds in more than one direction. Local businesses are the primary agents of transformation in any community — their reach extends to employees and their families, customers, suppliers, and service providers. A well-run business with a kingdom purpose is a discipleship engine. Pre-believers can be discipled too, so everyone inside the *oikos* of a business can be intentionally shaped.

Capital fills vacuums. That is not a metaphor — it is a description of what has been happening in Africa while much of the Western church has been debating whether commerce belongs in the mission conversation. The vacuum left by constricted kingdom thinking has been filled by capital that champion a very different cause. Islamic finance. Chinese infrastructure loans. Both are operating with a long-term vision for the continent. The question is whether faith-based capital will show up with equal seriousness, or whether it will continue to arrive in increments, apologetically, attached to aid conditions.

What does this mean in practice? Investments that prioritize enterprises addressing genuine societal needs — not handouts, but as Ed Silvoso says, "Good news to the poor is, 'You have a job.'" Businesses whose purpose extends beyond their own borders, into the community, into the systems around them. Faith-based ecosystems — Impact Networks — where businesses operate with scorecards that measure impact for today and for eternity. Patient, catalytic capital that builds ecosystems, not just individual companies. And yes, exits — there are times when a well-structured exit allows a business and its leaders to grow to the next level. Exits are not the enemy: exits designed to extract rather than release are.

What are we investing toward? Financial returns should testify to the investability of Africans and Africa. Relationships across the body of Christ go deeper than charity and donor-recipient dynamics.

Transformed towns, cities, and nations — not as a side effect, but as a stated objective. Resilient local economies. Institutions that strengthen over time. And ultimately, Africa becoming a sending continent — exporting faith-based entrepreneurship, bringing inspired innovations to market and deploying righteous capital to the rest of the world. That is not a distant dream. The trajectory is already visible in the founders and builders we will look at later in this book.

> *"Anti-capitalist intellectuals, both in Africa and abroad, endlessly repeat a victimhood narrative about Africa being poor due to slavery, colonialism, and ongoing exploitation. Yes, Africa has been victimized. But until and unless these same intellectual forces articulate and endorse the positive capitalist path forward—which will let us leave that past behind—they are part of the problem, not part of the solution. They are the bad guys."*
> *– Magatte Wade*[9]

She is right. And the corollary is equally true: faith-based investors who bring capital without a transformational framework, or who bring a transformational framework without capital, are also part of the problem. The thesis demands both.

## Good work is Good

Before capital can do its work in Africa, there is a more foundational question to settle: what do we believe about work itself?

This matters more than it might seem. In some parts of Africa, centuries of tribalism, colonialism, aid dependency, and the broken promises of

---

[9] The Heart of a Cheetah: How we have been lied to about African Poverty, and What that means for Human Flourishing, Magatte Wade

liberation movements have left a complicated relationship with work — entitlement in some quarters, exhaustion in others, and a persistent suspicion that the system is rigged against honest effort. Biblical principles around capital and investing only take root where there is a biblical view of work. And that view is more radical than most Sunday sermons suggest.

Work pre-dated the Fall. It was not a punishment handed down after Eden — it was the original mandate. God worked, called it good, and invited humanity into the same creative enterprise. Adam and Eve received a joint commission: work the earth, tend it, bring God's design and purposes to the planet. The pattern of heaven on earth was to be expressed through human hands. Work, in this framing, is not a necessary evil or a means to an end. It is worship. It is one of the primary ways human beings reveal the character and nature of God to the world around them.

Business, then, is not a secular category that faith occasionally visits. It is God's construct — "a fundamental structure of love in the Kingdom of God" as one theologian put it — whereby people serve each other, create value for each other, and build the conditions for communities to flourish. It is not the primary purpose of business to make money. Money is a consequence of business done well, not its reason for being. And when the ways God works are integrated into the processes of a business — its governance, its culture, its relationships, its decisions — that business becomes an effective instrument of discipleship. Not despite its commercial nature, but because of it.

This is the theological ground beneath the investment thesis. If it sounds unfamiliar, that is partly because we have spent generations separating Sunday from Monday and then wondering why our businesses don't feel like callings and our callings don't generate sustainable returns.

There is a second challenge worth naming. Investments — even by followers of Jesus — are sometimes more aligned to the economic policies and interests of the investor's home government than they are to kingdom economics. Capital often fosters the bidding a so-called first-world government rather than to the King of the Universe. It may then produce development statistics that look good in a report and cause damage on the ground that takes decades to undo. Discernment here is not optional. The faith-friendly language wrapped around an agenda does not change the agenda.

# 6. What about Risk?

## What About Risk?

Before we catalogue the risks of investing in Africa — and there are real ones — let's ask a prior question. How much of what we call "Africa risk" is actually the risk of applying a Western template to a non-Western context?

On March 24, 2026, African Merchant Capital published a piece titled *The Billion-Dollar Blind Spot: Why Standard Due Diligence Fails in African Financial Services.* Their argument was direct: the investors who will succeed in Africa are those who invest as much rigor in understanding the market as they do in modeling the deal. The developed-market overlay — the assumption that what works in London or New York works in Lagos or Nairobi — is not neutral. It is a source of risk in itself.

This is a worldview problem before it is a financial problem.

## Worldview Informs Risk

I have a friend with a master's degree in engineering who is building houses in India. He gives instructions to the foreman, who explains them in Tamil to the workers. They then do whatever they want to do. They hear the words, but they do not have the cultural, business, or technical framework by which to interpret them.

You could hand the same set of building plans to contractors in five different countries and end up with structures that look identical but perform radically differently in an earthquake. The skill sets vary. The building codes differ. Local knowledge causes adaptations — sometimes good, sometimes not. The weights and measures may not be equivalent. And the foundations — the underpinnings not visible to the naked eye — are different in each place. When I lived in earthquake-prone Northern California on a steep hillside, the pylons went eighteen feet or more into the ground. That is what made the house stable. You could not see them, but take them away and the house slides down the slope.

The same principle applies in finance — and even more so, because the products are less tangible. A Chinese banker reading an American banking code book will interpret that code through a Communist or Confucian grid. The outcome will not be the same as someone considering it through a Judeo-Christian framework. Likewise, a Christian who flies from Chicago with a Shari'ah banking handbook to do financing in Pakistan will not interpret that handbook the way her Muslim counterpart does. Same words. Different foundations. Different outcomes under pressure.

Darrow Miller defines worldview plainly: "A set of assumptions held consciously or unconsciously in faith about the basic makeup of the world and how the world works." That is the operating definition I work from and it has practical teeth.

I sat once with three businesspeople in India who were explaining to me why they did not need to do business planning. "Indians are so smart," they said, "we do not need to plan." I spent a night thinking about it and came back to them the next morning. "I want to suggest," I said, "that the three of you are Christian in your religion but Hindu in your worldview. You don't want to plan because your worldview is one of fatalism, not faith." One of them — a formerly devout Hindu — sat with that for a moment and said, "You are correct. There is a Hindu saying, 'whatever will happen, will happen.' And many Christians have it on the walls of their offices."

Worldview is not something you leave at the border. Every investor brings one into every market they enter. The question is whether they are cognizant of it.

What does this mean for investing in Africa? Before you assess the financial risk, assess the worldview gap — yours and theirs. Africa is not a single worldview, of course. It is tribally and culturally diverse in ways that colonial borders largely ignored and that Western due diligence frameworks still routinely underestimate. In some African nations, such as Rwanda and Mauritius, tribal identity has been deliberately subordinated to national identity — with measurable consequences for social cohesion and, by extension, for investment risk. In others, tribal, linguistic, and cultural identity is front and center, shaping everything from hiring decisions to contract enforcement to who gets paid first when cash is tight.

Diversity influences risk. The relationship, however, is not straightforward.

## Friction and Resilience

Some diversity is a strength — track the teams in the book of Acts and you find people from many nations traveling together, each bringing something the others lacked. But diversity is not automatically an asset. Whether it becomes friction or resilience depends on one thing: whether a country has built what I would call a trust architecture — shared language, functioning institutions, a common identity, and mechanisms for resolving disputes when they arise.

Rwanda is the clearest example I know. The genocide that tore the country apart in 1994 was, at its core, a catastrophic failure of trust architecture — tribal identity weaponized in the absence of anything larger holding people together. Rwanda's response was deliberate and radical: it is now effectively taboo to identify publicly by tribe. When we traveled there recently and asked people about their background, the answer was simply "Rwandan." That is not naivety. That is a nation that paid the full price for unmanaged diversity and decided never to pay it again. Mauritius has done something similar — ask anyone about their heritage and they will tell you they are Mauritian, even if their family came from India, France, or another part of Africa.

This is not true across the continent. In many African nations, tribal, linguistic, and cultural identity is front and center. It shapes hiring decisions, contract enforcement, political allegiances, and the flow of money when things get tight. The investor who does not understand this is not managing Africa risk. They are walking into it blindfolded.

When you overlay ethnic diversity against trust architecture, four zones emerge. (Warning: I will mention countries in each zone, but these are illustrative. A detailed country by country zone mapping is expanded on in the website.)

**Friction Zones** — high ethnic diversity, low trust architecture. Nigeria, DRC, Chad, Cameroon. Ethnicized politics, localized trust networks, high corruption risk, difficult scaling. This does not mean do not invest here — it means your strategy must be partner-first, your leadership must be deliberately multi-ethnic, and your relational costs will be higher than your model expects.

**Resilience Zones** — high ethnic diversity, high trust architecture. Tanzania is the gold standard. Swahili as a shared national language, strong national identity, distributed trust. Platform investments and replicable models work here. Scaling is genuinely possible.

**Transition Zones** — moderate diversity, low trust architecture. Ethiopia, Uganda. Strong identities, uneven cohesion, periodic instability. Region-specific strategies are essential. Align with the cultural power structures that actually operate on the ground, not the ones on the org chart.

**Opportunity Zones** — moderate diversity, high trust architecture. Kenya is the leading example. English and Swahili as bridging languages, a strong private sector, functional institutions. This is where you find your entry-point markets, your innovation hubs, your most scalable ventures.

These are generalizations, and Africa will always exceed its generalizations in both directions. But the framework gives you a starting point that is more useful than "Africa is risky" — which tells you nothing — or "Africa is opportunity" — which tells you almost as little.

Now here is the insight that does not appear in any standard due diligence framework: in high-diversity environments, churches often function as the missing trust architecture. A healthy, multi-ethnic local church extends trust across lines that nothing else in the society crosses. It is no accident that Jesus prayed in John 17 that his followers would be one — the unity of the church has economic consequences, not just spiritual ones. Where different groups within the body of Christ share a vision larger than their own subculture or denomination, it produces exactly the conditions that turn diversity into resilience rather than friction.

This is not theoretical. Over the last two decades a network of faith-based marketplace organizations has emerged across Africa that is quietly functioning as a trust infrastructure for investors who know how to engage it. Groups like Apostles in the Marketplace in Nigeria, Sinapis in Kenya, GoStrategic operating across multiple countries, Faith Driven Entrepreneur with its growing Africa focus, Ziwani — born in Africa and equipping the Christian business community continent-wide — and The Institute's own Repurposing Business program which has worked with hundreds of mid-market companies since 2003. The Kingdom Summit which Ben Akabueze and I established as an annual gathering of marketplace leaders in Nigeria is another node in this network.

None of these organizations was designed primarily as a risk-mitigation tool for investors, but that is partly what they are. They carry relationships across ethnic lines, embed local knowledge, form identity, and build the kind of trust that scales in diverse environments.

The table below maps how these different entities compare as trust-builders.

| Factor | NGOs | Investors | Churches | Marketplace Movements |
|---|---|---|---|---|
| Cross-ethnic trust | Medium | Low | **Medium** | **Highest** |
| Local embeddedness | Medium | Low | **High** | **Medium** |
| Identity formation | Low | Low | **High** | **High** |
| Scalability in diversity | Medium | Medium | **High** | **Highest** |

> *Diversity is a defining feature of Africa. Albeit not without its complications, it remains one of Africa's greatest strengths, and in its own unique way defines the region's identity. Africa's ethnic variety adds to a diverse cultural environment, with each group adding to the continent's vitality via varied modes of expression.*[10]

So, knowing there is a high probability of diversity in many African nations, let us get back to considering friction and resilience and how it maps to ethnic diversity. The table below lays out four zones: two have low-trust architectures and two have high-trust architectures. Two zones have high ethnic diversity, and two have moderate ethnic diversity. This gives rise to four zones with Edge Cases where there is a mix.

---

[10] https://africa.businessinsider.com/local/lifestyle/top-10-most-ethnically-diverse-countries-in-africa/5neyyfd

| | LOW TRUST ARCHITECTURE (Fragmented identity, weak institutions) | HIGH TRUST ARCHITECTURE (Shared language, strong identity, mediating institutions) |
|---|---|---|
| HIGH ETHNIC DIVERSITY | FRICTION ZONES **Characteristics:** - Ethnicized politics- Localized trust networks- High corruption risk- Difficult scaling **Implications:** - Partner-first strategy- multi-ethnic leadership essential- High relational cost | RESILIENCE ZONES **Characteristics:** - Shared national language (e.g., Swahili)- Strong national identity- Distributed trust- Scalable models **Implications:** - Platform investments- Replicable NGO/church models- Lower friction scaling |
| MODERATE ETHNIC DIVERSITY | TRANSITION ZONES **Characteristics:** - Strong identities, uneven cohesion- Periodic instability **Implications:** - Region-specific strategies- Align with cultural power structures | OPPORTUNITY ZONES **Characteristics:** - Bridging languages (English/Swahili)- Strong private sector- Functional institutions **Implications:** - Entry-point markets- Scalable ventures- Innovation hubs |

The point is not that faith-based networks eliminate risk. The point is that the faith-based investor who is genuinely embedded in these networks — not visiting them on a vision trip but known and knowing within them — is operating with a materially different risk profile than the investor who is not. There is the caveat, of course, that these networks do not become new fiefdoms.

Ethnic diversity is not the risk. Unmanaged diversity is the risk. Well-governed diversity is one of Africa's greatest assets. The investor who grasps that distinction is already ahead of most of the field.

## Real Risks

Before we look at how to reframe risk through an African lens, let us be clear about what the real risks are. Some readers will note that these are not unique to Africa — and they are right. But since this is the book we are writing, we should face them directly.

**Exchange control risk** is one of the first things an outside investor encounters. In practice it shows up as administrative delays, parallel market premiums, or outright inability to repatriate capital in hard currency. It is not always dramatic. It is often just slow and expensive enough to erode returns that looked reasonable on the model.

**OFAC compliance** catches investors who did not see it coming. The Office of Foreign Assets Control sits inside the US Treasury, and because most international transactions pass through US correspondent banks at some point, OFAC is effectively a checkpoint on much of the world's dollar-denominated commerce. Blocked transactions, reputational exposure, and increased due diligence costs are real consequences for investors who have not mapped this in advance.

**Beneficial ownership disclosure** is a double-edged sword. It helps investors understand who they are actually dealing with — which in Africa, where ownership structures can be layered through family trusts and political relationships, is not always obvious. The problem is that only about half of African countries currently require beneficial ownership disclosure. The absence of the requirement does not mean the ownership is clean. It means you have to work harder to find out.

**Government corruption** is documented and measurable. Sub-Saharan Africa scores the lowest of any global region on the 2025 Corruption Perceptions Index — an average of 32 out of 100. The practical effect is not always the dramatic bribe at the border. More often it is sand in the wheels: delayed approvals, disappeared licenses, unexpected fees at every stage of a process that should be straightforward. Budget for delays.

**Bank corruption** is less documented but I have observed it consistently over twenty years. Major banks are supposed to have clean reputations, and many do. But I have watched institutional behavior that amounts to the same thing as corruption — the refusal to release funds that must legally flow through a bank but that same bank has every incentive to hold the funds as long as possible. When large dollar values sit in an account subject to exchange controls, the incentive structure is not always aligned with the investor's interests.

**Worldview risk** deserves its own category and its own name. A friend of mine completed a large mining engineering project in a central African country for the government mining company. Getting paid took years — that much was expected and budgeted for. What he did not anticipate was the number of friends and family of his local director who, culturally, had to be taken care of because they had been faithful to the cause during the waiting period. Both directors were African. Both are followers of Jesus. But their worldviews about how obligations work — who is owed what, and by whom — were genuinely different. You can call it cultural risk or execution risk if you prefer. I call it worldview risk because that is what it is.

**Human capital risk** is relationship risk in a different register. Africa is, broadly, a relationship-based business culture. In larger corporates there is sometimes institutional knowledge that survives personnel changes. In many situations, the knowledge and the relationships are held by one or two key people — and when they leave, they take both with them.

**Execution risk** is simply the gap between the timeline your model assumes and the timeline Africa operates on. There is no Home Depot down the road. Improvisation and workarounds are normal, not exceptional. A three-year return of capital in the United States may well be five years in Africa, not because of corruption or incompetence, but because the supply chains, the infrastructure, and the regulatory processes were not necessarily built for speed.

**Religious risk** is real and underreported. Many Africans have learned to speak Christianese fluently. Investors on vision trips hear the language and assume the worldview. The stories they are told are often not untrue — they are simply not complete. Discernment is required. It is what it sounds like: knowing the difference between someone who is building in God's economy and someone who has learned to present in those terms because that is what the capital provider requires.

**Wineskin risk** — or operating model risk — is partly the gap between what a business looks like on Sunday and how it actually operates on Monday. The two can be further apart than any financial model will reveal. It is also a different modus operandi or way of doing business. The heart quotient may be there; the organizational quotient may not look Western.

## Perceived Risks: Americano vs Africano

When we first started taking teams of professionals to work with mid-market companies in South Africa in 2003 we carried large bags of our own coffee because, in our view, we could not find anything worth drinking in Cape Town. Today, South Africa and several other countries on the continent have a world-class coffee culture. Truth Coffee Roasting in Cape Town was voted the world's best coffee shop by multiple publications in the mid-2010s. Cape Town did not have bad coffee because it lacked the beans, the climate, or the skill. It had bad coffee because the market had not yet organized itself around what was possible.

On a recent trip I noticed some establishments no longer offering Americanos — only Africanos. Same product, different frame. Tongue in cheek, of course. But the reframe is the point.

Most Western investors bring an Americano grid to Africa. They measure risk against benchmarks developed in contexts where infrastructure is reliable, institutions are functional, timelines are predictable, and the rule of law operates roughly as advertised. Applied to Africa, that grid produces a risk assessment that is simultaneously too high in some dimensions and too low in others. It overstates some risks and misses others entirely.

| Americano says... | Africano says... |
|---|---|
| You don't have any outside investors; who believes in you? | I don't have any debt; I have proven it myself |
| This has no appeal in the international market. | I serve the African market, and it is big enough to get good returns |
| How quickly can you exit? | I am here to stay; I want to grow, not exit |
| Could this be a unicorn? | We have enough real animals in Africa to not depend on fake ones. |

| Americano says... | Africano says... |
|---|---|
| Your team needs the Big 3: CEO, CPO, CMO | We have the Big 5 and a set of competencies in a plural leadership structure with shared power. |
| Do these three key leaders have a track record? Have they raised capital and exited before? | I have potential leaders who will do well when given the opportunity. I have a faith-based trust network to support them. |
| How can you scale quickly? | How can I build permanently? |
| You need an independent board. | I need good governance including a network of relationships, connections |
| Investors are the key stakeholder and must be taken care of first. | I have a complex community that benefits if I do well, and this included investors |

Ryno Abrie is a serial entrepreneur who took his South African business to Texas looking for funding. His account of what happened is in the case studies on the website, but one line stays with me. He said: "The irony is that nothing about our business changed between Johannesburg and Austin. Only my understanding did."[11]

What he understood, on the other side of that trip, was this: what a founder calls commitment, an investor may read as overexposure. What a founder calls maturity, an investor may interpret as inflexibility. What a founder labels efficiency, an investor may see as fragility. Learning to translate your reality into an investable signal is not about changing who you are. It is about knowing which grid the person across the table is using — and being able to speak it without losing yourself in it.

The Africano grid works in the opposite direction too. The faith-based investor coming into Africa needs to be able to read what they are

[11] Check out Ryno's story on the website.

seeing through an African lens, not just translate Africa into Western terms. That is the work. And it is worth doing.

## Unpacking Challenges in Africa

Africa is both informal and startup-like in its economies, yet the regulatory burden in many countries exceeds what you would find in developed markets. That combination — loose structures, heavy rules — creates exactly the conditions where corruption flourishes. Magatte Wade puts it plainly: "Corruption is a natural consequence of too many senseless laws — laws that keep us poor."

The antidote to over-regulation is not under-regulation: it is better regulation. Rule of law that is consistent, predictable, and applied equally is what settles investors. Several countries are working on economic free trade zones that offer investors a degree of protection from the broader regulatory environment. These are worth understanding but they are not a workaround for doing proper due diligence. They are a starting point for structuring investments that have a chance of actually working.

Africa is 54 countries, each with its own political system and business environment. The mental model that treats the continent as a single risk category inflates perceived risk in places where it is genuinely low and misses it entirely in places where it is genuinely high. The four-zone framework above is an attempt to correct that. Use it.

Younger investors are approaching Africa differently from their predecessors, and the difference is structural rather than superficial. Rather than starting with asset class and yield, they begin with purpose — what problem does this investment solve, and does it align with their values? This makes them naturally oriented toward fintech, agri-tech, education, healthcare, and climate resilience — sectors where social impact and financial return are woven together rather than traded off. They are comfortable with political and currency risk but have very little tolerance for corruption, greenwashing, or storytelling that does not hold up under scrutiny. They want transparency, genuine local partnership, and a deal structure that invites them into the work rather than extracting their capital from a distance.

More seasoned investors are pushing in the opposite direction — not away from patience, but toward permanent capital vehicles that match the gestation period of infrastructure-scale investments. The argument from Africa Merchant Capital is straightforward: the extended runway changes what is possible. An investment that looks marginal over a five-year horizon looks different over fifteen. Adapting capital structures to the rhythm of Africa is not a concession. It is a competitive advantage.

> *"...we believe there is a compelling case for the industry to consider Permanent Capital Vehicles (PCVs) as a strategic complement to existing approaches. This is not about replacing what already works for some, but about introducing more adaptable, patient forms of capital that align more closely with sector mandates and provide portfolio companies with the extended runway needed to unlock their full potential, enabling managers to maximise investor returns." Africa Merchant Capital Advisory*[12]

One practical note on scale: the larger the capital investment, the more visibility it attracts from government bodies. In many African contexts it is prudent to structure your asset management or treasury function outside the investee country, infusing capital against project milestones or invoices rather than in a single tranche. High visibility, full

---

[12] The Strategic Evolution of African Private Equity: Why Permanent Capital Investment Vehicles Deserves Greater Consideration, Africa Merchant Capital, Co-Authored by Milko Škoro and Estiaan van der Walt

transparency, and documented pre-approvals from relevant authorities are not optional extras for large investments. They are part of the architecture.

## Can Technology Reduce Risk?

“I see how to get my money into Africa, but can I get my money out of Africa?” This is the question I hear quite often from investors who are serious about Africa but haven't made an investment commitment yet.

It is a fair question. Some banking systems — not only in Africa — are designed to be opaque. Transactions get held. Fees are not disclosed. Funds sit in correspondent bank accounts longer than they should, earning returns for institutions that have no right to them. The layers of bureaucracy around capital remittances in some African countries compound the problem.

But here is what the same investors often miss: the inefficiencies of traditional banking systems have driven some of the most significant financial innovation on the planet, and much of it originated in Africa. Fundamo, a mobile payments company we worked with in Cape Town, was eventually acquired by Visa for over $100 million. M-Pesa didn't emerge despite Africa's banking gaps — it emerged because of them. The constraint produced the innovation. That pattern is continuing.

Blockchain technology is now being applied across multiple layers of the cross-border investment problem — remittances, B2B payments, SME liquidity, tokenized investments, diaspora capital flows. The core value is not the technology itself but what it enables: end-to-end visibility, tamper-proof transaction records, near-instant settlement, and fee structures that can reduce traditional corridor costs of 7-10 percent down to 1-3 percent or less. For investors moving capital in and out of African markets, these are not marginal improvements but structural changes to the risk profile.

The specific platforms and partnerships evolving in this space — from Nairobi to Cape Town to Lagos — are documented in the appendices and on the website where we can keep them current as the landscape continues to move. What matters here is the principle: technology is actively reducing the friction that makes "can I get my money out?" feel like the decisive question. It is becoming less decisive every year.

### When Africa invests in Africa, risks reduce

There is a dimension of risk reduction that has nothing to do with technology and everything to do with ownership. When Africans with capital invest in Africa, several layers of risk recede simultaneously. The exchange control exposure is different. The worldview gap narrows. The relationships are already in place. The accountability structures are different when the investor is also a neighbor.

South African non-financial companies held R1.8 trillion in bank deposits as of mid-2025, and the number has not been decreasing. Some of that is understandable caution in an uncertain political environment. But it also represents an enormous pool of capital sitting on the sidelines of the continent's development. The question of what it would take to move that capital into productive deployment on the continent — through less red tape, better incentives, reduced political interference, stronger infrastructure — is one of the most important investment questions in Africa right now. It is also one that faith-based investors from outside the continent are well-positioned to help answer by building the kind of partnerships with African capital that turn outside investment into genuine co-investment rather than extraction with better branding.

## A Visual View of African Risk: Zones

Africa is not one market. It is four distinct operating environments, shaped not by geography alone but by the relationship between diversity and trust. The map below plots these zones visually — Friction, Transition, Opportunity, and Resilience — across the continent.

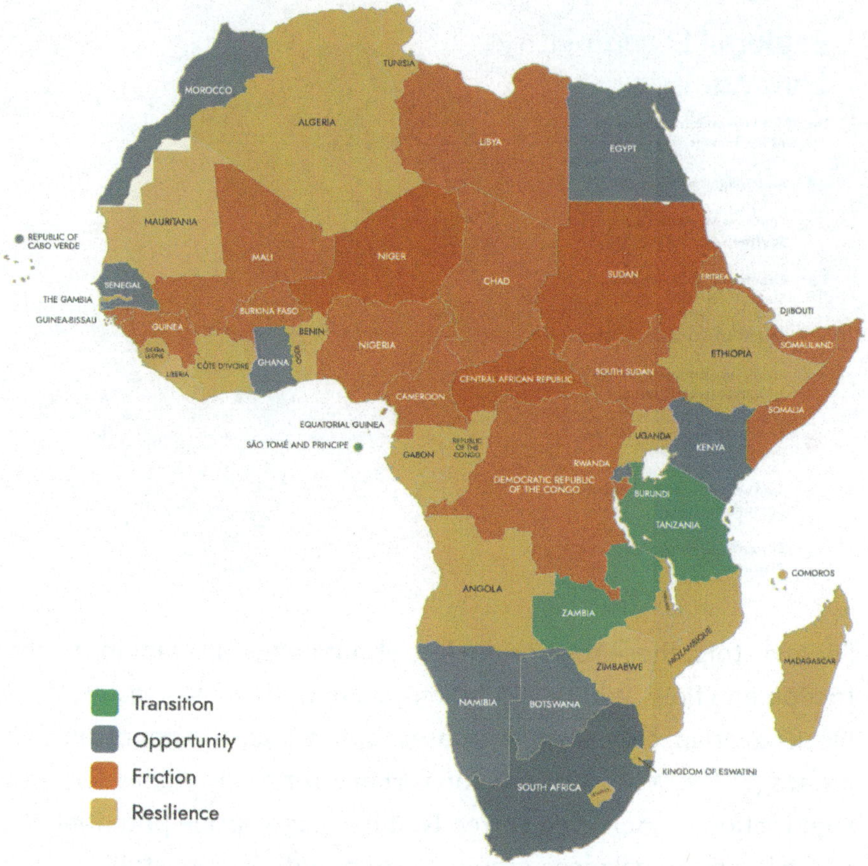


The full zone classifications, country-by-country analysis, and edge case breakdowns are in the appendix — see the Africa Master Zone Classification Table. The classifications are fluid and will be updated on the website as conditions shift. What the map gives you here is the orientation. The appendix gives you the working detail.

## A Visual View of African Risk: Regions

In Africa one will hear the language of Regional Economic Communities (RECs) that operate under the label of the African Union. From an investor perspective, the African Continental Free Trade Area (AfCFTA) sits above all of these areas.

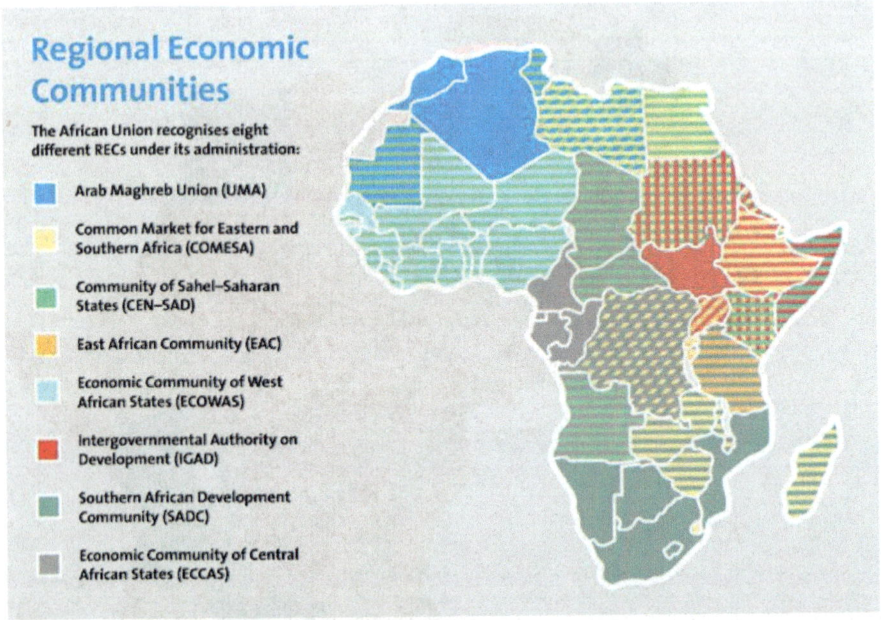


For investors, these regions are less about geography and more about friction and flow. Where regulations align, trade moves faster. Where blocks overlap, complexity increases, but so does the opportunity for arbitrage. The West Africa region is characterized by high energy and high friction. Understood correctly, it has huge upside potential. East Africa is a more balanced growth corridor with a more stable trajectory for the next 20 years. Southern Africa (SADC) generally has structural stability, but stability can shift at any time. More recently, Botswana and other African nations have been at odds with South Africa due to xenophobia. From an investor perspective, these flare-ups tend to be more political than economic. North Africa has relatively good cohesion but is not that well integrated with the rest of Africa. When I was working with a Chamber of Commerce in Casablanca they told me, "we have our roots in Africa and our branches in Europe."

North Africa is one of those areas where we need to be sensitive to the underlying worldview. When in Egypt in 2010 and 2012, we had a weekend retreat in the region where the Desert Fathers originated. This group of marketplace leaders often paid a price for being willing to be active Christians in a Muslim nation, so they were not lukewarm or half-hearted about their pursuit of God and business. To the contrary. What I did notice, however, was the impact of living in a society where, for whatever reason, business and entrepreneurship might be viewed as suspect by the Church. Happily, younger generations seem to have shaken this baggage.

## Investing Strategies by Zone

"If I want to start investing in Africa, where do I begin?" The four-zone framework is useful precisely because different actors belong in different zones — at least at the outset. The table below maps where each type of investor or organization should start, where they should move next, and where they can ultimately build a platform.

| | START | MOVE TO | PLATFORM IN |
|---|---|---|---|
| Kingdom Business | Start in Transition | Scale in Opportunity | Platform in Resilience |
| Investors | Start in Opportunity | Expand to Resilience | Partner in others |
| NGOs | Opportunities in Friction | Scale out in Resilience | |
| Churches | Lead in Friction | Elevate to Transition | |

The logic is straightforward. Conventional investors gravitate toward Opportunity Zones first because the infrastructure, institutions, and risk profile are closest to what their models assume. Churches and NGOs often find their most effective work in Friction Zones precisely because state weakness creates space for relational institutions to function as the missing trust architecture. Kingdom Business sits between those two — starting where there is enough brokenness to create meaningful impact, but enough stability to actually operate.

## Product-Zone Fit

When Lyn and I first visited Nigeria, we were struck by the sheer number of people selling things at the side of the road. Cell phone covers, washing powder, furniture, brooms, candy, snacks — if you were brave enough to eat them. When we asked our hosts about it, they told us that over fifty percent of all sales in Nigeria were informal, side-of-the-road transactions. We were genuinely puzzled. How could this be?

The answer, of course, is that the formal economy had never been built for the majority of Nigerians — so the majority of Nigerians built something else. They did not lack entrepreneurial instinct or commercial sophistication. Because the institutions, the supply chains, the credit systems, and the regulatory frameworks that formal commerce depends on had either never arrived or had arrived and then broken down. What filled the vacuum was something deeply relational, deeply decentralized, and deeply community-embedded. This something worked precisely because it did not require the infrastructure that was absent.

That observation points to a second axis in the zone framework that investor sequencing alone does not capture. Different product and business model types have structural affinities for different zones — independent of where an investor chooses to start or how long they have been operating in a particular context.

In Friction Zones, the business models that perform best are the ones that mirror what Lyn and I saw on those Lagos roadsides — relational, decentralized, community-embedded. A community micro-franchise network, a cooperative agriculture model, a vocational employment business built around multi-ethnic teams — these thrive precisely because the zone's conditions favor them. The absence of formal institutional infrastructure, the density of relational trust networks, and the community embeddedness that characterizes Friction Zones are not obstacles to these models. They are the conditions that make them work. A micro-franchise in the DRC does not succeed despite the friction. It succeeds because of it.

Businesses that require scale — standardized supply chains, institutional customers, regulatory predictability, and the kind of operational consistency that depends on functioning systems — will struggle in Friction Zones regardless of how patient or relationally sophisticated the investor is. The zone does not become more hospitable to scale-dependent models simply because the investor is well-connected or long-tenured. The structural mismatch is real and it compounds over time rather than resolving.

In Opportunity and Resilience Zones the relationship inverts. Scale-dependent businesses — fintech platforms, logistics networks, healthcare systems, education technology — find the conditions they need: functional institutions, talent pools, regulatory frameworks, and the kind of operational predictability that allows standardized models to replicate. Relational micro-models still work in these zones, but they are no longer the only viable entry point. The roadside economy still exists in Nairobi and Kigali — but it coexists with M-Pesa, with formal retail, with institutional supply chains. The zone has more options, and the investor's job is to match the model to the moment.

The practical implication is that due diligence in any zone should include a product-zone fit assessment alongside the investor sequencing question. The right zone for your capital and the right zone for your business model are related but not identical questions. Getting both right simultaneously is the goal. Getting only one right is a common and expensive mistake — and one that no amount of relational investment will fully correct if the structural mismatch is fundamental enough.

South Africa offers a vivid illustration of how this works over time. During Apartheid, city buses were segregated — white passengers at the front, black passengers at the back. When people of color boycotted the bus service, an informal taxi network emerged in response: Toyota Quantum vans, designed to carry ten passengers, packed to the roof with commuters circumnavigating a system that had excluded them. That informal solution — born entirely from friction, built entirely without institutional support — has since become one of South Africa's most established transport industries. The minibus taxi sector now moves millions of people daily across the country. It did not wait for the formal economy to include it. It built its own infrastructure and then became the infrastructure. That is what product-zone fit looks like when it is right — and it is a pattern worth understanding before you decide which business model belongs in which zone.

## Kingdom Business Strategy by Zone

Investors may follow the journey of a Kingdom Business across these zones. It is not random. Start where you can build trust, scale where trust already exists, embed carefully where trust has to be constructed almost entirely from scratch, and platform where the conditions allow what you have built to compound and replicate.

**Start in Transition Zones.** Business opportunities cluster where problems are not yet solved and where multinational firms have not yet arrived with capital and complexity that crowds out smaller entrants. A transition zone — Uganda, Ethiopia, Liberia, Senegal — offers enough stability to operate and enough brokenness to make your work matter. Employment-creating SMEs, agriculture value chains, healthcare and education enterprises, clean water and energy businesses — these are the sectors that reward integrity and long-term presence over short-term extraction. You are not just building a company in these environments. You are building culture. The two are inseparable.

My friend Amon Munyaneza has helped hundreds of people start businesses in Uganda. He identified pig farming as a rapid-growth entry point into the food security market. It is not glamorous. It is exactly right. He operates in a Transition Zone and understands what that requires — patience, relationships, and a willingness to stay long enough for trust to compound.

**Scale in Opportunity Zones.** Kenya is the leading example. Infrastructure that supports growth, talent pools that are real, regional scaling that is genuinely possible, and investors who are comfortable entering. This is where a Kingdom Business becomes proof of concept — not just that the model works in one location, but that purpose-driven business can outperform on financial metrics alongside impact metrics. If you can demonstrate that in an Opportunity Zone, you have something worth replicating.

**Embed carefully in Friction Zones.** Nigeria, DRC, Chad, Somalia, the Central African Republic. Do not start here unless you have deep local relationships already in place, you are partnering with churches or trusted networks, and you are genuinely prepared for slower growth and higher relational costs. What works in these environments is community-rooted — cooperative models, micro-franchise networks, vocational employment businesses that create multi-ethnic employment spaces and model reconciliation through the structure of the enterprise itself. The business is not separate from the ministry of trust. It is the ministry of trust.

Nigeria deserves its own sentence here because it defies easy categorization. Its dualistic economy — one segment genuinely world-class, the other still developing — makes it simultaneously a Friction Zone and a special Opportunity Zone. The optimism and intellect of Nigeria's upper-tier business community is, in my view, unparalleled on the continent. Plugging into existing marketplace networks like Apostles in the Marketplace offsets significant amounts of the low-trust dynamic. Nigeria rewards investors who are serious enough to do the relational work before deploying capital.

**Platform in Resilience Zones.** Tanzania, Zambia, Morocco, Egypt. Social cohesion that enables national scale. Lower relational friction.

Conditions where replication is genuinely possible. This is where you build the systems that outlast you — national supply chains, workforce development platforms, export-oriented businesses, multi-country expansion hubs. The Resilience Zone is not the starting point. It is what you build toward.

## Summary Deployment for Kingdom Businesses

By way of example, the deployment steps for a Kingdom Business across the zones could be:

| Step 1 | Step 2 | Step 3 | Step 4 |
|---|---|---|---|
| START IN | SCALE IN | EMBED IN | PLATFORM IN |
| **Build:**<br>• Culture<br>• Integrity<br>• Employment<br>• Trust | **Build:**<br>• Growth<br>• Efficiency<br>• Investor confidence<br>• Regional reach | **Bring:**<br>• Jobs<br>• Stability<br>• Cross-tribal collaboration<br>• Long-term trust | **Create:**<br>• National transformation<br>• Replicable models<br>• Training pipelines<br>• Multi-sector integration |

Rather than a one-dimensional approach where an investment goes in, generates a return, and then gets out, this mindset provides a path for growth for both the investor and the kingdom business. It hitches the investor and the business to a purpose that is bigger than just making money. It also challenges the investor and related businesses to grow beyond one organization to the systems in which that organization operates.

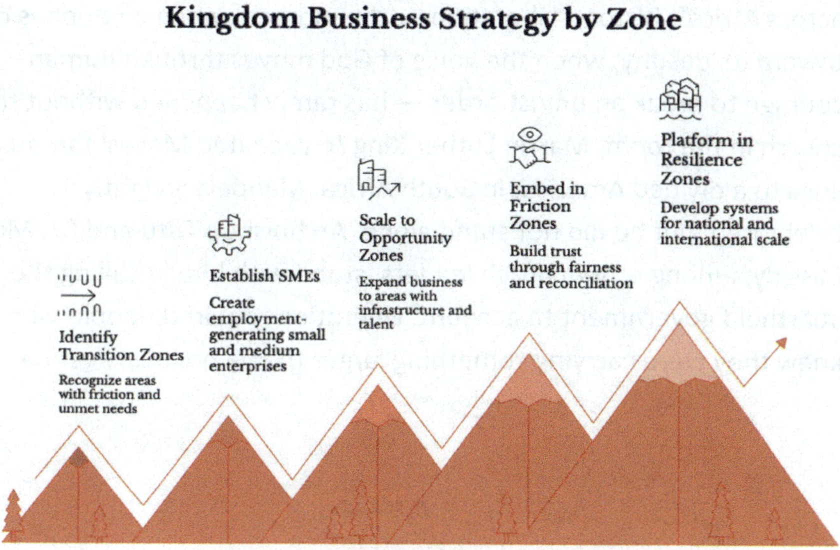


## Phases of Nationhood

Every nation is somewhere on a journey. In *Transforming Society* I identify the phases that nations move through — Defining, Disciplining, Liberating, Ordering, Self-Governing, and ultimately Transforming. They are not always sequential and they are rarely clean. But they are recognizable, and knowing where a nation sits on that arc changes how you invest in it.

God spoke identity and promise to Abraham, and a childless couple became a household. A household grew to a nation under the disciplining tutelage of the pharaohs. "Let my people go," and the liberating began. It took 40 more years of ordering, initially in the desert. God's goal was self-governance under a plural leadership-oriented theocracy. The idea was that individuals would know God and submit to his heart and ways. Israel opted for a king instead. They strayed. God used foreign nations to re-discipline them. This cycle repeated many times.

The church has played a decisive role in at least two of those phases across Africa's history. Liberation — the moment when a nation is called toward its destiny, when the voice of God moves through human courage to break an unjust order — has rarely happened without the church in the room. Martin Luther King Jr. repeated Moses' famous lines to a divided America. In South Africa, Mandela is rightly celebrated, but he did not stand alone. Archbishop Tutu and Dr. Michael Cassidy, among other church leaders, stood with him in calling the apartheid government to account. Liberation required people who knew they were carrying something larger than a political agenda.

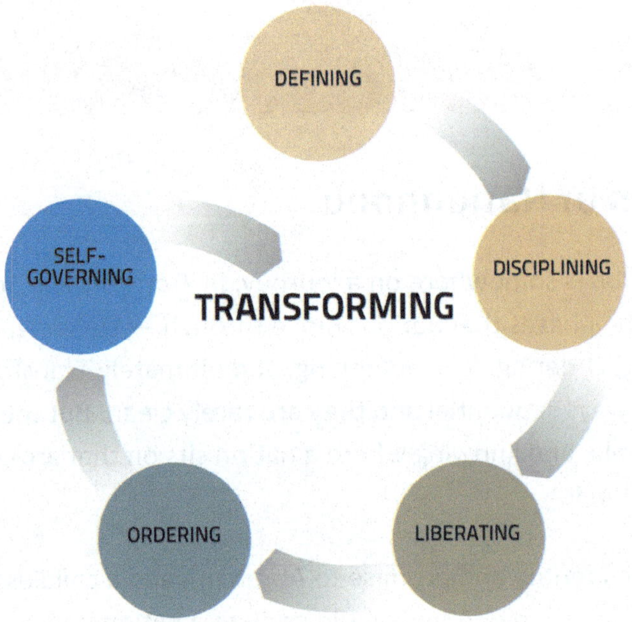


Ordering is the phase that follows Liberation and it is where the church's contribution could be the highest but is most often squandered. Paul told the Colossians he was rejoicing to see their "good order and the steadfastness of their faith in Christ" — he saw the two as inseparable. The book of Deuteronomy is essentially a manual for ordering a nation. A vibrant church builds personal identity and internal order in its people. But when a church has no vision beyond its own walls — no sense of responsibility for the city, the nation, the marketplace — the newly ordered people get pulled into service inside the institution rather than deployed into the world outside it. The church becomes a holding tank rather than a launching pad.

There is a warning embedded in this, and investors should hear it too. The cycle of national development can be broken. When a nation resists the ordering of God and throws off restraint, history suggests it cycles back to an earlier phase — sometimes at its own hands. Jerusalem has been attacked thirty-seven times. Nigeria's constitutional order succumbed to thirty cumulative years of military rule before democracy returned. Knowing where a nation sits in its development arc is useful. Knowing that the arc can reverse is essential.

The church that understands its role in this does not build an empire. It builds people. Pastors are drill sergeants, not emperors — their job is to get people ready for battle outside the four walls, not to consolidate influence inside them. Fortunately, a growing number of churches across Africa understand themselves as a steppingstone for marketplace people to do their best work in the world. That shift has direct implications for investors.

Which means the questions worth asking before you deploy capital are not only financial. They are also these: In what regions is God visibly on the move? Where is there a healthy, working relationship between local churches and marketplace leaders? Does the culture in this city or nation encourage people to carry their faith into their Monday work, or does it confine faith to Sunday? Is the church in this place sending people out, or drawing them in?

The answers will not appear on a term sheet. They belong in your due diligence, nonetheless.

# 7. Mechanisms to Optimize Investments

Risk and faith are two sides of the same coin. God is a risk taker. (I once had someone tell me that God is not a risk taker, and I suggested they go and look in the mirror.) If we eliminate risk, do we not eliminate the need for faith? The paradox is that we are cautioned in scripture to be prudent and wise and to not substitute faith with presumption. To me, "risk management" is a bit of an oxymoron, so I will settle for the phrase Optimizing Investments.

## World Class Biblical Governance

When you declare a business to be a kingdom business, you put a spiritual target on it. That is not a reason not to do it. It is a reason to take governance to a level that most investment frameworks never consider.

A governance structure that fuses biblical principles with world-class best practice is not a nice addition to a kingdom business. In a context like Africa — where the spiritual dimension of things is apparent on the surface, under the surface, and in the foundations — it is a survival requirement. I am not suggesting you put a pastor on your investment committee or an evangelist on your board, though neither of those is necessarily a bad idea provided they have the competence. What I am urging is a clear-eyed understanding of biblical governance principles, and in particular, plural leadership.

Much of Western leadership is built on hierarchical structures that have more in common with the industrial revolution than with the Old and New Testaments — or with Africa, for that matter. We have replaced biblical order with Deming, Drucker, and the org chart. We have titles like CEO, President, COO, and CFO, and we have relegated apostle, prophet, evangelist, and teacher to the realm of religion — as though these were spiritual decorations rather than functional offices with real organizational consequence. The disorder that results in many companies is a direct fruit of that dichotomy.

Here is the practical implication. If you have taken strategic counsel from someone gifted in wisdom, discernment, or prophetic insight and not compensated them because "that's their spiritual thing," you are most likely operating from a dichotomized worldview that is costing you more than you realize. Apostles and prophets have made companies millions and walked away unacknowledged. We then wonder why we lack the resources to complete our mandate.

I arrived at these convictions the hard way. At twenty-four I was a senior manager at Price Waterhouse in Cape Town and simultaneously leading a local church that had just come through a leadership crisis. To compound matters, I was consulting to mission organizations in Africa and traveling to Europe and Latin America to study best practices in missions. Managing three roles at once forced me to dig deep into biblical principles of leadership, the structure of local and trans-local churches, and the practical application of governance. What I found was that the most effective organizational structures — in business, in missions, and in the church — shared more in common than any of them were willing to admit.

Most churches would not recognize an apostle or prophet if they walked in with a sign around their neck. Businesses suffer from the same institutional blindness. Trans-local ministers — those who operate more broadly than the sphere of one local church or one company — are often the people with the clearest view of what is actually happening in an organization. If you have a smaller business, supplement your internal team with these voices from outside. Your board, if you have one, should include them.

The statistics of modern venture capital and private equity already tell the story of what happens without this kind of governance: a small number of winners, a large number of failures, and a structural assumption that this ratio is acceptable. It is not. It would not be acceptable in any other domain of life. ("I have five children, and only four of them are not making it." Never acceptable.)

So before you deploy capital — and before you accept capital as an investee — conduct a spiritual audit of the organizational structure. This is not a prayer meeting tacked onto a board meeting: it is a genuine assessment of how the key offices are represented, whether in-house or through outside relationships. One important caveat: if the person conducting the audit is not themselves a marketplace apostle, the result may be flawed. You do not send the wallpaper team to inspect the foundations. I am not advocating for a governance structure that requires people to carry the title of apostle or prophet. I am advocating for the discernment, the strategic wisdom, and the trans-local perspective that those gifts produce — whatever language you use to describe them in your context.

This may sound excessive to investors operating in a secular framework. In Africa, where business and the spiritual world are culturally less separated, it is simply realism. The discernment required to navigate governance, relationships, and authority structures in many African contexts is not merely human intelligence. It is a gift — and it should be treated as one.

## Offshore Treasury

Setting up an offshore treasury function is not about protecting yourself from your investee. It is about protecting the investment from entities that have developed an appetite for taking a piece of the action — sometimes government organizations, sometimes banks that have operated with impunity for so long that holding up the flow of capital has become a business model in itself. Financial services organizations have legitimate reasons to scrutinize unusual transactions. Profiting from the deliberate delay of large capital movements is another thing entirely.

There is a second reason that has nothing to do with external interference. Some investees — including well-intentioned ones — simply do not have the experience or the infrastructure to be accountable for large tranches of capital arriving at once. A friend of mine is a partner in a fund that invested in a business in the United Kingdom — a so-called Christian business with a compelling story. Once 80 percent of the agreed investment had been transferred, the CEO stopped returning calls. When investment agreements include proper governance and an out-of-country treasury capability with real teeth, that kind of situation becomes far harder to engineer — and the discipline it introduces tends to benefit the investee as much as the investor.

Over many years I have worked to establish entities in international jurisdictions that can provide exactly this function — offshore treasury combined with governance that enriches the experience of the investee and creates a meaningful, structured bridge for faith-driven investors from outside Africa to participate in what is happening on the continent.

What the offshore treasury structure does not protect you from is a sufficiently determined and creative counterparty. A CEO who came to one of our Executive Intensives was involved in trade finance in West Africa and asked me to look into a situation that had gone wrong. He had provided financing against commodities that were supposed to be moving from a warehouse to a European customer. The goods had not moved. His client — who presented as the head of a legitimate organization, had the backing of the state's governor, and had an independent inspector verifying the warehouse inventory — turned out to be running an elaborate fiction. A trusted advisor with genuine West Africa knowledge came back a week later with the full picture: the governor was corrupt, the warehouse contained a small fraction of the stated goods packed around lumber to create the appearance of volume, the inspector had been compromised, and the loan recipient had created a fake version of the legitimate organization specifically to run the transaction.

The structure was sophisticated. The relationships all looked right. The approvals were in place. None of it was real.

Trust. Verify. And build the relationships that give you access to the people who can tell you what is actually happening on the ground — before you wire the money, not after.

## Good Partnerships

Passion and shared purpose are not enough. I have watched partnerships form between people who genuinely love God, genuinely love Africa, and genuinely believe in what the other person is building — and still fail to meet expectations. Add a different continent, a different culture, and a different currency to the equation and the odds get worse, not better. Eighty-five percent of partnerships fail to meet expectations under normal conditions. Normal conditions are not what you are operating in.

That said, some of the most fruitful partnerships I have observed have formed in the least likely settings. At our annual Executive Intensive in Melkbosstrand just outside Cape Town, executives arrive from around the world carrying different competencies, different networks, and different pieces of a puzzle they have not yet fully seen. By the end of a week together, combinations emerge that none of them anticipated when they arrived. Shared purpose in a focused environment does something that a term sheet cannot.

But shared purpose still has to be tested. Before you make financial commitments to a potential partner — before the enthusiasm of a good conversation hardens into a legal agreement — conduct a Partnering Readiness Assessment. I know what you are thinking. (I can almost see your eyes glaze over as you contemplate a day-long workshop when you are a seasoned investor who already knows how to do this. Except that the statistics are against you.) The assessment is not designed to weed out unsuitable partners. It is a structured process — typically a day or two of working sessions — where you unpack expected outcomes, purpose, values, assets, and the many permutations for combining what each organization brings. When we use The 10-P Model® there are ninety-nine different ways two entities can team up to co-create impact. Most partnerships collapse because only a handful of those ninety-nine were ever examined.

I was asked by a company I was advising to conduct a Partnering Readiness Assessment with an organization that was proposing to bring a battery technology into a joint venture. The day went well. Toward the end of it we discovered, however, that the prospective partner had transferred the intellectual property crucial to the deal out of the target investment company into an offshore entity before the conversation had even begun. A day invested in a structured assessment saved my client a significant loss of capital and the far greater cost of trying to extricate themselves from a messy situation after the fact.

The right partner, properly assessed, is one of the most powerful risk-reduction tools available to a faith-based investor in Africa. The wrong partner, insufficiently examined, is how good capital disappears.

## Plural Leadership

I was at a function in Lagos celebrating a public holiday and my host said to me, "The king of Lagos is sitting behind you." My quick reply was, "I didn't know Lagos had a king." My friend quickly enlightened me: "Lagos has four kings."

Africa has kings, queens, princes, princesses, and chiefs in abundance. It also has, in the post-colonial era, a pronounced tendency toward strongman rule — near-patrimonial leadership with limited checks and balances, where institutional pluralism exists on paper while real authority concentrates in a small number of hands. This is not unique to Africa, but it is particularly pronounced there, and it has been reinforced rather than corrected by many of the governance structures that colonial powers left behind. The Ashanti, Buganda, Zulu, and Swazi kingdoms had hierarchical authority long before any European arrived. Post-colonial governments often inherited and amplified that hierarchy while stripping out the accountability structures that traditional leadership had built around it.

The investor who arrives in this context with a Western org chart and a CEO-at-the-top structure is not countering that tendency. They are reinforcing it with a different set of titles.

Kingdom culture must trump other cultures — and that includes both Ubuntu and Western capitalism wrapped in a Christian flag. Ubuntu has genuine wisdom in it, particularly around communal identity and mutual responsibility. It also has pitfalls that go unexamined when it is treated as automatically compatible with kingdom values. The question is not which cultural framework is superior. The question is which principles — drawn from Scripture, tested in practice, applied with humility — produce the outcomes that serve both investor and investee and honor God. Walking that line requires something more than good intentions. It requires a governance structure that models what it is asking of others.

Which means investment teams must embody plural leadership if they are to counter hierarchical organizations and winner-takes-all dynamics. In the LEMON Leadership Model I use five distinct leadership types: Luminary, Entrepreneur, Manager, Organizer, and Networker. A team that has all five represented — not just functional expertise, but genuine diversity of leadership wiring — is structurally different from a team built around a single dominant voice. It makes different decisions, catches different blind spots, and models a different culture to every investee it works with.

When investor and investee operate as one team — genuinely working together toward God's transcendent purposes rather than executing a transaction — the structure of the financing, the terms of the agreement, and the metrics of success all shift. They get shaped by the question of what produces a good return for all stakeholders, including God. That is not a soft aspiration. It is a design principle.

This is what it means to invest with Africa rather than in Africa or for Africa. The preposition is the whole argument.

## A Compelling "Why"

Purpose is the primary ingredient for innovation. It is also the primary driver of endurance — which matters more in Africa, where the timeline is longer, the friction is higher, and the moments that test your resolve will come earlier and more often than your model predicted.

Every investment has a why. The question is whether the why is large enough to hold when the circumstances get difficult. A why built around return on investment will not survive a currency devaluation, a governance crisis, or a partner who stops returning calls. A why built around the purposes of God — around what it looks like for a city or an industry or a nation to be ordered according to his heart — has a different tensile strength. It does not make the currency devaluation disappear. It changes what you do next.

This is why the "so that" in a purpose statement matters so much — not just what you are building, but what the building is for. It is not just the business plan, but the reason the business exists beyond its own survival and growth. When that "so that" is clear, compelling, and genuinely shared between investor and investee, it shapes everything downstream — how you structure governance, how you select partners, how you define success, how you handle the moments when the return is slower than the model said it would be.

Operating as stewards under the leadership of King Jesus is not a posture adopted for the pitch deck and abandoned in the board meeting: it is a working assumption that changes the texture of every decision. When both investor and investee carry it — when it is not one party's conviction being tolerated by the other — it produces something that neither could have built alone. It produces mutual discipleship. And mutual discipleship, over time, produces the kind of trust that no due diligence process can manufacture.

That is the prize that is bigger than ROI. It is also, in our upside-down kingdom, what makes the ROI more likely.

## Rethinking "Exits"

Some years ago I had a conversation with Chris Maclellan, who manages the impact investing side of the Maclellan Foundation. He made an observation that has stayed with me. When entrepreneurs placed a business plan in front of him for funding, the deal terms were structurally identical to what you would find in a secular transaction. Moments after someone had declared that they were called to do this business — that this was not merely a career but a vocation — the conversation turned to how and when they would exit from that calling. The term sheet put a wedge between the entrepreneur's calling, career, community, and creativity before the ink was dry.

In my book *Convergence* I make the case that these four elements — calling, career, community, creativity — are designed to operate together, not to be separated by the mechanics of a transaction. When a term sheet is structured to force either a sale or an exit on a predetermined timeline, it is worth asking whose agenda this serves. Jesus said: "The thief comes to steal, kill and destroy, but I have come that you might have life in abundance." When the terms of an investment structurally compel an outcome that severs a founder from their calling, their community, and the work God assigned them — are we not, however unintentionally, inking-in steal, kill and destroy?

That is a confronting question. It deserves a confronting answer rather than a polite qualification.

The standard venture capital and private equity exit model — up or out, five to seven years, return capital and move on — was designed for a specific context. It assumes that the founder's attachment to the business is a sentimental obstacle to value maximization rather than a sign that the business is embedded in relationships and community in ways that generate value the cap table cannot capture. It assumes that consolidation and buyout produce better outcomes than continuity and compounding. In many Western markets, in many sectors, that assumption has been tested enough to have some evidence behind it. In Africa, applied to kingdom businesses with long gestation periods and deep relational roots, it is frequently wrong.

I understand that investors need liquidity. Capital that gets permanently locked into a single company stops doing what capital is supposed to do — flow! The question is not whether investors should ever exit. The question is whether the exit structure assumed in a standard term sheet is the only way to create liquidity — and whether, in the kingdom business context, it is even the right starting point.

There are better questions to begin with. What does a return look like that honors both the investor's need for liquidity and the founder's calling and community? What structures allow capital to be recycled without severing the founder from the work? What would a term sheet look like if it was designed around the principle of life in abundance rather than the mechanics of extraction?

These are not ethereal questions. They are the design brief for a different kind of investing — one that produces fewer conglomerates built through forced consolidation and more mid-sized businesses with deep roots, strong cultures, and the kind of compounding impact that a five-year exit timeline will never capture.

The investors who figure this out will not just do well in Africa. They will build something worth pointing at.

# 8. Africa Investment Applications

Where would God invest in Africa?

It is a legitimate question. (If you are not imagining Jesus on your investment committee, try it.) The parable of the talents gives us a framework: look for good soil. Invest where there is capacity to grow, multiply, and produce a return that compounds beyond the financial. The question is where that soil exists on the continent — and where it could exist if the right capital arrived at the right time with the right intent.

Soil can be improved. The historical dynamic of the gospel says so. The Pentecostal revival of the early twentieth century spread to Chile and gave rise to a middle class that had not previously existed. Spiritual liberty and personal restoration change the conditions in which economic life takes root. Churches and NGOs have a role in that preparation — but the focus of this book is the investment layer that follows: the businesses, the supply chains, the industries, and the infrastructure that turn prepared ground into productive ground.

The areas I am highlighting in this chapter are not specific investment advice. They are an orientation — a map of the terrain organized into four categories: core infrastructure and energy, agriculture and supply chains, production and industry, and what I am calling NewGen Digipreneurs. Each category contains giants worth taking down and soil worth investing in.

**Where to Invest**

**Core Infrastructure, Energy**

- Housing and Real Estate tackle a giant: mass urbanization, Slum Economy
- Energy Access
- Transportation
- ICT access

**Agriculture & Supply Chains**

- Agriculture, Food, Environmental sciences
- End-to-end supply chains
- Ag education
- Cooperatives, incubators, critical mass-builders

**Production & Industry**

- Local beneficiation
- Reviving manufacturing
- Health & Education
- Core Corporations & Secondary industries
- Clean mining

**NewGen Digipreneurs**

- SME and Entrepreneurial Finance
- Digital economy talent
- Afrishoring

## Core Infrastructure, Energy

Africa needs investors willing to capitalize core infrastructure — housing, roads, bridges, airports, rail networks, energy grids. Up to 855 million people could be moving to urban areas in the next twenty-five years. In fewer than twenty years, every second person in Africa is likely to live in a town or a city. Without faith-based investing at scale, the slum population could triple by 2050. That is not a development statistic. This is a call to action with a deadline.

### Housing & Real Estate

Do not think about investing in real estate in Africa the way you would in a developed market. In Africa you are not just building a real estate portfolio — you are taking down a giant. Africa's demographic dividend will only be realized if mass urbanization does not result in hundreds of millions of people entering the slum economy. Right now, underdeveloped mortgage markets and a critical shortage of basic housing are driving the slumification of the continent at a pace that is outrunning most responses to it.

There are businesses in Africa exploring green building technologies — structures that are carbon negative, more soundproof, fireproof, and built for the climate they sit in. Coupled with rent-to-own or fractional ownership models, this approach could represent a genuine pathway out of poverty for millions of people who will never qualify for a conventional mortgage. Real estate in Africa is a solid investment area — not just because it produces grounded returns, but because it addresses one of the continent's most consequential giants. There is an appendix unpacking this in more detail, including the question of how to do property development for the benefit of local African populations rather than primarily for investors arriving from Europe, the Middle East, and the United States.

## Energy Access

Off-grid solar and clean energy investments do not just produce power. They unlock education, healthcare, and enterprise development while stewarding creation. The failure of central governments to deliver reliable energy has forced businesses and communities across the continent to develop creative solutions. In doing so, Africa has produced some of the most innovative distributed energy models in the world. When you have a cornerstone housing and real estate investment in Africa, it will almost certainly require its own clean energy solution. Plan for it from the beginning.

## Water Solutions

Africa is not water poor. It is water uneven and infrastructure poor. Central Africa has abundance. Northern and Southern Africa face genuine shortage. Most agricultural irrigation depends on rainfall across large parts of the continent, and rainfall is increasingly unpredictable. That is a challenge — and it is also an opening for creative thinking and large-scale solutions in water redistribution and management.

The careful and creative stewardship of water will be one of the defining investment themes of the next thirty years on the continent. Dr. Stephan Pretorius has shared a full case study on the website. His core argument is worth stating here: the strategic mobilization of groundwater and underutilized surface water has significant implications for rural agricultural development — enabling irrigation expansion without compromising national water security, maximizing existing public infrastructure, and supporting decentralized agricultural systems aligned with local economic realities.

## Transportation

Africa's transportation infrastructure is not just underperforming — it is underbuilt. Colonial-era rail was designed to extract raw materials to ports, not to integrate economies or connect people to markets. What exists is generally not interconnected, not interoperable across borders, and not built for the volume or the geography of a continent in rapid urbanization.

The return on transportation investments tends to look low in isolation. Modeled against the convergence of AfCFTA policy momentum, demographic demand, and emerging technology, however, the picture changes — non-linear growth becomes possible in ways that a conventional infrastructure model will not capture. The risks are real: regulatory instability, currency volatility, execution complexity, government weakness. These require a compelling tie to economic off-takers and a patient capital structure that matches the gestation period of the asset.

What is changing is the direction of ambition. In the last five years, Africa has seen a quiet shift from nationally siloed rail lines toward regional corridors — moving from extraction-oriented infrastructure toward connections between industrial zones, cities, and trading partners. The Lobito Corridor connecting Angola to the DRC copper belt, the Dakar-Bamako line in West Africa, and East African corridor projects are the early indicators of a continent beginning to build for integration rather than extraction. China led the first wave of this infrastructure development. US and EU-backed capital is now entering the same space. The trajectory is moving in the right direction, even if the pace is slower than the need.

## Information & Communication Technologies (ICT)

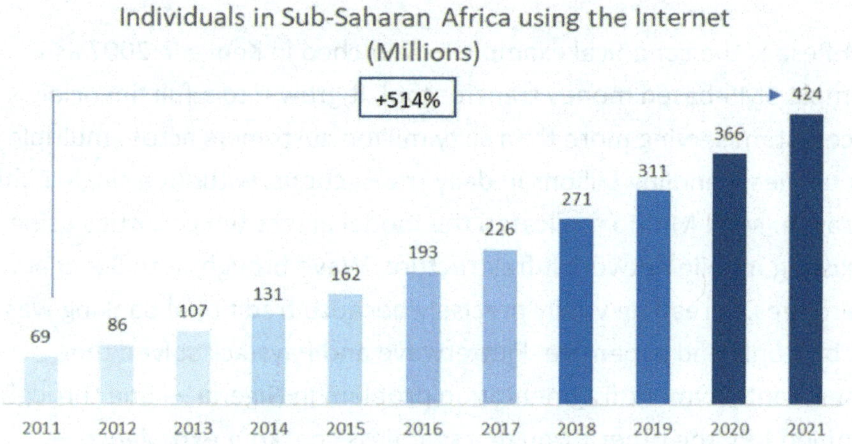

[13]

Andrew Dabalen, the World Bank's Chief Economist for Africa, put it plainly: the minimal usage of mobile internet on the continent is a lost opportunity for inclusive growth. Closing that gap, he argued, would boost Africa's capacity to create jobs for its growing population and support economic recovery in an increasingly digitalized world. He is right — and the entrepreneurs who did not wait for the gap to close are the ones who built some of the most significant financial infrastructure on the planet.

The pattern is consistent enough to be a principle. Africa's fintech pioneers did not succeed despite the continent's infrastructure gaps. They succeeded because of them. Sparse bank branches, unreliable electricity, limited ATMs, poor roads, low card penetration — these were not obstacles to innovation. They were the brief. When the existing system cannot serve you, you build a different system. And when you build it on mobile networks and local agents rather than

---

[13] https://www.worldbank.org/en/results/2024/01/18/digital-transformation-drives-development-in-afe-afw-africa

bricks and mortar, you build something that scales faster, costs less, and reaches further than the legacy model it replaced.

M-Pesa is the canonical example — launched in Kenya in 2007 as a simple SMS-based money transfer tool, it grew into a full financial ecosystem serving more than sixty million customers across multiple countries, handling billions in daily transactions, without a single bank branch. MTN MoMo replicated the model across ten countries using existing mobile network infrastructure. Wave brought it to Senegal with zero fees, spreading virally precisely because traditional banking was urban-only and expensive. Flutterwave and Paystack solved the merchant payment fragmentation problem in Nigeria — one through a unified API, the other through a seamless checkout experience — enabling digital commerce in a market where multiple incompatible gateways and cash-heavy culture had made it nearly impossible.

The result is that sub-Saharan Africa now accounts for around seventy percent (yes, 70%) of the world's mobile money accounts and transactions. That is not a regional quirk. It is a structural leapfrog — and it has lifted millions of people into the formal economy in less than two decades.

For the ICT investor, the primary infrastructure plays — telecoms, data centers, subsea cables — require significant capital and regulatory navigation, but the opportunity is real and the demand is not going away. The more accessible entry point is the layer that rides on existing ICT infrastructure: fintech, edtech, healthtech, and the growing ecosystem of platforms built for African market realities rather than adapted from Western models. If you understand the regulatory complexity and the infrastructure cost structure, this is one of the most dynamic investment environments on the planet.

I am currently working with solutions providers in Africa exploring closed-loop monetary and trading systems that can operate within existing regulatory frameworks in locations where we are conducting societal transformation initiatives. Digital capital is part of comprehensive capitalization — not a separate category, but an integrated layer of the same investment thesis.

The full profiles of Africa's leading fintech companies — M-Pesa, MTN MoMo, Wave, Flutterwave, Paystack, and the related innovators in payments and utilities — are on the website where they can be kept current as the landscape continues to move. What matters here is the principle: the infrastructure gap produced the innovation, and the innovation is now the infrastructure.

# Agriculture & Supply Chains

## Agriculture, Food & Environment

Africa holds sixty percent of the world's uncultivated arable land. It also has some of the highest rates of post-harvest food loss on the planet — not because African farmers lack skill, but because the infrastructure connecting farm to market is broken at multiple points simultaneously. Cold storage, processing capacity, transport, financing, market access — remove any one of these and the chain fails. Fix them together and the ripple effect is enormous.

Regenerative agriculture is not a Western concept retrofitted onto African farming. It is a return to a more ancient relationship between people, soil, and creation — one that colonial and industrial agriculture disrupted and that a growing number of African farmers and investors are working to restore. Richard Lackey of the World Food Bank describes it well: the regenerative lens brings farmers back to their original call, working with the soil and water to improve the ecosystem, creating more life in the soil, better nutrition for communities, and higher incomes as quality produce opens export markets and value-added processing. The investment opportunity sits not just in the farming itself but in the full chain that turns good farming into scalable economic impact.

## Supply Chains

The Hamara Group began its journey in 1987 as Sondelani Ranching, an ostrich ranching company working directly with rural farmers to service export markets. In those early years they set aside a percentage of profits to assist small-scale farmers trapped in poverty — effectively tithing their way toward a broader purpose. It did not take long to realize that God's call was far greater than a handout.

Over thirty-six years, Hamara attempted to build every part of the agricultural value chain themselves. What they discovered in the process is one of the most important lessons available to any investor in African agriculture: you cannot deal with a subset of the supply chain. If there is a breakdown anywhere — inputs, financing, logistics, processing, market access — the whole thing falls apart. Hamara has therefore built a platform that fills the gaps at any point so that the chain actually works. Today they work with over 150,000 small farmers who use the Hamara Platform to address different facets of agriculture across the value chain.

Joel Cunningham, who has worked closely on the Hamara model, draws the right conclusion: by integrating digital verification, real-time dashboards, and community accountability, it is possible to transform small-scale farming into a bankable and scalable system. The systemic thinking behind Hamara — recognizing that the goal is the reformation of the continent through self-sustaining, purpose-driven ecosystems — is what turns Africa's agricultural potential into agricultural performance.

The Hamara Platform case study is included in the case studies on the website and warrants reading for any investor considering the agricultural sector.

## Production & Industry

The idea that Africa was a religious, social, and economic backwater rescued by European settlers is not accurate — and it is worth saying so plainly before discussing what colonialism actually left behind. I have sat in the library in Alexandria, Egypt, which dates back to about 300 BC. It drew scholars from across Greece, Persia, and India to a city on African soil. At its height it held hundreds of thousands of scrolls. Africa was not a backwater receiving civilization from elsewhere. It was, for centuries, the place the world came to think.

Asian nations were trading with Africa before Europeans arrived. The early church thrived on the continent in its first centuries. What colonial infrastructure did produce — rail lines, ports, some administrative capacity — was designed primarily for extraction, not for the development of African productive capacity. Studies of colonial railroads show long-term effects on urbanization and cash crop production, but the infrastructure was oriented toward moving raw materials out, not toward building industries in.

China's more recent infrastructure investments have provided tangible improvements in transport and energy that colonial and post-independence efforts rarely matched in scale or speed. The costs — debt terms, maintenance obligations, questions about who controls the assets — have persisted into the long term in ways that the initial announcements did not always make clear. The pattern of extracting raw materials and processing them elsewhere is not unique to colonial powers. It is the default mode of outside capital in Africa, and it is one of the things that faith-based investors are specifically positioned to do differently.

Building world-class production capability in Africa is challenging, but it has been done. South Africa and Morocco have industries with genuine sophistication. And sometimes the most instructive examples are not the largest ones — they are the ones that got the model right.

## Boring but Beautiful

Kenya was the world's leading pyrethrum producer in the 1980s, supplying more than seventy percent of global demand for this natural, biodegradable insecticide derived from chrysanthemum flowers. By the 2000s the industry had effectively collapsed — policy failures, competition from synthetic alternatives, lack of processing capacity, and market liberalization challenges had left hundreds of thousands of smallholder farmers in the highlands without a reliable market for a crop they had grown for generations.

Kentegra Biotechnology stepped into that gap around 2017 with a model that is, by any glamorous standard, unglamorous. They supply high-quality planting materials, solar dryers, training, and agronomic support to smallholder farmers in the highlands. They buy dried flowers at fair prices, often with digital payments. And they built a modern pyrethrum processing facility first in Athi River Export Processing Zone then in the Naivasha Export Processing Zone to add local value rather than exporting raw flowers to be processed elsewhere. By 2025 they were exporting to over thirty countries around the world and providing livelihoods tens of thousands of contracted farmers, created hundreds of direct jobs, and positioned Kenya once again as a leading pyrethrin producer for the global organic farming and pest control market.

The financing mix — development finance from the US International Development Finance Corporation and Finland's Finnfund, patient equity, and structured debt — is worth noting. This is not venture capital chasing a unicorn. It is capital matched to the actual timeline of an agricultural value chain. The result is a business that compounds steadily, serves smallholders, restores a traditional Kenyan crop, and produces a product the world increasingly needs as it moves away from synthetic pesticides.

This is what I mean by boring but beautiful. Not every investment in Africa needs to be a fintech disruption or a continent-wide platform. Some of the most durable, most consequential, most kingdom-aligned investments are the ones that revive something that should never have been allowed to collapse, serve people who have been waiting a long time for someone to show up, and build quietly toward something that will still be standing in thirty years.

Similar stories are emerging across the continent. West Africa produces roughly fifty percent of global raw cashews but historically exported most of it unprocessed. Modern processing factories are now capturing local value and creating thousands of jobs, particularly for women and youth. Cooperatives and modern facilities in Ghana, Burkina Faso, and Mali are boosting shea butter refining for global cosmetics and food brands, supporting up to sixteen million women across the region. Tanzania's Lutheran World Relief has partnered with the Pyrethrum Company of Tanzania on a model similar to Kentegra's. The pattern is consistent — private-sector-led processing, development finance, smallholder focus, climate-resilient products, measurable income and employment gains.

The investment thesis is not complicated. Africa produces raw materials. Processing those materials locally rather than exporting them for processing elsewhere creates jobs, builds skills, retains value in the country, and produces businesses with genuine roots. The challenge is execution — the last-mile logistics, the off-take arrangements, the policy stability that makes a ten-year business plan credible. None of it is insurmountable. All of it requires staying longer than a standard fund term allows, which is, of course, the whole argument.

## Manufacturing & Light Industries

Africa has structural trade advantages that are underutilized. Ninety-seven percent of Africa's exports enter the EU tariff-free. The African Growth and Opportunity Act (AGOA) has provided similar access to US markets, with its extension through December 2026 under active discussion. Different regions have developed specializations — West and Central Africa in oil and cocoa, Southern Africa in precious metals and automotive components, East Africa in coffee, tea, and horticulture, North Africa in oil, gas, and textiles integrated into European supply chains.

The opportunity that is still largely unrealized is the shift from exporting raw materials to processing them closer to the source. Beneficiation — adding value at or near the point of extraction or production — is one of the most direct routes to job creation, skills development, and retained economic value. Moving processing from cities to rural areas where raw materials originate compounds the impact further. This is not a theoretical possibility. It is happening in pockets across the continent. The question is whether capital will show up at the scale and with the patience the opportunity requires.

## Health & Education Enterprises

Africa is not waiting for its public health systems to catch up. It is building around them.

I had the opportunity to visit a business incubator in Kigali where one of the first Zipline drones hangs in the lobby like a trophy. It deserves to. Zipline began operations in Rwanda in 2016 with a straightforward brief: deliver blood products to rural hospitals faster than road transport could manage in a mountainous country where over eighty percent of the population lives outside the cities. The roads were poor. The hospitals were understocked. The distances were real. And postpartum hemorrhage — one of the leading causes of maternal death in sub-Saharan Africa — was killing women who were dying, not from a lack of treatment, but from a lack of supply.

The solution was autonomous fixed-wing drones flying from central distribution hubs to hospitals across the country, dropping payloads by parachute with a median delivery time of around forty-one minutes. Blood wastage dropped by more than sixty-seven percent. Studies published in peer-reviewed journals documented reductions in maternal mortality from postpartum hemorrhage of roughly fifty percent at serviced facilities. The system now runs twenty-four hours a day, seven days a week, covering hundreds of health facilities and handling a significant share of blood supply outside Kigali.

By early 2026 Rwanda had signed an expansion agreement making it the first country with nationwide autonomous drone coverage — including urban delivery in Kigali itself, the first urban drone delivery network on the continent. The coverage now reaches over eleven million people. The US Department of State backed part of the expansion with a one hundred and fifty million dollar pay-for-performance award. Rwanda did not wait for a Western health system to arrive. It built something better suited to its own geography.

The investment lesson is not primarily about drones. It is about the model: a technology precisely matched to a specific constraint, built for African conditions rather than adapted from elsewhere, financed through a performance-based structure that aligns investor return with actual health outcomes. That alignment — capital structure matched to mission — is what faith-based investors should be looking for and building toward.

Drones are not limited to healthcare. Across African agriculture they are being deployed for crop monitoring and mapping, pest and disease detection, soil analysis, and precision application of fertilizers that cut chemical use by up to ninety percent in some cases. Livestock monitoring via satellite and drone integration is in its early stages. Drone-as-a-Service models are making the technology accessible to smallholder farmers who could never afford to own the equipment themselves. The infrastructure gap that made Zipline necessary in healthcare is producing the same pattern of innovation in agriculture — constraint driving invention, invention driving impact.

Affordable private solutions in education follow similar logic. Where public systems are constrained — and across much of Africa they are severely constrained — private enterprises are building models that extend access at price points that work for African households. The opportunity is significant. The execution challenges are real. And the faith-based investor who understands both is well positioned to build something that outlasts the investment horizon.

## Core Corporations & Secondary Industries

Every city and nation being transformed requires both primary and secondary businesses. The two are not independent — they are ecologically linked. A core business does not just employ people directly. It generates a network of secondary businesses that supply it, service it, distribute its products, and house and feed its workforce. Get the core business right and the secondary ecosystem follows. Miss it and the investment sits in isolation, disconnected from the economic fabric around it.

Dirk Oosthuizen's Carbon Smart Academy in South Africa illustrates the principle. The primary products are carbon-negative building structures and agricultural ingredients — including biochar, a soil amendment that sequesters carbon while improving soil fertility. Around each of those primary outputs, sixty-five secondary products and businesses spin off naturally. The core investment generates an ecosystem rather than a single revenue line. We are currently developing a plan to deploy the Carbon Smart Academy model in Mamre, a historic Moravian community outside Cape Town, alongside our Transforming Society methodology. The goal is not to build a business in Mamre. It is to build Mamre — with a business as the anchor and a community as the outcome.

But there is a deeper question underneath the economic one. Not just what does this company produce, but what is this company called to be?

In *Transforming Society* I describe what I call Called Corporations — entities that exist for a purpose larger than their own survival and growth, that shape the culture and language of the communities around them, and that carry an influence that outlasts any individual leader or product line. They are not always the biggest companies in a city. They are the ones that capture its heart. When you travel to Ireland, you quickly understand that Guinness is a Called Corporation — it has shaped the destiny of countless thousands, guided initially by a godly purpose. When in Silicon Valley I looked out from my study and pondered whether Google in Mountain View, Apple in Cupertino, and Cisco in San Jose carried something of this quality — whether they knew it, or not. The East India Company was a Called Corporation in India, and eventually believers got control of its board of directors. Company policy shifted from prohibiting missionaries to funding them.

Many Called Corporations do not know they are called — just as individuals and nations often do not. God sees the call on a company long before its leadership does. Part of the work of kingdom investing is exactly this: identifying the Called Corporations in a city or sector, praying for them, and working with those who have influence to bring out the characteristics that were always latent in the enterprise.

In *Transforming Society* I identify ten characteristics of a Called Corporation — what I call the 10-Cs. A Called Corporation is committed to a greater good. It is cleansed — having dealt honestly with its past and maintaining purity in its present practices. It is chiropracted — aligned in character and competence with Scripture. It carries a culture grounded in a biblical worldview. It understands itself as a community — a household in the fullest sense. It has centurions — watchmen and gap-bridgers looking out for the welfare of the city around it. It is a co-creator, developing products and services that actively meet the needs of the city, the nation, and the world. It commissions — it sends people out. It is capital-positive, a net creator of financial, human, spiritual, and relational capital. And it is city-changing — sometimes nation-changing, sometimes world-changing.

That is the investment brief. Not just a business with a faith-based founder. A Called Corporation — or one that could become one with the right capital, the right governance, and the right partners alongside it.

**The 10-Cs: Characteristics of Called Corporations**

1. Committed to a greater good. (The ultimate being, "to glorify God.")
2. Cleansed: dealt with past, and purity in present practices.
3. Chiropracted : aligned in aspects of character and competence with scripture.
4. Culture: a biblically grounded worldview.
5. Community—there is effective household understanding and experience.
6. Centurions: the corporation has watchmen, gap-bridgers, who are looking out for the welfare of their city.
7. Co-creators: the corporation develops products and services that actively meet the needs of the city, the nation and the world.
8. Commissioning: they send people out.
9. Capital-positive: they are net-positive capital creators—financial, human, spiritual, environmental… all forms of capital.
10. City-changing: including community and nation changing, sometimes world changing.

When you look at an investment opportunity in Africa through that lens, the due diligence questions change. You are not only asking what the return on capital will be. You are asking what this company is called to, whether it knows it, and whether your investment will help it get there.

When African Capital Alliance was contemplating the acquisition of Union Bank, I sat across the desk from Dr. Okey Enelamah and asked, "Is it possible that God has given you favor and success in your career because he wants his bank back?" You see, Union Bank used to be Barclays Bank, and Barclays Bank was started by Quakers to finance Christian businesses. He agreed. Some cold corporations need to be re-called.

## Clean Mining

There is a verse in Genesis chapter two that I have never been able to read past without stopping.

> *(The gold of that land is good; aromatic resin and onyx are also there.)*

It sits in parentheses, almost as an aside — God noting, while describing the rivers flowing out of Eden, that the land contains gold, and it is good. I cannot imagine God thinking "I will put gold in the ground, but these people will have to use arsenic and harmful chemicals to get it out." In my imagination, God already had clean mining processes figured out before the first ore was ever extracted. The problem is not the gold. The problem is what we have done to get to it.

Thankfully there are companies — some of them owned and led by followers of Jesus — that are applying microbiome technology to mining, using living organisms to extract minerals without the toxic chemistry that conventional processing requires. Dependence on harmful chemicals is being radically reduced. Yields are improving. The land is not being destroyed in the process of recovering what it contains.

There are other giants in mining that go beyond chemistry. At the micro level, child labor remains a persistent and documented problem. At the macro level, asset colonization — the extraction of minerals and metals without local beneficiation, the export of raw ore to be processed elsewhere and imported back as finished goods at a premium — is still one of the most consequential structural injustices on the continent. Mozambique's milled lumber, shipped to China and imported back as finished product, is one example. The minerals sector has versions of this story in almost every country.

There are believers working in mining who are taking these issues seriously — building companies that treat the land as a trust, the workers as full human beings, and the communities around the mine as stakeholders rather than externalities. That work is harder than conventional mining. It is also more durable, more defensible, and more aligned with the mandate that has been there since Genesis chapter two.

## NewGen Digipreneurs

Africa has somewhere between 300 and 500 million digital natives today. By 2050 that number could reach 850 million — young people who have grown up with mobile technology as their native language, for whom the smartphone is not a tool they learned to use but an extension of how they think and work. That demographic fact, combined with Africa's entrepreneurial energy and its structural need for locally-built solutions, is producing a generation of builders unlike anything the continent has seen before.

The question is not whether this generation exists: it is whether the investment infrastructure exists to deploy their energy productively — and whether it can do so in Africa rather than simply for Africa from a distance. A recent trip to Zimbabwe illustrated the tension sharply. Three years ago a qualified accountant could be hired for under a thousand dollars a month. Today the rate has tripled — not because Zimbabwe's economy has transformed, but because those accountants are working remotely for large accounting firms in the UK and the United States. The talent is real. The question of where it flows, and who benefits from it, is still being answered.

### Afrishoring

The remote work revolution has produced what I am calling Afrishoring — the deliberate routing of business process work, professional services, and operational functions to African talent pools. It is already happening at scale. South Africa serves UK, US, and Australian markets through call centers and operational hubs, helped by neutral English accents and genuine cultural affinity. Egypt and Morocco excel in multilingual support for European and Middle Eastern markets. Kenya and Ghana are growing as hubs for English-speaking and pan-African work.

The opportunity is significant and the risks are real. AI automation could affect up to forty percent of tasks in junior customer experience roles by 2030 — exactly the entry-level positions where Africa's youth are most heavily represented. The response is not to avoid the sector but to invest in it deliberately: in the upskilling infrastructure, the digital literacy programs, and the pathways that move workers from vulnerable entry-level roles toward the more resilient, higher-value work that AI augments rather than replaces. Many young African BPO workers are already using tools like ChatGPT and Microsoft Copilot with a natural fluency that their counterparts in other markets are still acquiring. That adaptability is an asset. It needs to be developed, not taken for granted.

## SME and Entrepreneurial Finance

The most durable investments in Africa's NewGen economy will not be in individual companies. Smart Investments will be in ecosystems — networks of interconnected businesses where a handful of core enterprises spin off hundreds of secondary businesses, supported by incubators, accelerators, and patient capital that understands the difference between a slow return and a bad investment.

David Livingstone's three-Cs — Christianity, Commerce, and Civilization — captured an interdependence that has not changed even if the language has. We might use different words today, but the relationship between the advancement of the gospel and the economic wellbeing of people and the improvement of their societies is as real now as it was when Livingstone proposed a Christian commercial highway through the Zambezi. The point was never that commerce saves — it was that commerce, rightly ordered, creates the conditions in which human flourishing becomes possible at scale.

Richard Lackey puts the investment principle plainly: regardless of geography or asset class, fully understanding and supporting the entire value chain — either directly or in partnership — is a practice that needs to be incorporated into every investment in developing markets. Sid Mofya, who has worked across African investment contexts for years, makes the same point from a different angle: in Africa, a spreadsheet is never the whole story. The emphasis on investing across interconnected spheres rather than isolating a single company reflects a centuries-long hope for Africa.

Initial investments in Africa's entrepreneur class — college-educated, tech-savvy, globally oriented — often target solutions that could be built in Africa and sold internationally. That is a legitimate starting point. It is not a sufficient endpoint. When investments are focused on the full portfolio of entities that can uplift a community — core businesses, secondary businesses, workforce development, local supply chains — they begin to address the deeper structural issues that decades of aid dependency have left behind. A collaboration of core businesses committed to a noble purpose carries a quiet but real moral authority with local governments. It is harder to ignore than a single well-funded company. And it is much harder to corrupt.

## Investing Strategies by Zone

The sectors covered in this chapter — infrastructure, energy, water, transportation, fintech, agriculture, production, health, education, clean mining, and the emerging digital economy — are not a random list of investment opportunities. They are the spheres of a society being rebuilt from the foundations up. Each one is a field of good soil waiting for capital that knows what it is doing and why.

The zone framework from Chapter 6 applies here as a practical organizing principle. Investors tend to start in Opportunity Zones where the infrastructure and institutions are closest to what their models assume, then expand into Resilience Zones as their relationships and track record develop. Churches and NGOs do their most effective work in Friction Zones, building the trust architecture that makes everything else possible. Kingdom Business sits across all four zones — starting where there is enough brokenness to make the work matter and enough stability to actually operate, scaling where trust already exists, embedding carefully where it has to be constructed from scratch, and platforming where the conditions allow what has been built to compound and replicate.

| | Start here | Expand here | Scale here | Partner here |
|---|---|---|---|---|
| Investors | Start here | Expand here | | Partner here |
| Churches | Start here | Expand here | | |
| NGOs | Start here | Expand here | | |
| Kingdom Business | Start here | Platform | Scale | Embed |

What the table cannot show — and what matters most — is the collaboration between these four actors when it is working well. Churches build trust, identity, and personal self-governance. Investors bring capital, expertise, and accountability structures. NGOs extend services into the gaps that neither business nor government reaches. Kingdom Business integrates all of it into enterprises that produce returns that outlast the investment horizon. When these four are aligned around a shared purpose in a specific city or sector, the outcome is not just a portfolio of investments. It is a community being transformed.

Africa is not a continent waiting to be rescued. It is a continent in motion — building, innovating, and compounding its own capital in ways that outside observers consistently underestimate. The faith-based investor who shows up with humility, with patience, with genuine partnership, and with a theological framework large enough to hold both the complexity and the opportunity — that investor is not just putting capital to work. They are joining something that was already in motion before they arrived.

That is the right posture. And it changes everything about how you invest.

## Zone-by-Zone Strategy

Before I offer this framework, let me preempt the mail I will inevitably receive. If I have placed your country in a zone that does not reflect your experience, I understand. I have a home in Cape Town, which is an exception within South Africa, which is itself an exception within Africa. The classifications below look at national economies as a whole, not at the exceptional neighborhoods, cities, or sectors within them. Pockets of excellence exist everywhere. I am trying to help investors who are looking at the continent as a whole find a starting point — not to write the final word on any country's potential.

**In Friction Zones** — low trust, high fragmentation — the counterintuitive entry point is the church, not the investor. Nigeria is the clearest illustration. One of the first missionaries to Nigeria was a Nigerian slave who had been freed, studied abroad, and returned to his own country. Missionaries from many nations followed and played a crucial role. They were not specifically targeting business development, but they laid a foundation — a critical mass of people coming into a personal relationship with Jesus Christ, building identity and personal order across the society. I believe Nigeria is reaping that dividend today. The church in a Friction Zone builds cross-tribal identity and relational infrastructure. It brings personal order and, to a degree, organizational order. That is the soil preparation without which business investment has nowhere to root.

NGOs play a supporting role in Friction Zones — humanitarian scaffolding, early system building. Kingdom Business enters differently from what most investors expect. Desperate countries are often highly entrepreneurial. Roughly half of the continent's entrepreneurs spring from Nigeria. The opportunity is not to parachute in with capital and a business plan. It is to find businesses that can move people from the informal sector to the formal sector, that are community-embedded, relationally anchored, and employment-first rather than scale-first. Agriculture cooperatives, local manufacturing tied to communities, micro-franchise models — these are the right entry points. There is also a second level: businesses that can operate effectively within a more developed economy while still located in Africa, providing incubators and business support for early-stage companies, and connecting Africa-born products to international markets.

Investors in Friction Zones should not go in alone. Invest through trusted operators. Accept longer timelines, lower early returns, and higher relational investment. It is tempting to visit an African country two or three times looking for opportunities. When you have been ten times and they have given you an African name and welcomed you as part of the family, the relational investment begins to bear fruit.

One more note on Friction Zones from our own experience: in our Repurposing Business work we have not led with capital — perhaps to our detriment in some cases — because when you arrive with a wallet full of money, you attract all sorts of people. Our rēp process has been described by someone in Johannesburg as a "laundromat for motives" — it requires an upfront commitment from potential investees to get trained in Kingdom Business principles before capital enters the conversation. The downside is that it takes time and commitment, and some investees will opt for lower-barrier alternatives. The upside is that the ones who stay are the ones worth backing.

**In Transition Zones** — trust is forming, systems are uneven — Kingdom Business really starts to shine. This is where businesses with strong values-based leadership and transparent governance become something more than commercial enterprises. They become visible alternatives to broken systems. A business that models integrity and breaks corruption norms in a Transition Zone is not just building a company. It is building culture.

Psalm 78:72 describes David leading his people "with skillful hands and integrity of heart." Investing in kingdom businesses should not require a trade-off between character and competence — it should not settle for one at the expense of the other. The front wheel of a leader's bicycle is character. The back wheel is competence. Both need to be turning for the thing to move forward. Dr. Stephan Pretorius captures the investment principle well: kingdom investment in Africa's water future — and this applies far beyond water — will not be defined by the scale of capital deployed, but by the depth of alignment between purpose, people, and leadership. When investment is rooted in Africa, led by people of integrity, and stewarded by a network of mature leaders operating from a kingdom identity, the infrastructure being built becomes a vehicle for the restoration of nations.

Investors enter Transition Zones selectively, backing proven kingdom operators. Churches shift from establishment mode to growth mode, shaping identity and influencing emerging leaders. NGOs strengthen education, governance, and health — building the systems that make the next phase possible.

**In Opportunity Zones** — functional systems, scalable environments — this is the sweet spot for investors. Capital flows more efficiently. Scaling is genuinely possible. Kingdom Business in an Opportunity Zone becomes a scale engine and, when done well, proof that faith-aligned businesses can outperform the market. Growth-stage companies in fintech, agriculture value chains, healthcare, and education — with a clear operating model, ethical and integrated leadership, kingdom-aligned purpose, and measurable social impact built into the business scorecard rather than tossed over the wall to an NGO — these are the investments that demonstrate the thesis. NGOs add technical depth and expand reach. Churches feed leadership pipelines into business, functioning as a steppingstone from personal order to organizational order.

**In Resilience Zones** — high cohesion, strong social fabric — Kingdom Business shifts from scale engine to platform builder. National-scale supply chains, workforce development systems, regional expansion hubs. Investors can deploy faster, replicate models, and build on lower friction. NGOs accelerate capability and shape policy. Churches sustain the ethical foundation and prevent the drift that comes with scale.

One nuance worth naming: two of the countries in the Resilience Zone category are Muslim-dominant. The cultural dynamics are different from the Southern African countries that share similar infrastructure profiles. That does not close the opportunity — it changes the approach. There are functioning businesses in South Africa, for example, that could be effectively planted in North African contexts with the right partnerships and cultural intelligence. The zone classification is a starting point, not a ceiling.

## Systemic Thinking for a Continent

When I arrived in California in June 1986 on a one-year assignment from Price Waterhouse in Cape Town, I went to get my hair cut about ten days after landing. Noticing my accent, the hairdresser asked where I was from. South Africa, I said. How long have you been here? About ten days. She thought for a moment and then asked: "So, did you drive or did you fly?"

Every immigrant has a version of this story. The reverse happens when I travel in Africa — many people have no concept of how vast and diverse the United States is, just as that hairdresser had no concept of how far

South Africa was from California. The point transfers directly to investing: small investments in Tulane or Timbuktu may make a real difference to that specific community. They will not rise to the level of what is needed to bring about systemic change. Africa requires systemic thinking — not because individual investments do not matter, but because isolated investments, however well-intentioned, seldom result in transformation on their own.

## Why Kingdom Business & Kingdom Economics Changes Everything

It is not hard to get lost when you look at the scale of what Africa needs. The capital required to transform systems and platforms, cities and nations, is genuinely daunting. But communities of faith are better positioned than any other actor to build flourishing societies — precisely because their engagement spans the entire value chain. As the gospel goes into all the world, identifying what is out of alignment with God's will and building the systems and organizations that reconcile all things to him, transformation happens not incidentally, but by design. The siloed approach — advancing the kingdom of God in one lane while deploying capital in another — does not achieve the objective. Africa has tremendous potential. Unlocking it requires clarity about what is actually happening on the continent right now.

The large investor groups operating in Africa are often pursuing asset colonization — extracting value rather than building it. China, the

Middle East, Europe, and Islamic finance are all playing long games with strategic intent. The NGO industrial complex, for all the good that individual organizations do, is structurally failing at systemic change. USAID, to name the most visible example, has never primarily been an aid organization — it has been an instrument of US foreign policy, often more focused on promoting particular governance outcomes than on genuine community upliftment. Aid is critical in some situations, particularly where states have failed or are failing. But it has more often made nations helpless than self-reliant. Poverty and unemployment remain the number one giant across much of Africa, and governments are structurally poor at genuine job creation. The era of Africa as a basket case requiring Western rescue is over. The era of Africa as a source of raw materials with no local beneficiation should be over — though there is still significant distance to travel.

Without kingdom businesses and enlightened investors in the picture, the dynamic is predictable. NGOs create dependency. Churches build communities but not economies. Investors struggle in low-trust environments. Governments are not pressured to change in ways that allow what might be called Promised Land economics.

With righteous, repurposed business and investing, something different becomes possible. Social good becomes self-sustaining. Impact scales without perpetual funding. Faith becomes economically viable. And Africa — which has been a receiving continent for centuries — begins to function as a sending continent, exporting business missionaries, inspired innovations, and kingdom capital to the rest of the world.

That is not a distant dream. The trajectory is already visible. The question is whether the right capital will show up in time to accelerate it.

## Native Advantage

I hesitate to use this table because it contains generalizations — and I can already anticipate the pushback from readers whose country has been misclassified. With that caveat clearly stated, the table may still be useful as a thinking tool rather than a final analysis.

| Zone | Investors | NGOs | Churches | Kingdom Business |
|---|---|---|---|---|
| FRICTION | Not a good idea to go in alone. | It might be a struggle, unless this is your focus. | Can do well here, first responders. | Only if you have a solid partner. |
| TRANSITION | Enter selectively | An area of good work: shifting from chaos to order | Shift from establishing mode to growth mode. | Take advantage of needs. Catalyze blessing. |
| OPPORTUNITY | Good place for investors to fuel growth. | Moderate: turn things over to self-sustaining organizations. | Limited value-add from TS perspective | Scale, engine for growth. |
| RESILIENCE | Good zone to promote upskilling and scale. | The strong zone provided is a shift from long-term dependence. | Add value if the church is a launching pad and not a destination. | Shift from profitability to Platform building. |

I can imagine much time being spent discussing the pros and cons of thinking through the zones, the players and sequence of work in Africa. So please consider this a thought-starter and not a final analysis.

## Final Synthesis on Investment Opportunities

The future of Africa will not be built by aid alone, nor by capital alone, but by a deliberate strategy that engages all three strands of David Livingstone's original vision — Christianity, Commerce, and Civilization

— in their contemporary forms. When it comes to the ordered systems, operating models, and supply chains of society, investing in the rising tide of kingdom businesses is the key lever. These ventures align economic value with God's purposes, turning trust into systems and systems into sustainable transformation.

The question is not whether to invest in Africa. It is how to align the right type of capital — financial, social, digital, spiritual — with the trust environment in which it is deployed. Whether the call is to Friction Zones or Resilience Zones, to Opportunity Zones or Transition Zones, the mandate is comprehensive capitalization — deploying the full range of godly resources for optimum impact.

Solving Africa's biggest problems requires more than money. It requires cross-national friendships forged in humility and honor. It requires a willingness to find and back what God has already been doing on the continent long before outside investors arrived. It requires, specifically, the discovery and support of the inspired innovations that African entrepreneurs and builders are already developing in response to the real problems of real people.

The innovations are already emerging. The question is whether the capital will show up to meet them.

INSPIRED
INNOVATION

FROM TOIL TO TRANSFORMATION

# 9. Partner on Inspired Innovation

Inspired Innovation™ is a term I coined to describe something I have observed consistently over two decades of working with businesses across Africa and beyond — solutions that emerge not primarily from market research or competitive analysis, but from moral imagination, proximity to need, and contextual understanding. When someone is close enough to a real problem, shaped by genuine faith, and willing to ask what God's solution might look like, they tend to arrive at answers that the standard innovation process would never have reached.

Africa is full of people doing exactly this. They are coming up with products and businesses that solve real problems — water, power, food, health, mobility, finance — because those problems are not abstractions to them. They live inside them. That proximity is an asset that no amount of venture capital can manufacture, and it is one of the primary reasons faith-based capital is uniquely positioned to partner with African innovation rather than simply fund it from a distance.

Rachel McDonough, who sees both the demand and supply sides of this clearly, puts it well: we are living in a season where heaven's strategies for redemption and blessing are being revealed to entrepreneurs at a pace that asset managers and investors have struggled to keep up with. The constraint is not the innovation. It is the capital structures willing to meet it. Innovations in products and businesses must be met with innovations in investing — patient time horizons, relational rather than transactional engagement, willingness to back early-stage or non-obvious solutions, and the imagination to see transformed towns, cities, and nations as a legitimate investment thesis.

## Africa Has Always Built Things

Before we look at the new wave of African companies, it is worth naming something that tends to get forgotten in the conversation about African innovation: the continent has been producing world-class breakthroughs for longer than most people realize.

Dr. Christiaan Barnard performed the world's first successful human heart transplant in Cape Town in 1967. Allan Cormack, a South African physicist, developed the Computed Axial Tomography — the CAT scan — and received the Nobel Prize for it in 1979. A digital laser was developed by researchers at the CSIR in South Africa in 2013. M-Pesa transformed mobile payments in Kenya in 2007. Arthur Zang's Cardio Pad, developed in Cameroon in 2011, brought cardiac monitoring to rural hospitals that had never had access to an ECG machine and has since influenced telemedicine solutions worldwide.

The battery technology story is worth a longer pause. The lithium-ion cathode innovations that now power electric vehicles and smartphones globally involved, among others, Moroccan scientist Rachid Yazami and South African-born Michael Thackeray, whose work at the CSIR is widely regarded as a missed opportunity for the country. The technology was licensed abroad, boomed globally, and South Africa saw little of the economic return. Thackeray's contribution is now being recognized internationally — but the industrialization happened elsewhere.

That pattern has a name. I call it invention colonization — the extraction of intellectual capital from Africa in the same way that raw materials have always been extracted, leaving the continent with neither the asset nor the return. It is the upstream version of the beneficiation problem. Without a network or systemic approach that creates an environment where African innovations can be developed and commercialized within Africa, the pattern will continue. The Global

Giants Trust, which I will describe later in this chapter, was built in part to interrupt exactly this dynamic — to sit between the inventor and the investor and ensure that both get a fair return, and that the excess flows back into an evergreen fund that keeps the cycle going.

## Africa's New Builders

Let me ask the question directly: is Africa a breeding ground for unicorns?

The honest answer is yes — but only if you're willing to update your mental map of what a unicorn looks like. As of early 2026, nine African startups carry valuations above $1 billion, with the bulk of them Nigerian fintechs. The ecosystem faced a funding hangover after 2022 that sobered a lot of Western investors who had arrived with Silicon Valley pattern-matching and left confused. But the companies that were solving real problems — not just chasing multiples — kept growing. New unicorns emerged in 2024. The trajectory is intact.

What is more interesting to me than the valuations is the story beneath the story. These are not companies built in garages by twenty-two-year-olds on Red Bull and venture capital optimism. They were built by Africans who understood the specific texture of African frustration — the cash-heavy economy, the absence of reliable banking, the farmer who can't get his produce to market, the ride-hailing driver who can never access vehicle financing — and decided to do something about it. That is a different starting point than building an app because you saw a gap in the U.S. market.

Here are some companies that deserve more than a line in a list.

### The Payments Revolution

**1. Flutterwave** (Nigeria, founded 2016, valuation ~$3B) was built to solve one of Africa's most maddening problems: payments. Not consumer payments. Business payments. The kind where a company in Lagos trying to pay a supplier in Nairobi had to navigate three banking systems, two currencies, and a form that required a fax. Flutterwave created a single API that abstracts the whole mess — mobile money, cards, bank transfers, cash — into one integration. Its co-founder and CEO GB Agboola once listed his priorities in public: family, faith, and Flutterwave, in that order. A man who puts his priorities in that sequence and then builds a $3 billion company is not an accident.

The other co-founder, Iyinoluwa Aboyeji, warrants a longer paragraph of his own. The son of a Nigerian reverend, educated at a Jesuit college and later at Waterloo, Iyin co-founded Andela before Flutterwave, left both companies at or near their peaks, and now runs Future Africa — a venture platform with a portfolio of over 100 companies valued collectively above $6 billion. He publicly identifies as a faith-driven investor, runs a Friday series on how his faith shapes his work, and has quoted John 12:24 to explain why he walked away from Flutterwave at its moment of greatest success: unless a kernel of wheat falls to the ground and dies, it remains only a single seed. He also said, without embarrassment: 'Like my Lord and Savior Jesus Christ, I have a commission to build and invest in businesses to save the world, starting with Africa.'

You can agree or disagree with his theology. What you cannot dismiss is his track record. He prayed on his twenty-fifth birthday, in a secluded cabin, fishing — and heard what he describes as a clear voice telling him his work at Andela was done. He walked away. The company subsequently hit unicorn status. Most investors would have stayed for the next funding round. He left because he believed he was meant to. The portfolio he built next is worth more than what he left. This is not the profile that shows up in most African investment reports. It should.

> *"When you pour your soul into something and work like everything depends on it... God just has a way of blessing your efforts and turning it into long-term success." — Iyinoluwa Aboyeji, co-founder of Flutterwave and Andela*

**2. OPay** (Nigeria, founded 2018, ~$2B+ valuation) went further than payments — it built the whole stack. Payments, lending, savings, bill payments, all in one app, for tens of millions of Nigerians who had none of these things before. The model is not unlike what WeChat Pay did in China: start with a narrow use case, earn trust, then expand the surface area.

**3. Wave** (Senegal, founded 2018, ~$1.7B) did something harder: it went after Francophone West Africa, where mobile money fees were crushing the people who could least afford them. Wave launched a near-zero-fee model backed by Stripe and others and built a product that spread virally because it was simply and obviously better. That is the kind of market disruption that looks inevitable in retrospect and impossible at the moment someone decides to try it.

**4. Moniepoint** (Nigeria, founded ~2015, unicorn 2024) is the company investors who were watching Nigeria missed — until suddenly they couldn't. It started as TeamApt, a software provider for banks, then pivoted into the field, literally: POS terminals and business banking for the merchants that Nigeria's formal banking system had largely ignored. By 2024, it was processing over $14 billion monthly. Its founder, Tosin Eniolorunda, put it plainly when he launched the company: "We didn't set out just to build a successful company. We set out to build an ecosystem." That framing matters.

**5. Paystack** (Nigeria, founded 2015) — acquired by Stripe in 2020 for over $200 million — is the story that announced Nigeria to the global fintech world. Shola Akinlade and Ezra Olubi met at Babcock University, a Seventh-day Adventist institution whose formation runs deep in its graduates. Paystack became the first Nigerian company accepted into Y Combinator. When Stripe came knocking, the founders sold not because they ran out of runway, but because the acquirer could give them global rails. The deal was a signal to every investor who thought African fintech was too risky: the exits are real.

## Banking the Unbanked

**6. TymeBank / Tyme Group** (South Africa, founded ~2018, ~$1.5B) became the first major South African unicorn, which is notable because

South Africa has the continent's most developed financial sector. The opportunity TymeBank found was not in the market's sophistication — it was in its gaps. Low-cost digital accounts, lending, and a distribution model that partners with retail chains to reach customers where they already shop. It was the first time a digital bank in South Africa genuinely made inroads with the underserved. The word 'first' matters here.

**7. Kuda** (Nigeria, founded 2019) is Nigeria's answer to TymeBank, and it grew faster. Zero bank fees. Free debit cards. An app designed for people who had been charged for every transaction by every institution that was supposed to serve them. Founder Babs Ogundeyi had spent years auditing Africa's largest banks at PwC — he understood the machine from the inside — before advising the Oyo State government and then building the thing he thought should exist. Kuda became famous during the 2020 #EndSARS protests when it was used to process relief contributions without interference. Sometimes the company that earns the most trust is the one that simply shows up at the right moment.

**8. Interswitch** (Nigeria, founded 2002, unicorn 2019) is the elder statesman of this list — older than most of the others, but its unicorn status arrived in 2019 and its infrastructure underpins much of what newer fintechs are building on. It is the proof point that African fintech is not a recent invention: someone was patiently building the rails for two decades before anyone started calling it a unicorn ecosystem.

## Energy, Mobility, and Supply Chain

**9. M-KOPA** (Kenya, founded 2011, major scale 2020s) is the company that proved pay-as-you-go wasn't just a clever pricing model — it was a financial product for people who had no other access to finance. Start with a solar panel and a basic phone. Pay daily in micro-amounts over your mobile money account. Build a credit history that did not exist before. Then unlock phones, fridges, motorcycles, school fees. The progression is deliberate and it is working: M-KOPA serves millions across Kenya, Uganda, Nigeria, Ghana, and beyond, and it has been profitable while doing it. Jesse Moore, its CEO and co-founder, is an American-born social enterprise leader who moved to Nairobi to build this. The servant-leader instinct here is not incidental — it is structural.

**10. Moove** (Nigeria, founded 2019) saw the problem that nobody else was naming: Africa has millions of people who want to drive for Uber, Bolt, or any of the ride-hailing platforms — but they cannot access vehicle financing. The formal credit system ignores them; the informal credit system is predatory. Moove finances vehicles through revenue-based repayment: drivers repay from their earnings, which the platform can see in real time. It is a financial product designed for the actual structure of gig-economy income, not for a salaried employee at a bank that serves a different kind of customer. Co-founder Ladi Delano, a serial entrepreneur who had previously built businesses in Asia, named his prior firm Grace Lake Partners — a quiet but telling signal about where he roots his purpose.

**11. Twiga Foods** (Kenya, founded 2014) tackled the supply chain problem that everyone in African agriculture knows and nobody had solved at scale: smallholder farmers who grow food that rots before it reaches the city, and urban vendors who overpay for produce that arrives inconsistently. Twiga built a cold-chain logistics network connecting the two — phone-based ordering for vendors, direct collection from farmers, same-day delivery. This is not a technology innovation; it is a logistics and trust innovation. The technology is the enabler.

**12. Husk Power** (pan-African, scaled in 2020s) is building mini-grids in rural communities that the national grid has never reached and probably never will. Its $100M+ funding rounds reflect a growing investor recognition that energy access in Africa will not be solved by waiting for governments to extend infrastructure — it will be solved by distributed systems that generate, store, and sell power locally. This is platform-reformer thinking applied to energy.

## The Wider Picture

The remaining companies on the list — **MNT-Halan** (Egypt's first fintech unicorn, microlending at scale), **Chipper Cash** (cross-border remittances built for the African diaspora), **PalmPay** (one of the fastest-growing payment apps in Nigeria), **Jumia** (Africa's NYSE-listed e-commerce giant, flawed but far-reaching), **Yoco** (South Africa's answer for SME payments), **Wasoko** (B2B supply chain for informal retailers), and **Planet42** (consumer lending fintech in Southern Africa) — all share a common DNA: they were built by people who looked at a structural gap in African economic life and decided to be the solution.

## What the Faithful Investor Should Notice

I want to name something that does not appear in the TechCrunch coverage of these companies. Nigeria, which dominates this list, has one of the most faith-saturated cultures on earth. The Redeemed Christian Church of God (RCCG) has 40,000 branches in 190 countries. Lagos has more mega-churches than most countries have churches. When you build a company in that environment, you are drawing from a talent pool that has been shaped — consciously or not — by decades of formation in communities where faith and hustle are not in tension. They reinforce each other. I had the privilege of partnering for many years with a good friend, Ben Akabueze, in hosting an annual conference called The Kingdom Summit at RCCG Kings Court in Lagos.

Some of the founders on this list have talked about faith explicitly. Iyin Aboyeji runs a public series on faith and investing. GB Agboola lists his faith before his company. Shola Akinlade and Ezra Olubi met at Babcock University, a Seventh-day Adventist institution whose graduates carry its formation with them. Others have not said so publicly — Tosin Eniolorunda, Babs Ogundeyi, Ladi Delano are not known for faith-forward public statements — but the cultural DNA is present whether they articulate it or not.

The point is not to claim these companies for the Kingdom as if faith were a membership card. The framing is simpler: when Western investors arrive in Nigeria with their Americano assumptions about secular markets and secular founders, they are misreading the room. The people building the most consequential companies in Africa are not building in a spiritual vacuum. When I ran a LEMON Leadership Workshop at the Central Bank of Nigeria before I even started, the host asked, "Who's got the prayer?" A Muslim man stood up and opened in prayer. At the end of the workshop, a Christian prayed, not some seeker-sensitive, non-offensive prayer either.

The question for the faith-aligned investor is whether they will engage that reality — or walk past it on the way to the cap table. Africa's most successful founders are not building despite the continent's faith formation. In many cases, they are building because of it.

Fintech dominates this list for an obvious reason: financial exclusion is a giant that camps upstream from most other problems in African economic life. Fix payments, fix credit, fix savings, and you unblock agriculture, education, healthcare, energy access, and mobility simultaneously. The investors who understand that infrastructure logic — not just the returns it generates, but the systems-level leverage it creates — are the ones best positioned to partner well with the people building it.

Nigeria leads. South Africa, Kenya, Egypt, and Senegal follow. The ecosystem took a funding hit in 2022 and 2023 as global capital retreated from risk. It came back. New unicorns arrived in 2024. The builders did not stop building just because Western investors got nervous. That is worth remembering when the next correction comes.

## Challenges and Opportunities

Africa's innovation problem is not primarily a lack of ideas but a lack of the conditions in which ideas can become businesses, and businesses can become industries. The story of the Joule illustrates the point with painful clarity. Engineers at Optimal Energy in South Africa developed a five-door electric car with a range of 150 to 300 kilometers, unveiled in 2008 — ahead of the Tesla Model S. It was not a concept car. It was a viable product. The South African government's insistence on owning a large percentage of the company (40%), combined with a mandatory Black Economic Empowerment allocation on top of that (10%) meant the project was structurally doomed before it could get to the production line — not technically, but financially. The story is documented in *Hope Arising* by Gerhard Swart, for which I wrote the foreword. The thought that stayed with me after reading it: the financial capital sucked the life out of the intellectual capital. That is a precise description of what happens when the wrong capital structure meets a genuine innovation.

We have worked with more than 200 companies in Africa since 2003. A meaningful percentage of those companies have brought inspired innovations to market — products and business ideas that emerged from genuine creativity, proximity to need, and in many cases what I can only describe as divine prompting. Several of them could scale globally with the right support. Most of them have not, for the same reason the Joule did not — not because the idea was wrong, but because the capitalization was insufficient, misaligned, or simply absent.

Let me give you four examples from that portfolio, many of which are covered in my book, Inspired Innovation: from Toil to Transformation.

A South African inventor developed an organic process for oxygenating and purifying water using locally sourced plant materials — no chemicals, no infrastructure dependency, replicable at community scale. It has not reached the market it deserves.

A colostomy bag attachment developed nearly thirty years ago uses a unique adhesive that bonds reliably to skin in ways that existing products do not, with associated wound-care properties that accelerate healing. The South African government will not purchase it from the local inventor. The reason given is that he does not have the right skin color. That sentence should not exist in 2026. It does.

Mannabrew is an espresso alternative made from mesquite pods — a superfood with genuine health benefits, produced from alien vegetation that is simultaneously an environmental problem across large parts of southern Africa. A business built around it creates local jobs, addresses an ecological challenge, and produces a product with legitimate international market potential. They have had amazing favor yet are still moving towards the capital to scale to their full potential.

A lightweight carbon-smart cement has been developed with no Portland cement in its composition — made instead from alien vegetation, biomass, ash, waste material, and a proprietary binding agent. It carries a four-hour fire rating. It is bulletproof. It deadens sound. It is carbon negative in its production. The construction industry in Africa — and well beyond Africa — needs this product. It is not yet at scale.

These are not marginal ideas. They are the kinds of solutions that emerge when people with moral imagination, proximity to real problems, and genuine faith ask what God's answer might look like. The gap between where these innovations are and where they could be is a capital gap — but not only a financial capital gap. It is a gap in organizational support, relational networks, market access, and the kind of patient, comprehensive capitalization that most investment structures are not designed to provide.

That is the problem the Global Giants Trust was built to solve. More on that shortly.

## From Africa, for the World

I want to be clear about something before we go further. This book is not an Africa-only argument. I am not proposing that investors focus exclusively on Africa, nor that African solutions should stay on the continent. A kingdom business and a kingdom investment should carry both a planted and a pilgrim perspective simultaneously — rooted deeply enough in a specific place to produce genuine transformation there, and oriented outward enough to carry what has been built into adjacent and stretch markets. Not planted first, then pilgrim. Both at once.

The commissioning verse in Acts 1:8 has always struck me as more than a geographic sequence. Jerusalem *and* Judea *and* Samaria *and* the ends of the earth. That word — *and* — is doing significant work. In Hebrew the equivalent is the letter Vav, one of the most common words in the ancient text, and it carries a both-and weight that English conjunctions tend to flatten into sequence. Jesus was not giving his disciples a four-stage rollout plan. He was describing a posture: immediate, adjacent, regional, and global all at once, held in tension, pursued simultaneously. The investor who is deeply embedded in one city in Kenya while simultaneously thinking about what that model means for East Africa, for the continent, and for the world is not being unfocused. That investor is operating in the spirit of the commission.

This does not mean every business scales in every direction at once — execution still requires sequence and prioritization. But the orientation, the imagination, the "so that" of what you are building — that should be global from day one, even if the first customer is local. South Africa has the highest GDP on the continent at the time of writing. There are remarkable businesses there that are genuinely needed in the rest of Africa. The step from South Africa to the continent is sometimes more achievable than the step from South Africa to the world — and that intermediate stage of continental scaling is currently underutilized as an investment thesis and underappreciated as a risk-reduction strategy. But the vision that drives it should never be merely continental.

When it comes to deploying capital, the most useful frame may be a continuum rather than a binary choice between startup and unicorn. Mezzanine financing, scaling capital, and growth equity for companies moving between stages of the step-scaling model are underserved categories in the African investment landscape. The investor who understands that continuum — and is willing to deploy across it rather than only at the endpoints — is operating with a structural advantage.

One more thing worth stating plainly: Africa should not be about Africa alone. The power of the kingdom of God flows through unity and interdependence. We grow as people through mutual encouragement and honor — and that applies to continents as much as to individuals. Africa has things to learn from Latin America, Southeast Asia, Europe, and North America, just as those regions have things to learn from Africa. Simply reinventing the wheel so that we can say "we built this in Africa" is not wisdom. It is a smaller version of the same nationalism that has held the continent back. If Africa wants to have genuine global impact, it must be part of an Impact Network that is larger than itself.

Building that network is not a nice idea. It is a structural requirement. And it starts with understanding what an Impact Network actually is.

# 10. Build Impact Networks

I remember it like it was yesterday. We were in Mexico on vacation when we got the news of the tsunami that rocked Southeast Asia in late 2004. Many organizations scrambled to respond to the devastation in Banda Aceh, Indonesia. In May 2005 I traveled with a team from Jakarta to Banda Aceh. Half the town had been wiped out as if it had been scraped off the surface of the earth. Ships that had been out at sea were now sitting in local neighborhoods. Only the foundations of homes remained. The scale of the devastation was a surprise — or was it?

In Matthew 24, Jesus told his disciples they would hear of wars and rumors of wars, of nations rising against nations, of famines and earthquakes in various places. He did not say these things might happen. He said they must. The scale of need that arises from man-made and natural disasters is such that an individual business or NGO operating alone will not be able to cope with it. In fact, investing in individual businesses without a supporting network may well be foolish. The Banda Aceh moment crystallized something I had been thinking about for years: we do not just need better businesses. We need businesses that are part of an Impact Network.

## What is an Impact Network?

In the late 1990s I had the opportunity to work with Gary Daichendt, who at the time was EVP of Worldwide Operations at Cisco Systems. We researched 600 companies looking for the winners and losers in the emerging digital economy. One of the areas we examined was partnering — how the most effective organizations were building networks of relationships that multiplied their reach and impact beyond what any single entity could achieve alone.

> *In 1997, The Institute developed a term to describe this new type of partnering; we called it an Impact Network™. This is the subset of organizations that you pull from the universe of players to repeatedly help you have an Impact. The rationale then was that it takes a network to create an impact. This is even truer today. Clients or customers no longer believe that one company has it all. Customers therefore expect that their suppliers will work together to develop the solutions that they need. The Impact Network has four cardinal points: customers, competitors, contributors (or suppliers), and complementors.*[14]

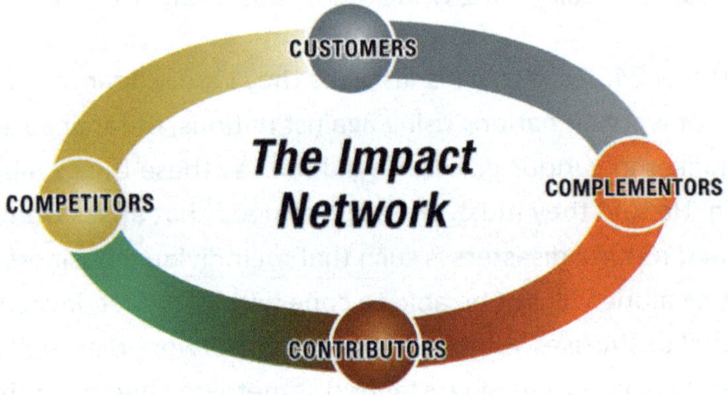


The relationships between these four points are not fixed. A competitor can become a contributor on any given day — a private equity fund that raises capital from the same family offices you target might take money

---

[14] I-Operations: How the Internet can Transform your Operating Model, Daichendt and Johnson, Indaba Publishing 2002

away from your fund one day and invest in businesses in your network the next. A competitor can become a complementor, creating demand for your own product. The NGO that offers free training — competing with your paid offering — becomes a complementor when its graduates become suppliers to your business. When you encounter an investment opportunity that is too large for you alone, or where you want to spread risk, a competitor becomes a co-investor. The categories are fluid. The network is the constant.

One of the reasons the church is a decade behind the rest of the world in defining and measuring impact in Africa is its reluctance to partner. The Impact Network framework is a practical corrective to that reluctance — it names the categories of relationship that need to be built and maintained, and it makes the case that the most significant investments are rarely made by a single actor operating in isolation.

As you have already seen from the discussion of zones and actors, investment risk is materially reduced where there is a defined Impact Network. This is not a soft observation. It is a structural one.

## The Impetus for Impact

What's the starting point for a kingdom adventure in Africa? This is the question I hear most consistently from investors who are serious about Africa and ready to move from conviction to action.

One answer is to put the fund together first and then go looking for investment opportunities. This makes genuine sense — you do not raise hope and then leave it without the capital to underpin it. Henry Kaestner's Solving the World's Greatest Problems initiative is a good example of this approach: define the capital structure, build investor conviction, then deploy toward problems that matter.

A second answer is to build the network first — a collective of leaders, intellectual property, and businesses that work together — and then find the funding to support what is already forming. The Nehemiah Africa Impact Network, headed by Francois Steyn, is the clearest example I know. It builds trust capital and deep relationships over time as complementary solutions providers learn from each other. The funding follows the network because the network has already demonstrated what it is capable of.

A third answer is to find the end-use project first and pull the network and funding in behind it. The Hope Estate Project in Bulawayo is tackling the giant of mass urbanization in Africa by building cities on the edges of cities. It requires a network of players to be part of the solution — so it has pulled in the Nehemiah Africa Impact Network for building technologies, the Hamara Group for agricultural competencies, property development partners, and funders. The project defines the network rather than the other way around. And the project finds its "Why" in the context of a Transforming Society plan for Bulawayo, its host city. Nehemiah was a man who sought the welfare of a city. God made a promise through the prophet Jeremiah and it was specifically for those who were rebuilding cities.

> [7] *Work to see that the city where I sent you as exiles enjoys peace and prosperity. Pray to the Lord for it. For as it prospers you will prosper.'* [11] *For I know what I have planned for you,' says the Lord. 'I have plans to prosper you, not to harm you. I have plans to give you a future filled with hope.* [12] *When you call out to me and come to me in prayer, I will hear your prayers.* [13] *When you seek me in prayer and worship, you will find me available to you. Jeremiah 29:7-13*

Typically, we read verse 11 as a personal promise, yet it was made to those who were seeking the flourishing of cities.

In practice, you probably need all four legs of the stool working simultaneously: funding, networks, projects, and end customers or off-takers who create the demand that makes everything else viable. A stool with three legs is unstable. Four legs, properly placed, hold the weight.

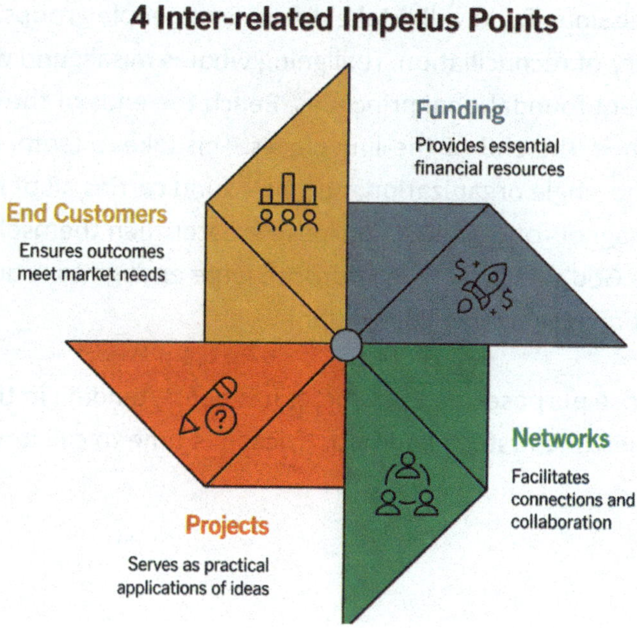


The Mergon Foundation, founded by South African entrepreneur François van Niekerk and led by CEO Pieter Faure, has become one of the most significant aggregators of faith-aligned philanthropic capital for Africa — pulling together resources from multiple sources and deploying them strategically across the continent. It is a working model of what the orchestrator role looks like when networks are built intentionally rather than discovered accidentally.

## Know your value-add as in Investor

I am not suggesting you stay in your lane if you want to make a difference in Africa. I am not suggesting you narrow your niche to the point of irrelevance. What I am advocating is that you know your purpose and the specific value you bring — whether that is the structuring of finance, operational excellence, industry expertise, governance capability, or relational networks that open doors nobody else can open. Know it precisely. Name it clearly. Then bring it fully.

The commission we have received is threefold and simultaneous — the Vav commission, if you will. Make disciples of people groups. Exercise the ministry of reconciliation, realigning what is misaligned with transcendent foundational principles. Reach the ends of the earth, the least reached, the end-of-the-line places. This takes a team. No single investor, no single organization, no single fund carries all of it. The aligning magnet for teams is a purpose greater than themselves, firmly hitched to God's purposes — a purpose large enough to require collaboration rather than competition.

One of those purposes has a name. It has been standing in the room since Livingstone first walked into Africa. It is time to call it what it is.

## 11. Invest to tackle Global Giants

When David Livingstone went to Africa in the 1840s, his primary vision was to spread Christianity, open legitimate trade routes, and encourage civilization — in nineteenth-century terms. The slave trade was a concern, but it was not yet his defining focus. Everything changed when he personally witnessed the horrors of the East African slave trade: caravans crossing Central and East Africa, people chained, starved, and brutalized, entire villages destroyed by raiders. He described scenes of indescribable misery and mass suffering. What he saw broke something open in him that never closed again.

By the 1860s and 70s, during his final expeditions, his mission had sharpened to a single defining purpose: end the slave trade. His approach was strategic rather than merely moral. He believed slavery would not end through outrage alone — it would end when legitimate commerce made it economically redundant. Open the Zambezi. Build trade routes. Connect Africa to global markets in ways that gave communities an economic alternative to the slave economy. In today's language, he was trying to shift from exploitative extraction to sustainable economic systems.

He raised global awareness through his reports, shocking Britain and Europe and catalyzing anti-slavery sentiment that strengthened British resolve against the trade. His efforts contributed directly to the 1873 closure of the Zanzibar slave market — the largest slave market in the world at the time.

It was not an easy task. Livingstone operated in what we would now call a Friction Zone — high ethnic diversity, low trust architecture, and a massive, entrenched giant in the form of the exploitative slave system. His missionary presence and relational engagement built trust across communities that had every reason not to trust an outsider. His advocacy and exploration brought moral pressure at the policy level. His commercial vision created an economic alternative. And indirectly, through influencing British trade and policy, he brought capital to bear on a giant that had resisted every previous effort to dislodge it.

Three strands. One coherent strategy. A global giant brought down. While Livingstone was not a business-first person, the concept of commerce taking down giants was inherent in his strategy.

## What is a Global Giant?

The year is 2026. We have had over 2000 years to address the ills of society since Jesus Christ left the planet. There has been good progress on some fronts. The charts do tell a story worth telling. But the benefits have not been evenly distributed, and the question is no longer whether transformation is possible. The question is why, after two millennia and all the resources the church has accumulated, so much remains undone.

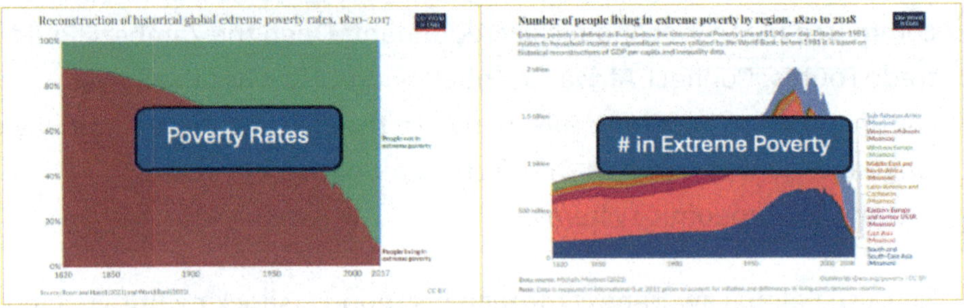

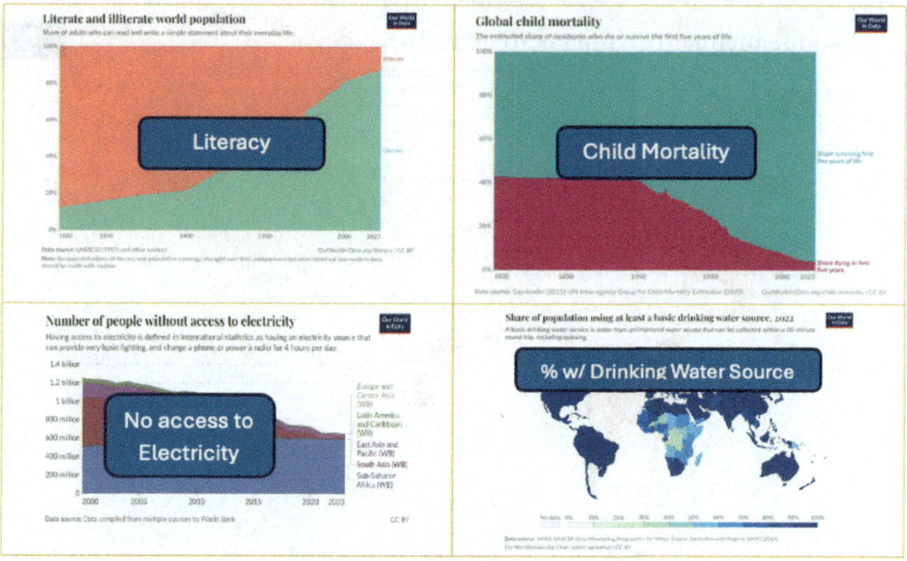


In a world with the capacity to feed everyone, children still go to sleep hungry. In a civilization that outlawed slavery centuries ago, human trafficking is the fastest-growing criminal enterprise on the planet. Child labor persists in supply chains that serve consumers who prefer not to know. Billions lack adequate healthcare — not because the medicine does not exist, but because the systems to deliver it have never been built and the economic incentives serve the over-served, not the poor.

Underemployment — the quiet giant, the failure of people to meet their God-given potential — may be the most pervasive and least visible of all. Migrant workers remit money to families they rarely see, serving people who live in relative luxury, rarely asking where their services come from. The gap between those who have and those who do not is widening, not closing, in most of the world.

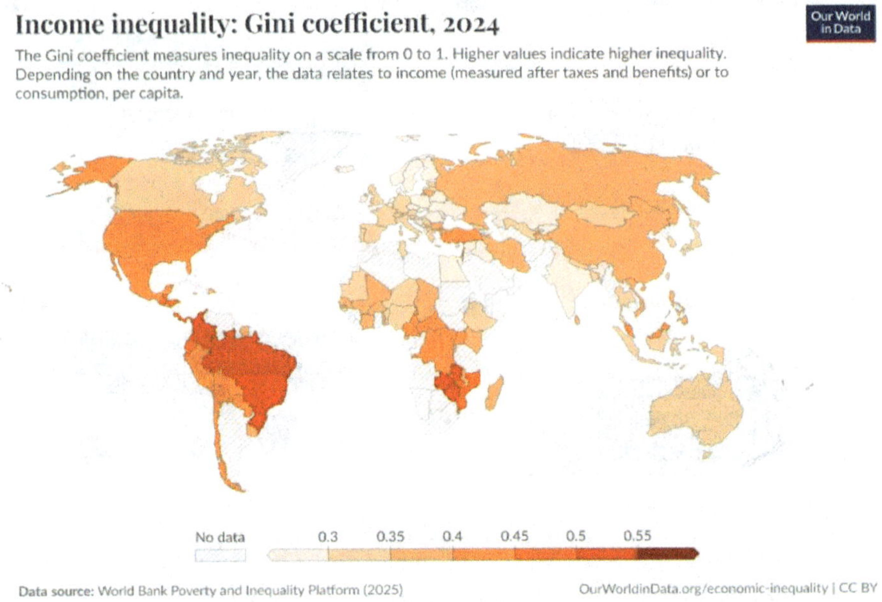


These are not problems confined to one country or one region. They cross borders, cultures, and continents. They are structural, systemic, and deeply resistant to the solutions that well-intentioned people keep applying to them.

These are the global giants. And they are still standing.

## Why do we still have global giants?

Why are the giants still standing? You might point to the sinfulness of man — the straightforward answer that we are not walking in the laws, ways, precepts, and instruction of God, and the giants are the consequence. You would not be wrong. But there is something else going on, and God put it in parentheses in the book of Judges so we would not miss it.

> *These are the nations the Lord left to test all those Israelites who had not experienced any of the wars in Canaan* ***(he did this only to teach warfare to the***

***descendants of the Israelites who had not had previous battle experience):*** *the five rulers of the Philistines, all the Canaanites, the Sidonians, and the Hivites living in the Lebanon mountains from Mount Baal Hermon to Lebo Hamath. Judges 3:1-3*

Read that carefully. God left the giants. Not because he forgot about them, not because he lacked the power to remove them, but because his people needed battle experience. The giants were not an oversight. They were a curriculum.

God has not called us to a country club life of ease and peace. Isaiah tells us that "of the increase of his government and peace there will be no end." Meanwhile, we are conscripted into an army to contend for the things that are on God's heart and to right the wrongs counter to His intentions. To fulfill this assignment we must understand warfare, and we must have battle experience. It requires that we stop treating the giants as someone else's problem.

By and large, the Western Church avoids giants. We must identify the ones that are our assignment, understand them clearly, and get ready to tackle them — with every form of capital at our disposal.

## Who will face the giants?

We left Tel Aviv at 3 a.m. It was a cold December morning as we flew into Marseille. As is my habit, I looked out of the plane window and contemplated the giants in the nation to which we were going. In my 5 a.m. fatigue, I whispered, "God, I don't have the strength to fight every giant in every country." As quick as anything, he replied, "Yes, but you can't fight the same giant in every country." There is no room for pity parties in the kingdom of God.

If you have been blessed with financial resources and have had the privilege of building capital, you have a privileged opportunity — not just to preserve that capital or multiply it, but to direct it toward the giants that oppose God's purposes. Money finds its meaning in pursuit of those purposes. Capital deployed toward a global giant is not philanthropy. It is warfare by other means.

For centuries the secular-sacred dichotomy has sidelined the people best positioned to do this work. Businesspeople were told their job was to make money and hand it to churches and charities who would then do God's real work. The implication was that commerce was a necessary evil — tolerated, not celebrated — and that the marketplace was a place you left as quickly as possible on your way to something more significant. That line of thinking is not just wrong. It has been catastrophically costly. The giants are still standing partly because the people with the resources and the competencies to tackle them have been sitting in the stands watching the game played by religious professionals rather than suiting up to play.

The truth — the self-evident truth, as the Founding Fathers might have said — is that God works, work is good, work is worship, and we work with God. Business is ministry. Business is a calling. The marketplace is not a compromise; it is a commission. The vast majority of people are called to it, which means the vast majority of kingdom resources flow through it. Recognizing these truths is not the hard part: acting on it at scale still is.

God has a business. Our businesses should be subsidiaries. Think of it as God Unlimited holding a portfolio of companies — Head Office with a transcendent purpose, and each subsidiary aligned to that purpose rather than running its own agenda. When that alignment is genuine, a business stops being merely a wealth-generation vehicle and becomes a giant-tackling machine.

The question is not whether you have the resources to engage. If you are reading this book, you probably do. The question is whether you are willing to direct those resources toward something large enough to matter — and whether you understand that tackling a global giant requires more than financial capital alone.

## Business tackles Giants

In 1976 a group of Christian leaders gathered in South Africa for something called the South African Christian Leadership Assembly — SACLA. They identified six giants that were tearing the country apart: poverty and unemployment, breakdown in family structures, violence against women, sexual immorality, children born outside of stable homes, and the spiritual vacuum underneath all of it. They also named the gorilla in the room — the giant that caused all the others to follow: Poverty and unemployment. Take that one down and the others become more tractable. Leave it unaddressed and everything else is symptomatic treatment.

Fifty years later the same giants are still standing in South Africa — and across most of Africa, and in many parts of the world that would not describe themselves as developing. The gorilla is still in the room.

Now here is the question that follows from that observation: who is going to bring it to its knees.?

Not governments. Governments are good at redistributing money. They can create the policies and infrastructure that support business. But job creation — genuine, dignity-restoring, family-sustaining employment — is not something governments do well. The record is clear enough that this is not a controversial claim. It is simply a description of what governments are structurally equipped to do and what they are not.

Business tackles giants. A well-purposed business is focused, efficient, capable of generating the profits that make it sustainable, and able to create an upwardly positive domino effect that ripples through a community in ways that no aid program or government initiative can replicate. When a business employs people, it changes families. When it changes families it changes neighborhoods. When enough neighborhoods change, a city changes. When cities change, a nation changes. While the domino falls a long way from where you tipped the first one, the chain is not automatic. The societal value-adding chain must be architected, or it will be lost in little projects and small investments.

Many of the world's biggest problems today will be solved by businesspeople — IF. That IF carries significant weight. Small problems can be solved by local businesses operating in relative isolation. Global giants will only be tackled if they receive what I call comprehensive capitalization — financial capital, yes, but also human capital, relational capital, intellectual capital, organizational capital, and spiritual capital, all deployed together toward the same giant. Change the cap table. Change the financing structure. Change what you count as a contribution to the deal.

Without comprehensive capitalization, inspired innovations stall, promising businesses plateau, societal transformation ends up on an NGO scorecard, and giants remain standing. With it, something different becomes possible. The structure that makes comprehensive capitalization operational is what the Global Giants Trust was built to be — the mechanism that sits between the inventor and the investor, ensures fair returns for both, and channels the excess into an evergreen fund.

Which brings us to July 4th, 2006.

## The Global Giants Trust

It was July 4th, 2006. Lyn and I were about to meet with a couple whose stated aim was to give away a billion dollars. Before the meeting I went for a long walk and had a conversation with God about what I was seeing in the world.

By that stage we had worked with hundreds of companies in Africa, Southeast Asia, India, and the United States. The model was a ten-day Repurposing Business Venture — we would take a team from somewhere like Silicon Valley, land in a place like Jakarta, and work intensively with ten businesses to get those businesses into God's business. The tagline we used then is the one we still use: *Repurposing Business — Transforming Society.*®

The thesis was simple: if we could get a critical mass of mid-market companies in a particular market genuinely repurposed, we would start to see the needle move in terms of societal flourishing.

As the work progressed, a pattern emerged. A subset of these businesses carried what I started calling Inspired Innovations — products and business ideas that had certain qualities I could not fully account for through conventional innovation theory. They had arrived through a different process. The full account of what I mean by that is in my book *Inspired Innovation: from Toil to Transformation.* What matters here is the problem that became clear as I watched these innovations: the inventors who carried them and the investors who wanted to fund kingdom work were consistently failing to find each other — and when they did find each other, the language they spoke and the terms of engagement were usually wrong for both of them.

I have sat across the table from inspired inventors who were passionate about what God had given them — sometimes fiercely protective of it — but who had a low organizational quotient and an unexamined assumption that since God had given them the idea, the funding would follow automatically. And I have sat across the table from godly, well-intentioned investors who genuinely wanted to deploy capital to advance the kingdom of God, but whose grid was standard Western venture capital or private equity — IRR, ROI, exit strategies, return multiples. In extreme cases, the inventor decided the investor was a greedy capitalist. The investor decided the inventor was nuts. The capital never moved. The innovation never scaled. The giant remained standing.

On that July 4th walk, God spoke to me clearly. The instruction was specific: set up the Global Giants Trust — an entity that would sit between the inventor and the investor, keep purpose at the center, ensure the investor received a fair return, ensure that the inventor received a fair return with IP protection, and channel the excess into an evergreen fund that would keep deploying capital toward the next inspired innovation tackling the next global giant.

When Lyn and I sat down with that couple in Silicon Valley and shared the concept, they endorsed it immediately. The wife had watched close-up as her father — a professor with genuine innovations — had seen his work taken over by those providing the capital. He saw no return. She understood viscerally why a structure was needed that protected both sides of the table.

That conversation was twenty years ago. The structure is now built.

## Comprehensive Capitalization

The purpose of Global Giants is stated plainly in its founding mandate: *Comprehensively capitalizing inspired innovations to tackle global issues.™*

Two entities have been established on the Isle of Man to operationalize that mandate. Global Giants Trust is a registered UK charity — those who wish to deploy charitable capital, including from donor-advised funds, can direct it here. Global Giants Limited is the commercial vehicle — those who want to make direct investments in businesses tackling problems God cares about can do so through this entity. A two-page Executive Summary is in the appendices.

The word "comprehensively" is doing the most work in that mandate and it deserves unpacking. We define capital too narrowly. Ask most investors how many categories of capital they work with and the answer will be three at most — financial, human, maybe intellectual.

The actual number is larger, and the categories that tend to be underweighted are often the ones that determine whether a faith-forward business. succeeds or fails.

Financial capital is the one everyone counts. But an inspired inventor with abundant financial capital and no relational network, no organizational infrastructure, no spiritual discernment about timing and partnerships, and no intellectual framework for scaling what God has given them — that inventor will fail with the money in hand. Conversely, an investor with a purely financial grid who cannot recognize spiritual capital, who has no framework for assessing the organizational quotient of an early-stage kingdom business, who applies standard exit terms to an enterprise with a calling — that investor will consistently back the wrong things and structure deals that damage what they were trying to build.

Comprehensive capitalization means every form of capital is identified, valued, and deployed deliberately. Financial capital. Human capital. Intellectual capital. Relational capital. Organizational capital. Spiritual capital. The cap table expands. The financing structures change. The metrics of success include the eternal ROI alongside the temporal one.

The future of transformation belongs to models that do not just fight problems but replace broken systems with ones that sustain life, dignity, and flourishing. Global Giants was built to be that model — the structure that makes comprehensive capitalization operational, that protects the inventor and rewards the investor, and that keeps the evergreen fund flowing toward the next giant on the list.

If that is a structure you want to be part of, the conversation can begin here.

## Give me the giants

Who doesn't love the story of Caleb?

When Israel finally entered the Promised Land after forty years of circling the desert, the giants were still there. The same ones the spies had seen four decades earlier — the ones that had caused ten of the twelve to come back with a bad report, the ones that had made grown men feel like grasshoppers — they had not gone anywhere. And Caleb, now eighty-five years old, walked up to Joshua and asked for his assignment.

When Israel finally entered the Promised Land after forty years of circling the desert, the giants were still there. The same ones the spies had seen four decades earlier — the ones that had caused ten of the twelve to come back with a bad report, the ones that had made grown men feel like grasshoppers. They had not gone anywhere. And Caleb, now eighty-five years old, walked up to Joshua and asked for his assignment.

> *The people of Judah came to Joshua at Gilgal. Caleb son of Jephunneh the Kenizzite spoke: "You'll remember what God said to Moses the man of God concerning you and me back at Kadesh Barnea. I was forty years old when Moses the servant of God sent me from Kadesh Barnea to spy out the land. And I brought back an honest and accurate report. My companions who went with me discouraged the people, but I stuck to my guns, totally with God, my God. That was the day that Moses solemnly promised, 'The land on which your feet have walked will be your inheritance, you and your children's, forever. Yes, you have lived totally for God.' Now look at me: God has kept me alive, as he promised. It is now forty-five years since God spoke this word to Moses, years in which Israel wandered in the wilderness. And here I am today, eighty-five years old! I'm as strong as I was the day Moses sent me out. I'm as strong as ever in battle, whether coming or going. So give me this hill country that God promised me.*

*You yourself heard the report, that the Anakim were there with their great fortress cities. If God goes with me, I will drive them out, just as God said." Joshua 14, The Message translation*

The Anakim were not metaphorical. They were a race of formidable warriors inhabiting southern Canaan — tall, organized, occupying fortified cities. Historians believe Goliath and his fellow giants may have descended from them. These were the people that had made the original spies lose their nerve. And Caleb, at eighty-five, said: give me the hill country where the giants live.

Forty-five years of waiting had not diminished his appetite for the assignment. He had no thoughts of retirement. The delays had sharpened his resolve.

I have long believed that as leaders advance — as they move beyond building their own businesses into attempting to solve problems in the world — something in them either expands or contracts. The ones who expand begin to see the global giants as their assignment. The ones who contract build larger barns and/or chase little white golf balls. (I am not opposed to golf; I just mention this as an example of a retirement-oriented diversion.)

There are current-day initiatives that seek to tackle societal giants with genuine seriousness. The Millennium Development Goals, which morphed into the Sustainable Development Goals, represent the world's best attempt at coordinated, measurable action against poverty, disease, inequality, and environmental degradation. They are worth knowing. They are worth engaging with critically — not dismissing because they are secular, but asking whether the targets are right, whether the mechanisms are adequate, and where faith-based capital can accelerate what is already moving. The Grameen Foundation and HOPE International have done serious work in microfinance. The Faith Driven Entrepreneur and Investor movement's Solving the World's

Greatest Problems initiative is asking faith-based investors to rank the giants they care most about and then put capital behind solving them. These are meaningful efforts.

And then there are the initiatives that should exist but don't — or that exist in embryonic form and need the kind of comprehensive capitalization that could take them to scale. The tech billionaires who have decided that the fortune they made in one narrow domain qualifies them for wisdom across every field are not entirely wrong to believe their capital can move mountains. They are sometimes wrong about which mountains need moving, and wrong about what moving them actually requires. Capital without discernment is not enough. It never has been.

## Our Unfinished Mandate is a global giant

In 2010 I was facilitating a workshop on transforming society in Northern California. That is where I met John Anderson — shortly after he had obeyed God's challenge to walk away from a CEO role at a major corporation to pursue a mandate that had not yet been fully defined. As we talked about transforming society, relaying foundations, stewarding assets, repurposing spheres of society, and restoring the glory of God, John asked a question I have kept pondering: "What does finished look like?"

I told him to figure out the answer for himself. He has been on a quest to do so ever since. Every Monday we host a Kingdom Business Community online call where we discuss this and related questions in depth. One does not need to be a rocket scientist to observe that we have not yet completed the Great Commission. The question John asked is not rhetorical. It is the most important strategic question the church has not yet answered with sufficient precision.

When we lived through the dot-com boom around 2000, something struck me that I have never fully shaken. Billions of dollars of wealth —

on paper at least — sat in the hands of Christ followers. Many began forming foundations and family offices, putting staff in place, developing criteria for deployment. They built barns called foundations, trusts and family offices. And then it was gone. I have a suspicion — one I intend to ask God about directly when I see him — that we had, at that moment, sufficient resources in the hands of his people to complete the Great Commission. We built barns instead.

We are living through another such moment. The Web 3.0 wave. The explosion of artificial intelligence. The potential for returning to the Genesis 1 mandate of co-creating with God is genuinely extraordinary right now — more so than at any previous point in history. The tools are extraordinary. The capital is concentrated. The innovations are emerging faster than the investment structures can absorb them.

The question is not whether the opportunity exists. It is whether we will be intrigued by the shiny new thing — chasing the next technological wave for its own sake — or whether we will pursue impact that connects to eternity. Whether we will build barns again, or whether this time we will actually deploy. If we fail to do so, capital in the hands of Christians will continue to grow, and a crisis of meaning will accelerate in parallel.

Caleb did not ask for the easy territory. He asked for the hill country where the giants lived. At eighty-five.

What is your hill country?

## 12. Take Impact to New Heights

Will the SDGs rescue Africa? The honest answer is no — not on their own, and not without a fundamentally different understanding of what drives sustainable change. That is not a reason to dismiss them. The Sustainable Development Goals represent the world's most coordinated attempt to measure and address the giants of poverty, disease, inequality, and environmental degradation. We have been mapping the SDGs to Scripture, to biblical principles, to critical success factors, and to metrics aligned with biblical truth — not to throw stones at the effort, but to find where it aligns with God's intent and where it diverges from it. The divergences matter. So does the alignment.

The better question — the one that reframes the entire conversation about impact metrics — is this: what does "it is finished" look like when you are working toward the triple-braided Great Commission?

> *I have fought the good fight, I have finished the race, I have kept the faith. 2 Timothy4:7*

I believe we must reimagine the full restoration of the glory of God in every facet of society. Before there was a Bible or a formal synagogue or a church, the ancients contemplated creation and concluded that nature declared the glory of God. They could see order, beauty, structure, intention, and purpose in what was made. We live in a world with floods of information, avalanches of distraction, and countless competing claims on our attention. The challenge is not access to ideas about God's glory but the capacity to re-comprehend it — to see it freshly enough that it becomes the organizing principle of how we invest, how we build, and how we measure whether we are winning.

In the framework I lay out in *Transforming Society*, there are four movements in the work of societal restoration: relaying foundations, stewarding societal assets, repurposing spheres of society, and restoring glory. They are sequential by nature but not always in practice. Today our best approach is to start at the end — to imagine what it would look like if the glory of God was fully restored in this industry, this city, this nation — and then work backward to what needs to happen first. If we cannot see it in our minds and spirits, we will not see it in practice.

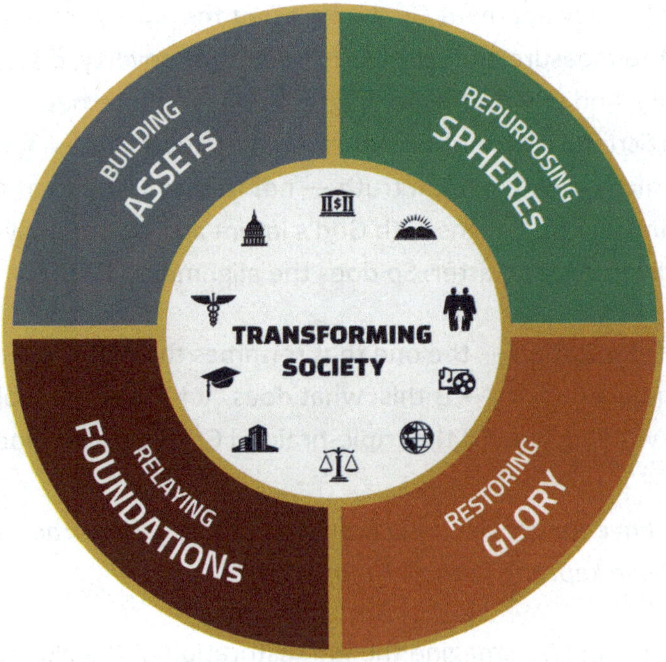


Of what relevance is this to an investor? More than it might seem. Many investors are rightly concerned about sustainability — they do not want to deploy capital only to find that the investee is back at the well twelve months later. What I have observed consistently is this: if an investee is shooting for anything less than the full restoration of what God intends for their sector and community, the chances are that their business will not be sustainable. Small vision produces fragile businesses. Vision calibrated to the glory of God produces enterprises with the roots to survive the storms.

## Scorecarding for Today & Eternity

The last thing anyone wants is a Kingdom Business Scorecard that simply relocates the secular-sacred dichotomy rather than resolving it. And yet that is precisely what tends to happen.

First we separated career from calling — as though the way you earned a living had nothing to do with what God had called you to. Then we separated career from community and kept a home life and a work life in different compartments. Then the Seven Mountains philosophy became a thing and we relocated the dichotomy again, asking "what mountain am I from?" — as though we were from this domain or that, rather than from the mountain of the Lord. And when it comes to business, we took our cue from the corporate world which long ago decided that social responsibility belonged in a separate department, funded by a separate budget, measured by separate metrics. Corporate Social Responsibility might more accurately be called Outsourced Social Responsibility — most corporates simply hand money to charities and call it done. Entrenched corporate dichotomy.

For more than thirty years we have contended that there should be no separate scorecard for social impact and for business results. If business is ministry, then doing good should show up in the key performance indicators of the business itself — not in a footnote, not in an annual CSR report, not in a separate line item where philanthropic activity gets isolated from the essence of the enterprise. The business either produces abundant life or it participates in steal, kill, and destroy. Jesus said so in John 10:10, and it applies to the P&L as much as to anything else.

This is the logic behind The 10-P Scorecard we have used for decades at The Institute. It records strategies, action items, and key performance indicators and then maps those business strategies to the ten spheres of society and to the societal giants that each strategy is actively addressing. Not every business strategy maps to a giant — that would be forced and artificial. But the goal is for more and more of the organization to be deliberately connected to the problems it is solving and the advancement of the kingdom it is serving. As the business advances, the society improves. The aggregate of a collection of repurposed companies in a city gives some genuine indication of the health of that city — not as a separate set of metrics, but as an integrated outcome.

## A Spiritual Audit of Corporate Giving

Remember — it is not the devil who is in the details. It is God who is in the details. Which means if you want to find out whether a business is genuinely integrated or merely performing integration, you go to the line items in the P&L. The symptoms of dichotomy are almost always hiding there.

The faith-based investing world has developed three distinct postures toward this challenge, and it is worth understanding how they differ.

The first is negative screening — avoiding companies whose products or practices conflict with biblical values. This is where most faith-based investing began, and it remains a legitimate starting point. It is not, however, a complete answer. Knowing what you will not own is different from knowing what your ownership is producing.

The second posture is shareholder activism — using the tools of ownership to change corporate behavior from the inside. Robert Netzly and the team at Inspire Investing have developed one of the most systematic approaches to this in the faith-based world. Their model combines ownership, voting rights, and sustained engagement — filing shareholder proposals at major corporations, voting against resolutions that conflict with biblical values, and applying what Netzly calls a viewpoint diversity engagement model that pushes companies toward neutrality in their giving and advocacy. In their 2026 shareholder proposal campaign alone they filed thirty-eight proposals at major corporations. The full methodology is documented on the Inspire Investing website and warrants careful study for any investor with listed equities in their portfolio.

The third posture — and the one that goes furthest — is positive engagement: actively seeking out and backing companies whose products and services genuinely serve human flourishing, and whose business model is itself an expression of the kingdom rather than merely a funding source for it. This is the ground that Robin John and Finny Kuruvilla have been developing at Eventide Asset Management. Their framework moves beyond asking "does this company avoid harm?" to asking "does this company create genuine value for all its stakeholders — customers, employees, suppliers, communities, and society?" That is a different analytical grid, and it produces a different portfolio. Eventide's research has also made the case that businesses genuinely serving human flourishing tend to outperform over the long term — that the integration of biblical values into investment analysis is not a concession to conscience at the expense of return, but a more complete picture of what drives durable business performance.

The broader principle connecting all three postures is this: ownership carries responsibility. If you own shares in a company, you have a voice in what that company does with its profits, its influence, and its brand. Most faith-based investors have never fully exercised that voice. A spiritual audit of charitable giving starts not with what you give away but with what you own — and what your ownership is actively producing in the world.

## The problem with SDG and similar scorecards

The inherent logic of most SDG-aligned corporate initiatives follows the same pattern: take excess profits, or dip into assets, and transfer the resources to NGOs or social sector organizations to do good with money that the corporation made doing something else. It feels virtuous. It generates good press. And it systematically disconnects a corporation from its actual calling.

We have no right to outsource our calling. When a scorecard separates a corporation from its purpose by routing its good works through a third party, it is not solving the problem — it is institutionalizing the dichotomy in a new form. The corporation continues doing what it does, the NGO continues doing what it does, and the two never have to reckon with the question of whether the corporation's core business is itself producing life or producing harm.

The SDG framework, whatever its merits as a coordinating mechanism for global attention, largely reinforces this separation. It asks corporations to measure and report on their social and environmental contributions often as a category distinct from their business operations. That framing is the problem. A kingdom business does not have a separate social responsibility budget. It has a single purpose — and that purpose shows up in everything, including the P&L.

There is a harder edge to this worth naming plainly. If money has been made in a suspect way, giving it away does not make it good. Laundering bad capital through charitable giving is not generosity. It is a more socially acceptable form of the same problem. The audit has to go all the way to the source.

## The failure of the NGO industrial complex

The NGO industrial complex deserves its own book — and I am writing it. The short version is this: NGOs were never meant to replace families, businesses, markets, or governments. At their best they serve as catalysts — temporary scaffolding that enables people and systems to heal, stand, and flourish on their own. At their worst they have become permanent intermediaries, professionalizing dysfunction and unintentionally undermining the very communities they exist to serve. Compassion has not failed. The delivery mechanism has.

It is worth being precise here because the zone framework we developed earlier in this book is relevant. In Friction Zones — where trust architecture is low, state capacity is weak, and the conditions for sustainable business are still forming — NGOs often do their best work. They build the relational infrastructure that makes everything else possible. Churches and NGOs are frequently the only institutions with the reach, the trust, and the community embeddedness to operate effectively in these environments. The problem is not NGOs in Friction Zones. The problem is NGOs that never leave — that set up permanent operations in Resilience Zones and Opportunity Zones where functional markets and capable institutions should long ago have made them redundant. A scaffold that becomes a permanent structure is no longer helping the building stand. It is preventing it from being finished.

The strategic response is what I call bypass surgery. Rather than continuing to route capital, training, and opportunity through institutional arteries that are partially blocked by bureaucracy, ideology, and misaligned incentives, the goal is to move resources directly to people, households, and enterprises — as close to the coalface as possible. Link makers to markets. Resource entrepreneurs and families rather than defaulting to NGO funding. Measure success by value created rather than money spent.

Some activities will always require charity — rescue operations, emergency relief, temporary aid in genuine crisis. Temporary, however, must remain temporary. The moment a temporary solution becomes a permanent institution, it has begun to work against its own purpose. The Repurposing NGOs book will make this case in full. For now, the relevant point for investors is this: know which zone you are operating in and let that determine the role of the NGO in your impact network. In a Friction Zone, fund the NGO. In an Opportunity Zone, fund the business — and let the NGO walk into its sunset or find a new Friction Zone.

## Over-regulating charity

There is a genuine tension here worth acknowledging. On one side, the US tax code does something right: it creates meaningful incentives for generosity, encouraging individuals and corporations to direct resources toward causes that serve the common good. That is worth appreciating and worth protecting. On the other side, the system has been abused. An immigration officer told us fifteen years ago that a third of nonprofits in the US were fake. The more recent fraud scandals suggest the problem has not improved with time.

The tendency of African governments to over-regulate does not stop with businesses — it extends to charities as well. The instinct is understandable. The execution is often counterproductive. The amount of compliance paperwork that nonprofit organizations face in many African countries routinely outstrips both their organizational capacity and their founding passion. Many give up within a few years — not because the mission was wrong, but because the regulatory burden was designed for institutions far larger and better resourced than a community-rooted faith-based organization trying to serve its neighborhood.

The Nonprofit Center estimates that more than fifty percent of nonprofits fail or stall within a few years of founding. That number is probably understated, because many organizations do not formally close — they simply drift, shrink, and go quiet. The cause is rarely a lack of passion. It is almost always a structural problem: organizations that are financially orphaned from the beginning, dependent on grant cycles that reward reporting over results, and disconnected from the communities they were meant to serve.

Faith-based organizations tend to survive longer than their secular counterparts — not because they are better managed, but because they are relationally embedded. The community is both the constituency and the accountability structure. Foundations persist because they are capitalized — but capitalization without accountability produces its own pathology, and missional drift is most common.

The real problem is not nonprofits versus for-profits but the alignment of capital structure and mission. The closer a nonprofit is to earned or embedded capital — community ownership, endowment, social enterprise revenue — the higher its survival rate and the deeper its impact. The further it is from those sources and the more dependent it is on external grants with attached conditions, the more fragile it becomes. That is not a criticism of generosity. It is a description of what generosity needs to be structured around if it is going to produce lasting change rather than temporary relief.

## Household Economics

The optimum solution is not a better NGO model or a more sophisticated CSR framework. It is businesses that take genuine ownership of their responsibilities toward their households and communities — and stop outsourcing those responsibilities to third parties who were never equipped to carry them. Your child should not be raised by a nanny. Your "charity" should not be handled by a charity.

The language of the Sustainable Development Goals, whatever its intentions, tends to overlay a nonprofit mindset onto the business world — coercing corporations to "do good while doing well" in a way that produces greenwashing rather than genuine transformation. The framing separates the good from the doing, the impact from the enterprise, the calling from the career. It is the secular-sacred dichotomy in a green suit.

We have worked with businesses across Africa since 2003 and have consistently advocated for a single scorecard that deals simultaneously with the success of the business and its impact on the society around it. Not two parallel tracks. One integrated pursuit. This is more often a question of the heart than of the budget. The moment a CEO or managing director genuinely believes that employees, their families, suppliers, customers, and the community surrounding the business are all part of their household — their oikos — something shifts. They begin to ask God for strategies to support the wellbeing of that household. They stop asking "how much should we give to charity?" and start asking "how should we run the business so that the people in our household flourish?"

That shift changes everything downstream. It changes hiring. It changes supplier relationships. It changes how profit is deployed. It changes what success looks like and how it is measured. And it changes the timeframe — because a household thinks in generations, not quarters.

Kingdom business is a household-to-household model. When businesses operate as households — taking genuine responsibility for the wellbeing of everyone in their oikos — and then connect with other businesses doing the same, the aggregate effect is a community being transformed from the inside out. This is discipling not as a side effect of commerce but as its intended purpose. The returns it produces are temporal and eternal simultaneously — and that is the only kind of return worth building a portfolio around.

## 13. Context is Key: What's God doing in the World?

I shudder at my own arrogance when I catch myself saying "this is what God is doing in the world." The honest truth is that connecting the dots of geopolitics, economics, technology, and the shaking of institutions that have stood for decades is genuinely difficult. Culture wars. The capitalism versus socialism debate. Climate and environmental stewardship. International food security. Captured narratives blanketing emerging generations in uncertainty and suspicion, with hopelessness as the downstream consequence. The list is long and the picture is complex.

And yet. We live in the light of recorded Scripture. Proverbs 25:2 says "it is the glory of God to conceal a matter — and the glory of kings to search it out." Since the Garden of Eden we have been invited into collaboration with the Divine. That invitation has not been withdrawn. It means we are not left to the mercy of worldly interpretations of what is happening on earth — but it does require that our antennae be tuned to God rather than to the ambient noise of the age. So let me offer not a definitive account of what God is doing, but some informed observations about where his fingerprints seem to be most visible.

## The Kingdom of God is advancing

In Iran, war rages, men make plans, and the kingdom advances. The fastest-growing church in the world at the time of writing is in a country where following Jesus can cost you everything — which, historically speaking, is exactly the kind of soil in which the church has always grown fastest.

Across the Muslim world, a supernatural awakening is underway driven in significant part by dreams — Jesus and angels appearing to people who had never opened a Bible and who had every cultural reason to resist the gospel. This is documented, widespread, and accelerating. In China, estimates of the number of Christ followers are staggering — the figure may now exceed the entire population of the United States, driven by networks of house churches that have multiplied under pressure rather than in spite of it. In India, an indigenous church planting movement I consulted with was establishing multiple new churches every week — not through Western missionary programs but through locally rooted, culturally embedded communities of faith.

In the United Kingdom, after decades of declining church attendance, the trends have reversed. The demographic driving this is NewGen — the generation that was supposed to have abandoned faith entirely is returning to it, and doing so on its own terms. In the United States, recent Barna and Lifeway data shows a surprising resurgence in church attendance among Gen Z and Millennials — the highest rates since tracking began — with nondenominational and larger churches seeing particularly strong growth.

Globally, nearly seventy percent of all Christian growth worldwide is now occurring in Africa alone — a figure that Operation World researcher Jason Mandryk described at the 2025 World Evangelical Alliance General Assembly as "astonishing." In 1900 there were approximately ten million Christians on the continent. Today there are an estimated 734 million. That trajectory — from ten million to 734 million in 125 years — is one of the most remarkable movements of faith in human history. The center of gravity of world Christianity has shifted — not gradually, but dramatically, within a single generation.

## God is moving in the Global South

For hundreds of years there have been prophetic words about revival breaking out at the southern tip of Africa and spreading northward through the continent and then to the world. It is easy to dismiss such words when decades pass without obvious fulfillment — or to give up on them entirely when the centuries accumulate. But there is a remnant of Africans who have stewarded these proclamations with patience and faith, and the current trajectory of African Christianity gives those words a different quality of resonance than they had even twenty years ago.

My friend Andre Baard has compiled and analyzed these prophetic words in a free booklet called *The Southern Tip of Africa Fire Prophecy* — a collection of visions, words, and historical accounts centered on a recurring theme: a powerful spiritual revival beginning at the southern tip of Africa and spreading across the continent and then to the world. The earliest entry in his compilation dates to 1908. The pattern, as Baard notes, is perennial and widely accepted in Cape Town and South African charismatic circles. I commend it as a resource for anyone investing in Africa who wants to understand the spiritual history they are stepping into.

But should prophetic words influence our investing? That is the question worth sitting with.

I think the answer is not naively. Prophetic words are not a business plan. They do not replace due diligence or substitute for sound capital structure. What they do — when held with maturity and tested against what is actually happening on the ground — is orient our attention. They tell us where to look. And what we see when we look at Africa right now, from the perspective of both the data and the spiritual reality, is a continent in motion in ways that no purely secular framework can fully account for.

Which brings us to the question that every investor in Africa eventually has to answer for themselves: why are you here?

Is it because Africa is a new frontier that could produce higher than normal returns? That is a legitimate reason and there is nothing wrong with saying so. Is it because investment capital has a bigger impact here than almost anywhere else — that a dollar deployed in Africa creates more value, employs more people, and changes more lives than the same dollar deployed in a saturated Western market? Also legitimate, and also true. Or is it because God is visibly at work on this continent — because the trajectory of African Christianity, the hunger for integration of faith and work, and the quality of the builders and innovators emerging from this soil all suggest that something significant is happening here — and you want to co-invest with what God is already doing?

The best answer, in my experience, is yes to all three. And when those three motivations align — return, impact, and divine partnership — you have the conditions for the kind of investing this book has been arguing for from the first page.

## Bring your Distinct Value-Add

In April 2003 a team of us traveled from Silicon Valley to Cape Town. One of our consultants, Susan Gibson, was applying her Harvard MBA and pharmaceutical expertise to help a local company. She asked her client what he wanted to do with the business. "I want to double it," he replied with evident pride. She asked: "How often?"

In Silicon Valley, doubling every six months or a year was a reasonable stretch goal. In Cape Town in 2003, doubling the business at all — in a lifetime — was considered a significant achievement. Neither perspective was wrong. Both were products of context, formation, and the particular way that capital, culture, and ambition had been shaped in each place. The cross-pollination that happens when God's people travel intentionally from one nation to another — bringing different assumptions, different timeframes, different definitions of what is possible — can be genuinely life-giving and accelerating for both parties. Susan's question did not embarrass her client. It expanded his imagination.

God's business involves every tongue, tribe, and nation — and not just for the sake of reach. There is a surround-sound quality to the worship and the work of a genuinely multinational kingdom community that no single culture can produce on its own. God receives glory when the Father of all humanity is recognized across every nation, and when his people come together in unity to serve his purposes. The practical implication for investing is this: every nation brings something that the others need. God is just — which means every people group has assets and a contribution to make, not just needs to be met.

If you are coming from a Western nation, lean into what God has specifically formed in you. Bring your Judeo-Christian values — the deep historical roots of property rights, contract law, and institutional trust that your culture inherited even if it has largely forgotten the source. Bring your fiscal discipline and your structured processes — the organizational order that turns good intentions into scalable outcomes. Bring your faith that believes God can do the impossible, because Africa will test that faith in ways that a comfortable Western context never will. Bring your friends — investors who share your values and who can spread both the risk and the relational load. Bring your measurement frameworks and your KPIs — but chase them down with the Africano, not an Americano. And bring the willingness to receive as well as give — because the African church has things to teach the Western investor that no MBA program covers.

Kingdom culture is not the imposition of one culture's best practices onto another. It is the weaving together of what God has deposited in each — a fabric stronger than any single thread. The goal in investing is not to superimpose the ABC way of doing things on the XYZ. High impact investing happens in a culture of mutual honor and joint learning. The giving and receiving of investment is an opportunity for mutual discipleship — and mutual discipleship, compounded over time, produces something neither party could have built alone.

## Livingstone: A Cautionary Tale

David Livingstone arrived in Cape Town on March 14th, 1841. He did not intend to become an explorer. He intended to preach the gospel, open legitimate trade routes, and bring what he called civilization — in nineteenth-century terms — to the interior of Africa. What he became was something more complicated, and more instructive.

His legacy has genuine and lasting positives. He trusted God's promises through hardship, disease, isolation, and physical suffering that would have broken most people. He walked tens of thousands of miles. He fought lions. He used exploration, medicine, and anti-slavery advocacy to open doors for the church across a continent that had been largely closed to it. In Malawi, Zambia, and other regions he is still remembered with genuine affection as the pioneer who brought the gospel. And though it is said he had very few direct converts — some accounts say just one — at his funeral a new wave of missionaries was launched into Africa. His single notable convert, Chief Sechele, went on to spread Christianity regionally, adapting it to local contexts in ways that Livingstone himself could never have managed. The seeds he planted outlasted him by generations.

The cautions are equally real and equally instructive. Some argue that his Christianity, Commerce, and Civilization framework — however sincerely held — opened the way for colonialism and unwittingly provided a moral vocabulary for imperialism. The Eurocentric narrative embedded in his accounts erased indigenous knowledge and agency in ways that are still felt. Renaming Mosi-oa-Tunya as Victoria Falls is the small symbol of a much larger pattern: the assumption that the Western observer's name for a thing is the real name, that the Western arrival at a place constitutes its discovery, that the African reality only becomes legible when it has been translated into European terms.

Today, colonization is rightly considered unacceptable. But asset colonization is still taking place across Africa — minerals, precious metals, and gemstones stripped from the ground and processed elsewhere, hardwood forests felled in Mozambique and shipped to China to be milled and imported back as finished products at a premium. The form has changed. The logic has not. Faith-based investors arriving in Africa with genuine intentions need to be clear-eyed about the history they are stepping into — and equally clear-eyed about whether the structures they are using to invest might be replicating that logic in a new form.

Here is the uncomfortable truth about where we stand in 2026, 185 years after Livingstone's first arrival. Africa's population is now ten times what it was then. The average age on the continent is under twenty years old. The market is growing dramatically. Whole countries are open to a faith-based approach to their national challenges. Vast amounts of under-stewarded assets sit across multiple asset classes. The window is real and it is open.

And yet when it comes to capital, the Protestant church is lagging dramatically behind the Catholics, the Muslims, the Chinese, the Russians, and the Middle Easterners. The University of Zurich Center for Sustainable Finance and Private Wealth puts it plainly: faith-based investor engagement has been characterized by a focus on negative screening and shareholder engagement, with proactive investment for impact still limited in breadth and scope. If Protestant and Evangelical investors do not break out of traditional patterns — which in Africa have been either charity-oriented or Western VC and private equity-oriented — they will miss the wave. Not just a financial wave. A kingdom wave. The kind that does not wait for the slow to catch up.

The NGO world has lost both capital and credibility. Africans are increasingly distrustful of Chinese intentions and pushing back against Islamic radicalism and have some anti-US sentiment as well. The geopolitical ground is shifting in ways that create a specific opening for faith-based capital that is genuinely transformational rather than extractive, genuinely partnering rather than colonizing. That opening will not stay open indefinitely.

This is the time for the people of God to step into the gap — with meaningful, comprehensive, and substantial capital investments that come from the heart of God and operate in the ways of God.

Let me be direct about who I have been writing for.

This book is for foundations, family offices, and faith-aligned institutional investors in Europe, the United Kingdom, and the United States who are serious about deploying capital for long-term societal transformation without abandoning fiduciary discipline. It is for investors from Africa who are ready to expand their footprint into other parts of the continent. And it is for anyone who has sensed that there is a more integrated, more purposeful, more kingdom-aligned way to invest — and has been looking for a framework to make that instinct actionable.

The framework I have attempted to build is grounded in *Kingdom Economics* and *Repurposing Capital*, operationalized through the *Transforming Society* ten-sphere model, and oriented toward the inspired innovations that are already emerging from African soil. Africa is not approached here as a charitable cause or a speculative frontier. It is approached as a strategic environment where capital, faith, and innovation can converge to restore broken systems, unlock human potential, and generate returns that are sustainable financially and significant eternally.

Henry Kaestner, founder of the Faith Driven Investor movement and Sovereigns Capital, put it simply when I asked him why he invests in Africa: "For me it has to do with faithfulness and calling on one hand, and market opportunity on the other." That combination — faithfulness and market opportunity held together without apology — is the posture this book has been arguing for from the first page.

If you have read this far, you probably still have some "what abouts" running through your mind. Some of those questions I hope are now in clearer relief. Others may require a conversation rather than a chapter. What I want to name plainly before we close is this: Africans are rightly allergic to colonizing ways, and those of us who know Jesus Christ personally are part of a kingdom that is larger than any fund, any nation, and any investment thesis. The question is not whether faith-based capital belongs in Africa. The question is whether we will bring it with enough humility, enough patience, and enough genuine partnership to deserve the invitation.

How then do we press through the barriers and invest with Africa — not in it, not for it, but with it?

That is what the final pages of this book are for.

## 14. A Call to Apostolic Asset Deployment

The parable of the talents makes clear that disengagement from stewardship — burying what we have been given rather than putting it to work — is a failure of faithfulness. Risk in the service of the master's purposes is expected, not optional. That is not a comfortable observation for legacy asset managers who have built careers on capital preservation and risk avoidance — but it is what Jesus said. The University of Zurich Center for Sustainable Finance and Private Wealth identified this bottleneck precisely: most assets under management are held by legacy asset managers with little exposure to or interest in impact investing, producing a lack of impact-related deal flow and a predominant business-as-usual attitude. That attitude, applied to kingdom capital, is not prudence. It is the one-talent response.

People will last for eternity. Investments that bring about the order, the intentions, the beauty, the structure, and the purposes of heaven on earth are surely good investments. Is this potentially risky? Yes. But God is a risk-taker — and he invites us to partner with him thoughtfully, intelligently, and boldly. Those who have generated wealth through hard work and measured risk-taking already know this instinctively. The question is whether they will apply that same boldness to investments oriented toward eternal as well as temporal returns.

Partner on Inspired Innovations | Take Impact to new heights | Add Value in Context of God's doings

God's people have a mandate: go into all the world — eschatos — and make disciples of all nations — ethnos — and reconcile everything to Christ — cosmos. That is a three-dimensional commission. It requires a three-dimensional response. Not just missionaries. Not just churches. Not just charities. Apostolic Asset Deployment — the deliberate, coordinated, comprehensive deployment of capital in all its forms toward the purposes of that commission — is the response this moment requires.

## Practice Promiscuous Partnering

About thirty years ago I was a speaker at a conference titled "What is the Church doing with technology?" I informed the organizers this was the wrong question — the real question was what technology was doing and going to do to the church. Mark Kvamme, a venture capitalist on the same platform, gave the faith-based organizations in the room a piece of advice that has stayed with me ever since: "Practice promiscuous partnering."

His point was direct and it has only become more relevant in the decades since. Faith-based organizations are not just siloed — they are partnering-averse. The reasons are familiar: theological differences, own-kingdom-building dressed up as branding or thought leadership, doctrinal disputes, spiritual superiority, cultural supremacy. Insert your own excuse here. (Usually it is about money — scarce donor money.) None of them survive honest examination. We will only be free to partner effectively when the kingdom of God is genuinely bigger than our stuff.

In Jakarta, some of our team recommended we partner with Dr. Jakoep Ezra. Both of us were cautious — cautious enough that we agreed to spend a day doing a Partnering Readiness Assessment before committing to anything. Toward the end of the day he needed time to consult with his team, so we took a break. When we bumped into each other in the hallway, he looked at me directly and asked: "What do you sense the Spirit is saying?" I replied: "If I were God looking down from heaven at our two organizations, I would tell us to partner." I like to think God has a heavenly portfolio of organizations and he sees how, if they teamed up, they could have far more impact together. The question is whether the organizations themselves are willing to see it.

The Impact Network we described in Chapter 10 is the structural expression of promiscuous partnering. A kingdom fund sourced from the EU, US, and UK, with its asset management function outside Africa and its deployment within Africa, blended governance, and fiduciary disciplines executed from jurisdictions with genuine financial teeth — that is what apostolic asset deployment looks like in practice. JVs, SPVs, term sheets, and deal structures can be designed to optimize impact rather than minimize risk. The evergreen fund model — which Neuberger Berman's research suggests may generate return multiples of 3.2x compared with 2.7x for traditional structures — matches the patient, compounding nature of kingdom investment more naturally than the standard closed-end fund with its forced exit timeline. Global Giants Trust and Global Giants Limited were established precisely to operationalize this model.

## Partner to Send, not just Receive

I first went to Nigeria in 2008. I told the leaders I met there: "Faith-based entrepreneurs could become Nigeria's best export." Look at what has come out of Nigeria in the last ten years — the fintech founders, the diaspora investors, the business missionaries carrying kingdom principles into markets across the continent and beyond. The trajectory was already visible in 2008. It has accelerated dramatically since.

Investing in Africa is not just deploying capital into local businesses. It is partnering in sending. The nation of Israel was designed to be a billboard to the nations — a demonstration of what life under God's governance looks like, compelling enough that other nations would look and say: their God must be remarkable. There is precedent in that pattern for what Africa could become — not a continent receiving missionaries and capital from elsewhere, but a continent sending both.

Investment dollars deployed in Africa get stretched efficiently; missionaries from Africa yield a similarly good return. It stands to reason that African-born businesses (that are self-funding missionary bands) should produce a great kingdom ROI. Putting it another way, isn't it high time we thought about partnering with our African brothers and sisters to "go into all the world" and produce outsized returns together?

The nation of Israel was designed to be a billboard to the nations, a poster child of God's wisdom, goodness, provision and protection. Nations should have looked at Israel and said, "their God must be amazing since they are doing well." So, there is precedent of pattern. Why, then, should we not lift our eyes higher and co-invest in African nations with an eye to teaming with them to go to other nations?

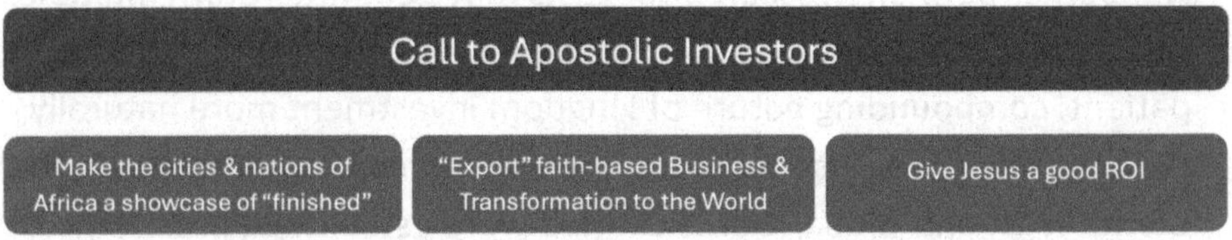


Of course, we should not be spreading darkness at the speed of light. Transformed nations transform nations. African nations must themselves be on a path to flourishing. The confluence of factors mentioned in this book are the ingredients that make many African nations "good soil." Jesus is not indifferent to returns. The parable of the talents, the servants put in charge of the master's property, the steward called to account — the expectation of fruitfulness is built into the commission. Capital deployed in the right way at the right time in the right place can generate Jesus-deserving returns.

## Recapture Apostolic Investing

Apostolic investing is cross-city and cross-national capital flow fostered by spiritual fathers who see beyond local and facilitate purposeful and structured engagement.

The apostolic giving that Paul describes across three chapters of 2 Corinthians was not personal generosity — it was cross-national capital flow, organized and urged by a spiritual father who understood that the body of Christ is not a local institution but a global network with mutual obligations. These generosity chapters are primarily about cross-community, cross-national capital flows — the Gentile churches supporting the Jerusalem church in a moment of need. The principles Paul articulates apply to individuals, but the primary unit of his argument is the community and the nation, not the individual donor. That is worth recovering.

My estimate is that ninety-eight percent of church funds are spent inside the local church, with roughly two percent reaching the ends of the earth. That ratio is not stewardship. It is hoarding — with excellent branding and perhaps good intentions. Apostolic Asset Deployment inverts that ratio as its aspiration. It urges investees to be more than receivers — to become empowered co-laborers with a "so that" that reflects God's heart for every tongue, tribe, and nation.

> *These men have turned the world upside down and have come here also, and Jason has received them, and they are all acting against the decrees of Caesar, saying there is another king, Jesus—Acts 17:6-7*

The opponents of the Apostles said that they had turned the world upside down. What will be said of our generation? Is it not time that the world was turned upside down, or right-side up, again?

## How then Shall We Invest?

Psalm 22 ends with a vision that still stirs me since I first read it with investor eyes:

> *All the ends of the earth will remember and turn to the Lord, and all the families of the nations will bow down before him. For dominion belongs to the Lord, and he rules over the nations. All the rich of the earth will feast and worship; all who go down to the dust will kneel before him. Psalm 22:27-29*

The ends of the earth — eschatos. All the families — households and businesses and cosmos. All the nations — ethnos. The three strands of the commission are all present in the psalm, woven together into a single vision of what the full return on God's investment in humanity looks like: they belong to Him.

And then the feast.

The rich of the earth feasting and worshipping simultaneously — not despite their wealth, but through it, in the presence of the One who gave them the ability to produce it. Before we start thinking about the world's billionaires, let us remember that those of us holding this book are probably in the top few percent of the world's wealthy people. God does not condemn the rich. He gives them the privilege of feasting and worshipping at the same table. And he reminds them — gently, but unmistakably — that they will end up as dust, and that the only investments that survive that transition are the ones made in things that last.

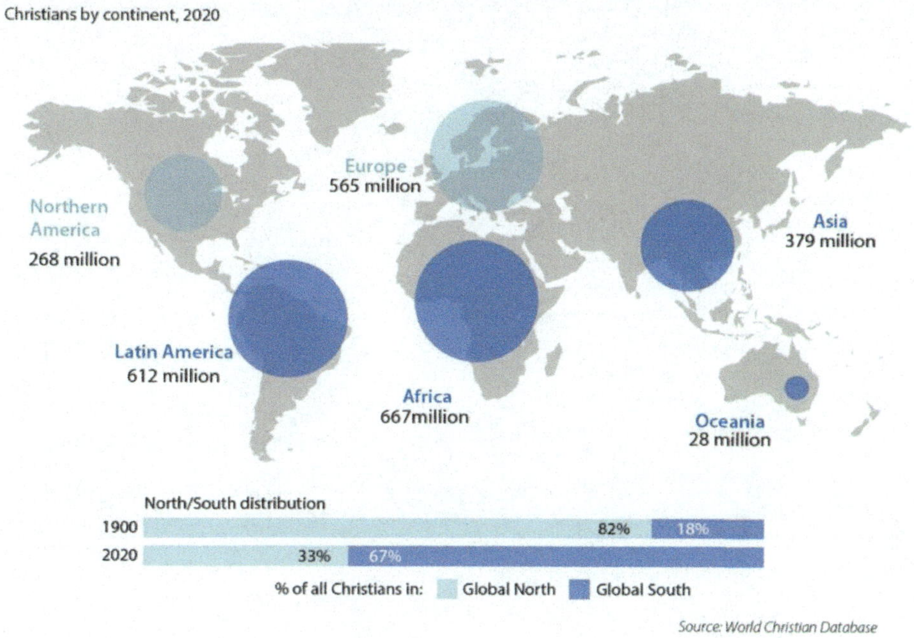


This book focuses on investing in Africa. In truth it is a book about the strategic deployment of capital to advance the kingdom of God. The Universal Church across the planet needs to partner in doing this. We have a window — not unlimited, not unconditional, but real — to rediscover North-South collaboration in a season when Africa's spiritual capital, its demographic energy, and its hunger for integrated faith and work make it one of the most significant investment frontiers in the history of the kingdom.

How then shall we live? How then shall we invest? How then shall we partner to comprehensively capitalize what God is doing in the earth?

> *Your kingdom come, your will be done on earth as it is in heaven. — Jesus Christ.*

# 15. APPENDICES

- Throughout this book, I have referred to other writings, and I have therefore included one-page snapshots of Kingdom Economics, Repurposing Capital and Transforming Society for ease of reference.
- Since much of my thesis is built upon the three strands of the Great Commission, I have unpacked this idea in a separate appendix for those who are theologically inclined.
- I have also mentioned ideas for a fund of funds or capital aggregation to address the ecosystem needs to support effective investments and the capital required for Platform Reform. I have therefore included a two-page overview of the Global Giants Trust and Global Giants Limited, which is a vehicle that might be used to accomplish these purposes. I am sure we will see a growing number of similar structures in the near future.
- Most of the workings behind the models are included on the website, http://InvestingWithAfrica.com I have given small insights into the rationale for the zones in an appendix. Readers should of course make their own assessments of things and modify with my categorizations.
- For more resources, case studies and details behind Zones and more, visit http://investingwithafrica.com

# Kingdom Economics – One Pager

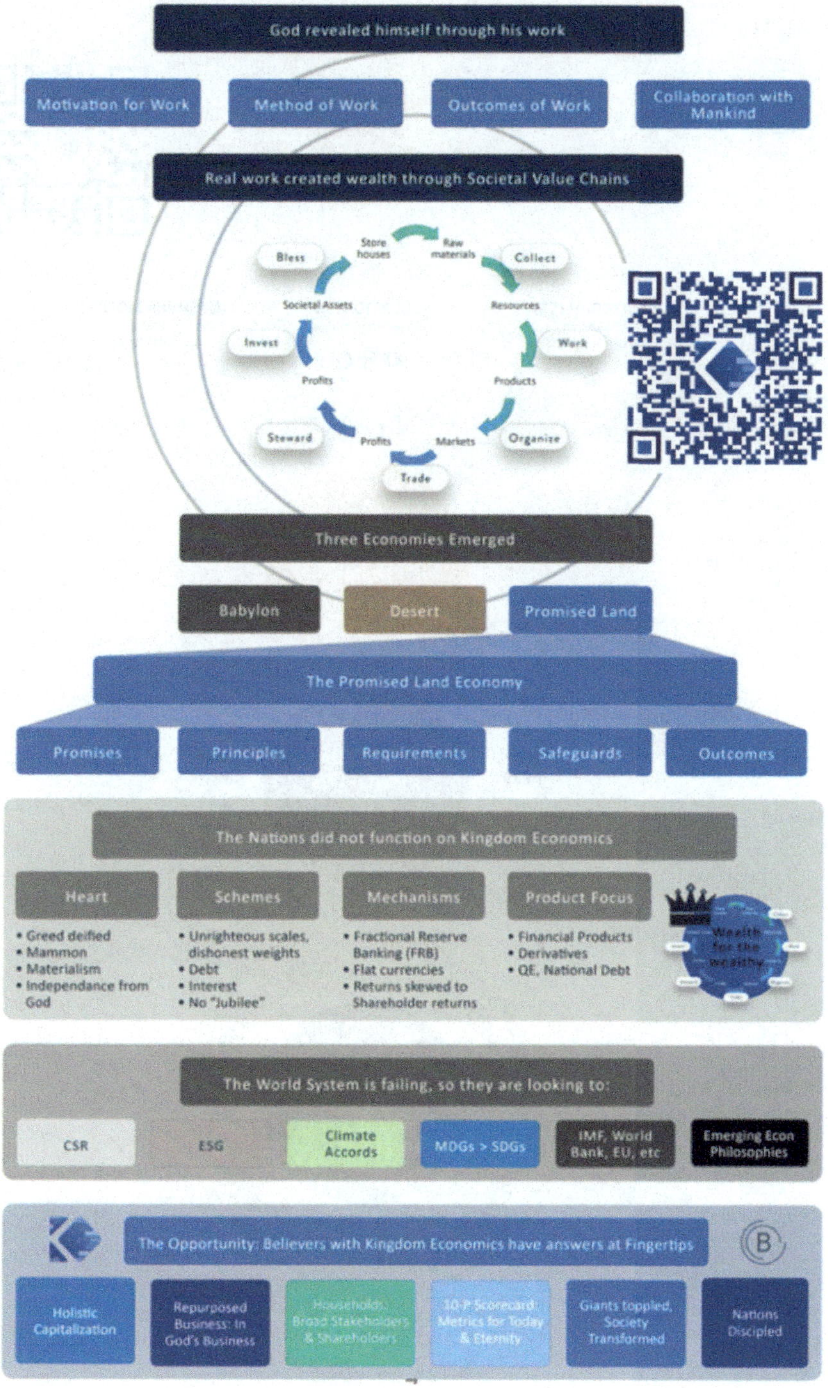

# Repurposing Capital – One Pager

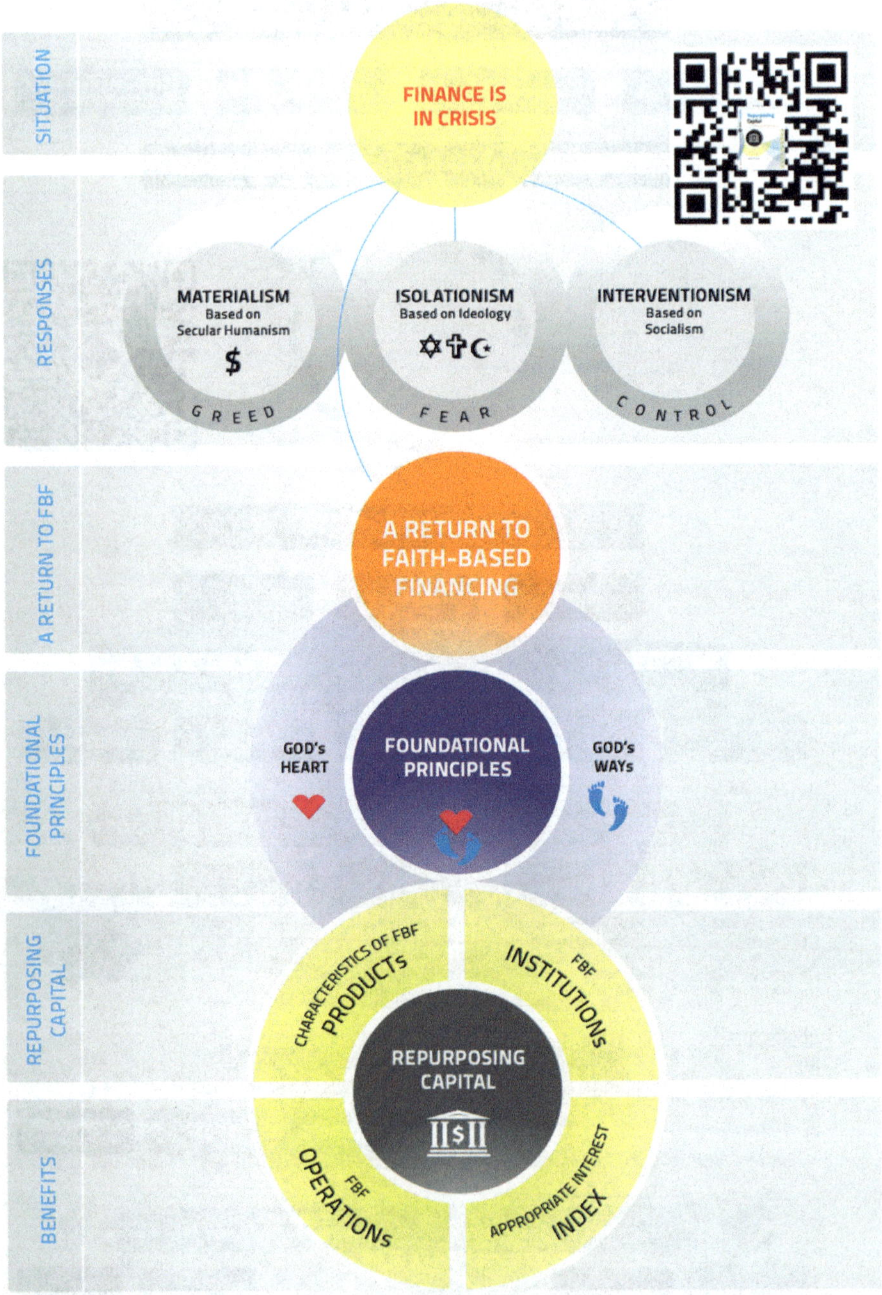

# Repurposing Capital

SITUATION

The world will never be the same again after the financial crisis that became evident in the first decade of the 21st Century.

RESPONSES

The three main responses:

1. **Materialism**: prop up existing systems with debt; leave motivations or mechanisms intact; keep capital markets vibrant. The basis is greed; the driver—materialism, touted as capitalism
2. **Isolationism**: insulate group based on religious affiliation, or a cause such as Zionism, Islamization or Dominionism. The basis is fear; the fruit is radicalization and dualism (decrying the systems they rely on).
3. **Interventionism**: intervene with funding, regulation and/or government control; cap gains and redistribute wealth. The belief: few (usually government) know better than many.

A RETURN TO FBF

Faith is the opposite of fear. The positive principles of capital and finance can only be exercised, for good, in an atmosphere of faith.

FOUNDATIONAL PRINCIPLES

Faith is based on truth. The Universal Foundational Principles of finance and capital must therefore be rediscovered, codified, and considered. The wellspring for such Universal FBF principles is the heart of God, the ways of God, and the thoughts or mind of God (not the laws of man and the schemes of religious, state or other groups).

REPURPOSING CAPITAL

Once the FBF principles have been set, the basis is laid for Repurposing Capital—getting capital back to its intended temporal and eternal purpose. This has four elements: Products with FBF characteristics, Appropriate Interest, FBF-compliant Operations, and FBF Institutions.

BENEFITS

The result of a Return to FBF will be stability, savings, character improvement, transparency, collaboration, wealth creation, prosperity, poverty alleviation, community-oriented investments, and infrastructure improvement.

# Transforming Society – One Pager

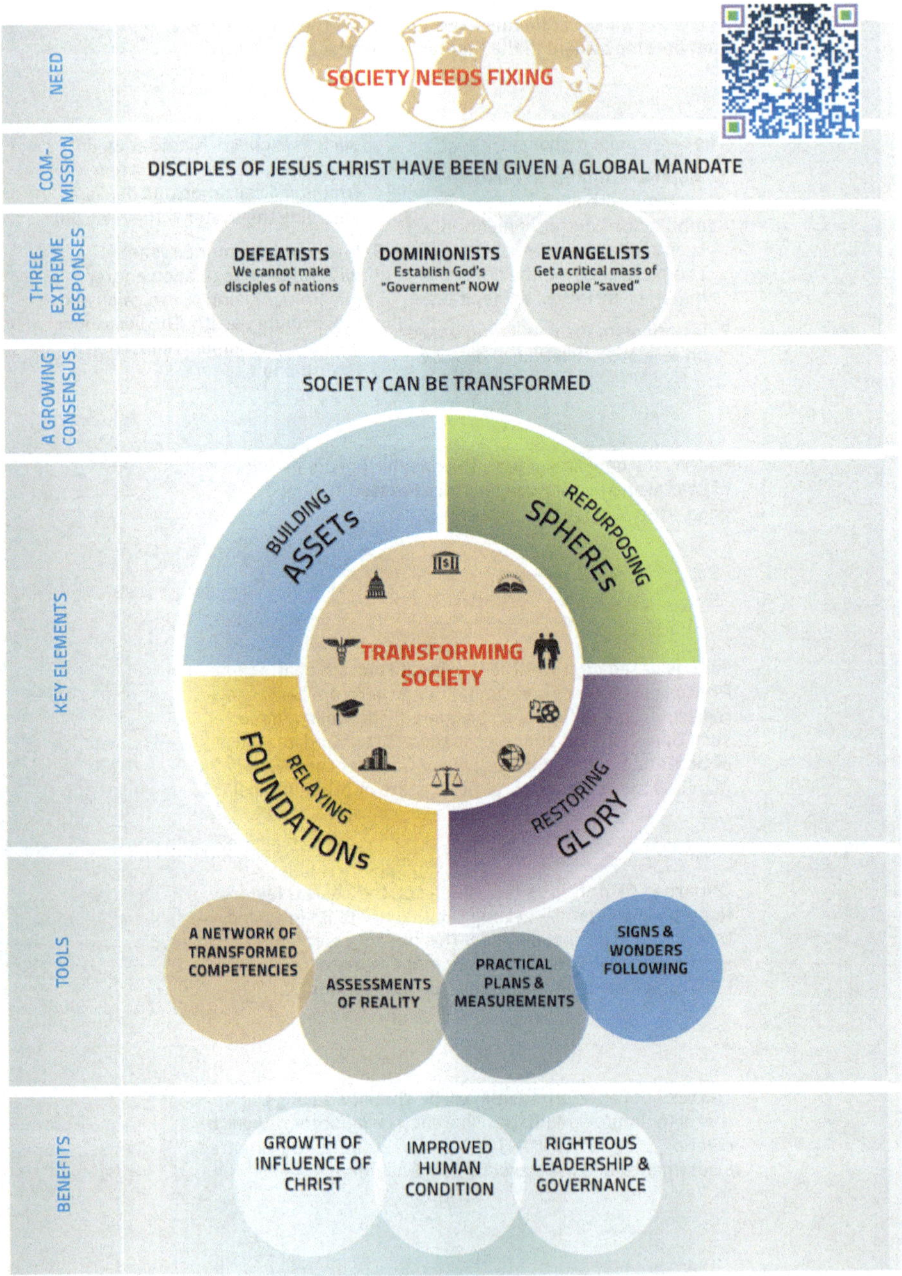

# The Three Greek Words of the Great Commission

A lexical and exegetical note for **Investing with Africa**

## Introduction

The phrase "Great Commission" is typically applied to Matthew 28:19–20, but the full commissioning mandate of the New Testament spans at least three distinct texts, each employing a different Greek term to describe the scope of the mission. These terms are not synonyms. Each carries a distinct semantic range, and reading them together produces a mandate considerably broader than any single text conveys in isolation.

This appendix examines the three Greek words in their textual and lexical context:

*ethnos* (Matthew 28:19), *eschatos* (Acts 1:8), and *kosmos* (Mark 16:15). The analysis draws on Strong's Concordance, standard Greek lexica, and the distribution of each term across the New Testament corpus.

| Text | Greek term | Strong's ref. | Primary gloss | Scope |
|---|---|---|---|---|
| Matthew 28:19 | ethnos (ἔθνος) | G1484 | Nation, people group | Cultural / ethnic |
| Acts 1:8 | eschatos (ἔσχατος) | G2078 | Uttermost, farthest end | Geographic / spatial |
| Mark 16:15 | kosmos (κόσμος) | G2889 | World, created order | Systemic / total |

## 1. Ethnos (ἔθνος) — Matthew 28:19

**Matthew 28:19** Go therefore and make disciples of all the nations [ethnos], baptizing them in the name of the Father and of the Son and of the Holy Spirit.

Lexical range

*Ethnos* (Strong's G1484) derives from a root denoting custom or habit (*ethos*), and refers to a body of people defined by shared culture, language, or ancestry — a nation, tribe, or people group. In the Septuagint it frequently renders the Hebrew *goyim* (the Gentile nations), and in the New Testament it appears 164 times.

The term carries three distinguishable senses across the New Testament corpus:

**(a) Gentiles in contrast to Israel.** In much of Paul's usage, *ethnos* functions as a technical term distinguishing non-Jewish peoples from the Jewish nation — as in Romans 1:5, "obedience of faith among all the Gentiles [ethnos]."

**(b) Nations as political entities.** In prophetic and eschatological contexts, *ethnos* designates the nations of the world as collectivities — as in Revelation 21:24, "the nations [ethnos] will walk by its light."

**(c) People groups defined by cultural identity.** In missionary and missiological usage, particularly in Matthew 28:19, *ethnos* functions as the defining unit of evangelistic scope: every identifiable people group, defined by cultural and linguistic distinctiveness, is within the commission's purview.

Exegetical significance

The force of *panta ta ethne* ("all the nations") in Matthew 28:19 is qualitative rather than merely quantitative. The commission does not simply assert geographical breadth; it asserts cultural comprehensiveness. No people group — however remote, however politically marginal, however linguistically distinct — is outside the scope of the mandate.

In missiological practice, this text has grounded the unreached peoples movement, the discipline of ethnolinguistic mapping, and the "10/40 window" framework. Its primary analytical unit is the culturally defined human community.

## 2. Eschatos (ἔσχατος) — Acts 1:8

**Acts 1:8** But you will receive power when the Holy Spirit has come upon you, and you will be my witnesses in Jerusalem and in all Judea and Samaria, and to the end [eschatos] of the earth.

Lexical range

*Eschatos* (Strong's G2078) is a superlative adjective meaning "last," "uttermost," or "farthest." Its primary semantic field is spatial and temporal extremity. It appears 52 times in the New Testament, most frequently in eschatological contexts ("the last day," "the last trumpet"), but in Acts 1:8 its application is explicitly geographic.

The phrase *heōs eschatou tēs gēs* — literally "to the uttermost of the earth" — is a direct echo of Isaiah 49:6, where the Servant of the Lord is appointed as a light to the nations "that my salvation may reach to the end of the earth." Luke's use of this phrase in Acts 1:8 is therefore not merely geographic description but deliberate intertextual allusion: the mission of the church is the fulfilment of the Servant's vocation.

Exegetical significance

Acts 1:8 structures the missional geography of the book of Acts in concentric circles: Jerusalem → Judea → Samaria → ends of the earth. This is not a sequential program so much as a description of simultaneous expansion. The "ends of the earth" functions as the outer boundary marker — the furthest conceivable point — ensuring that no geographic frontier constitutes a limit to the commission.

Whereas *ethnos* names the cultural unit of mission, *eschatos* names the spatial boundary: there is no place on earth beyond the commission's reach. The two terms together create a mandate that is both culturally exhaustive and geographically unlimited.

## 3. Kosmos (κόσμος) — Mark 16:15

**Mark 16:15** And he said to them, "Go into all the world [kosmos] and proclaim the gospel to every creature."

Lexical range

*Kosmos* (Strong's G2889) is the most semantically complex of the three terms. It appears approximately 186 times in the New Testament — far more frequently than *ethnos* or *eschatos* — and carries a range of meaning that no single English rendering captures adequately. Strong's Concordance identifies four primary senses:

**(a) The created universe.** In its broadest application, *kosmos* denotes the totality of created reality — heaven and earth together, the sum of all that exists. This sense underlies John 1:10 ("the world was made through him") and the repeated New Testament references to events occurring "before the foundation of the world" (*pro katabolēs kosmou*) — as in Ephesians 1:4, John 17:24, and Revelation 13:8.

**(b) The inhabited earth and its people.** More frequently, and especially in John's Gospel and the Johannine epistles, *kosmos* refers to the human family — the community of persons for whom Christ died. This is the sense operative in John 3:16 ("God so loved the world"), John 6:51 ("the bread I will give for the life of the world"), and 2 Corinthians 5:19 ("God was reconciling the world to himself"). Here *kosmos* functions as a synonym for humanity in its totality.

**(c) The system opposed to God.** This is the most theologically freighted sense, and it dominates the Johannine corpus. *Kosmos* in this usage designates the organized structure of human society insofar as it operates in rebellion against God — its value systems, its power arrangements, its philosophical frameworks, and its economic incentives. This sense is operative in John 15:18–19 ("if the world hates you..."), 1 John 2:15–17 ("do not love the world"), 1 John 5:19 ("the whole world lies in the power of the evil one"), and James 4:4 ("friendship with the world is enmity with God"). The ruler of this *kosmos* is identified as Satan (John 12:31; 14:30; 16:11).

**(d) Order and adornment.** The root meaning of *kosmos* is "arrangement" or "ornament" — a harmonious ordering of parts into a beautiful whole. This sense is preserved in 1 Peter 3:3 (where *kosmos* is translated "adornment" in reference to outward decoration), and in the verbal cognate *kosmeo* (to arrange, adorn) used of the temple in Luke

21:5. The English word "cosmetics" preserves this original sense. This root meaning underlies the term's application to the created universe: the *kosmos* is creation understood as ordered beauty.

Exegetical significance

The semantic range of *kosmos* makes Mark 16:15 the most expansive of the three commission texts. Where *ethnos* defines the mission's cultural scope and *eschatos* defines its geographic boundary, *kosmos* defines its systemic depth. The commission is not only to all peoples (*ethnos*) and to all places (*eschatos*), but into the totality of created reality and human organization (*kosmos*) in all its dimensions.

This is reinforced by the Johannine parallel in John 17:18, where Jesus grounds the disciples' sending in the pattern of his own incarnation: "As you sent me into the *kosmos*, so I have sent them into the *kosmos*." The incarnation itself becomes the structural template for mission. Christ did not engage the human system from outside it; he entered it fully. The *kosmos* commission carries the same logic.

The eschatological trajectory of the *kosmos* commission is established in Revelation 11:15: "The kingdom of the world [*kosmos*] has become the kingdom of our Lord and of his Christ." The *kosmos* is not ultimately abandoned or destroyed; it is transferred — brought under the full sovereignty of God. This eschatological frame gives the commission its ultimate horizon: mission into the *kosmos* is participation in the process by which the created order is reclaimed for its Creator.

## 4. The Three Terms in Synthesis

Read in isolation, each commissioning text produces a partial mandate. Read together, they constitute a comprehensive one. The following observations emerge from comparative analysis:

| Term | Unit of analysis | Dimension | Question answered | Missiological tradition |
|---|---|---|---|---|
| Ethnos | People group | Cultural | To whom are we sent? | Church planting, unreached peoples |
| Eschatos | Geographic frontier | Spatial | How far are we sent? | Frontier mission, cross-cultural outreach |
| Kosmos | Created order / human system | Systemic | Into what are we sent? | Cultural mandate, marketplace mission |

The *kosmos* commission in particular has historically received less systematic attention in Western Protestant missiology than *ethnos* or *eschatos*. This is partly a function of the long-standing sacred/secular dichotomy in evangelical thought — the tendency to define "mission" in terms of personal evangelism and church planting, while treating economic, cultural, and systemic engagement as secondary or instrumental. The *kosmos* commission challenges this dichotomy at its root. If the created order, the human family, and the organized systems of society are all within the scope of the mandate, then mission that does not engage those systems is operating on a truncated commission.

For investors and business practitioners operating in Africa, this has direct implications. The deployment of capital into African economies is not merely an economic act that may have spiritual significance as a secondary effect. Under the *kosmos* commission, it is a primary act of obedience — participation in the mission of reclaiming the *kosmos* for its Creator.

**Notes on Sources**

Strong's Concordance entries referenced: G1484 (*ethnos*), G2078 (*eschatos*), G2889 (*kosmos*). Strong, James. *The Exhaustive Concordance of the Bible*. 1890.

For the Septuagintal background of *ethnos* as a rendering of *goyim*, see Liddell, H.G. and Scott, R. *A Greek-English Lexicon*. Oxford: Clarendon Press, 9th ed., 1996, s.v. ἔθνος.

The intertextual echo of Isaiah 49:6 in Acts 1:8 is widely noted in Lukan scholarship. See in particular: Bock, Darrell L. *Acts*. Baker Exegetical Commentary on the New Testament. Grand Rapids: Baker Academic, 2007, pp. 62–65.

The fourfold semantic range of *kosmos* follows Kittel, Gerhard, ed. *Theological Dictionary of the New Testament*, vol. III, s.v. κόσμος (Hermann Sasse). Grand Rapids: Eerdmans, 1965, pp. 867–895. Sasse distinguishes the Hellenistic-philosophical, Jewish, and distinctively Johannine uses of the term.

The identification of *kosmos* with the systemic "ruler of this world" in Johannine theology is examined in: Carson, D.A. *The Gospel According to John*. Pillar New Testament Commentary. Grand Rapids: Eerdmans, 1991, pp. 488–491.

The New Testament occurrence counts cited (*ethnos* 164x, *eschatos* 52x, *kosmos* ~186x) are derived from standard concordance data and may vary by one or two instances depending on textual tradition consulted.

# Executive Summary: Global Giants Initiative

The Global Giants Trust
& Global Giants Limited

## Vision

Global Giants exists to comprehensively capitalize inspired innovations to tackle the world's most pressing societal ills—called "Giants"—which stand in opposition to God's ways and human flourishing.

## Problem Addressed

Despite inspired, faith-driven innovations and rising impact investing, efforts are often fragmented, niche-focused, or motivated by financial returns. Large-scale societal transformation demands a united, purpose-driven framework that channels diverse capital toward tackling Giants such as:

- Poverty, poor infrastructure, healthcare inequity
- Exploitation in industries (e.g., bonded labor, environmental plundering)
- Suppression of novel solutions
- Societal "-isms" and mass urbanization

## The Solution: A Two-Part Structure

1. Global Giants Trust (Isle of Man-based charity)

    - Receives donations and grants ($2M initial target)
    - Focuses on governance, purpose alignment, education, and accountability
    - Acts as an evergreen foundation to steward capital in all forms (intellectual, spiritual, monetary, etc.)

2. Global Giants Limited (Isle of Man-based company)

    - Receives investment capital (initial target $100M)
    - Deploys transformation, search, and growth capital to fund businesses tackling Giants

- Invests in initiatives vetted through the rēp process to ensure biblical alignment and measurable impact

## Strategic Process

- Evaluate the Context in light of the Great Commission, societal transformation: Identify possibilities, future glory, assets, needs and contextual giants through fieldwork (Transforming Society Ventures)
- Identify Opportunities: Source investable projects from rēp community and global partners
- Capitalize Comprehensively: Leverage ecological, financial, human, intellectual, social and spiritual capital
- Collaborate for Impact: Encourage ecosystem-building and transformation around value chains and domains such agriculture, energy, housing, food security, clean mining, and sustainable city development

## Purpose

Promote human flourishing through enterprises built to grow and to last, infused with biblical principles and aligned with—but deeper than—UN SDGs.

## Current Status

- Global Giants Trust has been formed and registered as a UK charity in the Isle of Man (Charity Number 1377)
- Investment arm, Global Giants Limited, is active and open to qualified investors
- Leadership team and solution collaboratives are growing.

## Call to Action

- Donors & Foundations: Seed the Trust for long-term governance, stewardship and framework & metrics enhancement
- Investors: Join in funding transformation-capable businesses that are tackling Giants

- Innovators: Propose ventures that align with biblical impact and in the context of societal transformation.

## Conclusion

"Who fills the void if we fail at this strategic opportunity in history?" It is widely held that Africa is the next opportunity-continent. Right now investors and governments representing Islam, the Middle East, China and the Catholic church are well underway with funds and initiatives. Mainstream Christianity is fragmented and relatively small in its thinking and initiatives. There are expressions of interest, some level of investment, but generally these are in point solutions. By focusing on the transformation of towns, cities and nations Global Giants aims to bridge donors, investors and societal transformers so that the Kingdom of God can advance in meaningful, sustainable and measurable ways.

The website

For donors

# AFRICA: Master Zone Classification Table

Framework: Diversity × Trust → Operating Environment

The Master Zone Classification Table is intended to be dynamic and receptive to the inputs of readers and investors. By making this available to a cohort that is interested in investing with Africa, members of the cohort can make adjustments as they see fit. The zones represented in this book are not intended to be static but a thinking tool for those who can apply their own insights and analysis. The workings are available on the website and will change periodically. http://investingwithafrica.com

With that caveat in mind, examples of early reflections on the zones are covered below. You will also notice that the confidence levels in the table are not reflected in the shading of the maps. You will also see some countries, such as South Africa, appearing in both the opportunity zone and in the edge case.

## Zone Scoring Methodology

The purpose of including extracts from the underlying spreadsheet is to show you that the analysis exists, not to test your eyesight! The table below unpacks the trust and diversity scores and gives some examples.

| SCORING METHODOLOGY · Trust & Diversity Framework | | | |
|---|---|---|---|
| **TRUST SCORE (1–5)** | | | |
| **Score** | **Label** | **Indicators** | **Examples** |
| 1 | Very Low | Collapsed institutions; contracts unenforceable; pervasive corruption; active conflict or coup | DRC, Libya, Sudan, CAR, South Sudan |
| 2 | Low | Institutions weak but present; high corruption; politicized judiciary; currency instability | Nigeria, Zimbabwe, Mozambique, Angola |
| 3 | Moderate | Improving trajectory; inconsistent rule of law; functioning but unreliable bureaucracy | Egypt, Algeria, Ghana pre-2020 |
| 4 | High | Consistent rule of law; contracts enforceable; corruption relatively contained; predictable | Kenya, Senegal, Morocco, South Africa |
| 5 | Very High | Africa benchmark governance; minimal corruption; institutional excellence; investor confidence | Rwanda, Botswana, Mauritius |

| DIVERSITY SCORE (1–5) | | | |
|---|---|---|---|
| **Score** | **Label** | **Indicators** | **Examples** |
| 1 | Very Low (Homogeneous) | Single dominant ethnic group (>80%); national language unifier; low inter-ethnic tension | Rwanda post-genocide, Botswana, Lesotho, Eswatini |
| 2 | Low-Moderate | 2-3 major groups; bridging language (English/French/Swahili); manageable tension | Morocco, Zambia, Ghana, Namibia |
| 3 | Moderate | Multiple significant groups; some tension but institutional management; regional variation | South Africa, Kenya, Tanzania |
| 4 | High | Many ethnic groups; active tension; identity politics significant; federalism strained | Uganda, Ethiopia, Mozambique |
| 5 | Very High (Fragmented) | 250+ ethnic groups; no dominant group; institutional capture by one ethnicity; systemic risk | Nigeria, DRC, Chad, CAR, South Sudan |

Next, we can see a Logic for classifying the different zones in different ways. In other words, you can see the range of scores that put a particular country into a zone. The sources noted go into the thinking around the current classifications as of the date of publishing of the different countries.

| ZONE CLASSIFICATION LOGIC | | | |
|---|---|---|---|
| **Zone** | **Trust** | **Diversity** | **Rationale** |
| Friction | 1-2 | 4-5 | High fragmentation + low trust = systemic friction. Relational entry only. |
| Transition | 2-3 | 3-4 | Building systems not yet trusted. Watch inflection; can shift either direction. |
| Opportunity | 3-5 | 1-3 | Functional trust + manageable diversity = predictable entry. Best for scalable investment. |
| Resilience | 3-5 | 3-5 | High diversity but strong unifying layer (language, identity, faith). Platform-building. |

**SOURCES & NOTES**

This classification draws on:

· Transparency International Corruption Perceptions Index 2024-2025
· World Bank Governance Indicators (WGI) 2024
· Ethnologue / Alesina et al. Ethnic Fractionalization Index
· Fragile States Index (Fund for Peace) 2024
· EIU Democracy Index 2024
· Brett Johnson, Investing with Africa (2026) Zone Framework
· Author's contextual knowledge from 20+ years of Africa engagement

**DISCLAIMER**

This classification is analytical and educational. Country positions are fluid and sub-national variation is significant.
Do not use as the sole basis for investment decisions. Seek qualified local partners and current due diligence.

## Investment Zone Summary

I have kept the Edge cases listed as a category, even though they aren't marked on the map, because they represent areas where there are specific opportunities and where thoughtfulness is needed.

| INVESTMENT ZONE SUMMARY · 54 African Countries | | | | |
|---|---|---|---|---|
| Zone | Definition | Trust Level | Diversity Level | Countries |
| Friction | Trust has collapsed at system level but survives relationally. Informal relationship-driven economies; people function but systems do not. Risk is structural, not occasional. | Low (1-2) | High (4-5) | Burkina Faso, Burundi, Cameroon, Central African Rep., Chad, DRC, Equatorial Guinea, Eritrea, Guinea, Guinea-Bissau, Libya, Mali, Niger, Nigeria, Somalia, South Sudan, Sudan |
| Transition | Systems are being built but not yet trusted. Institutions uneven; identity still contested. Often one election or reform away from major shift in either direction. | Moderate (2-3) | Moderate-High (3-4) | Algeria, Angola, Benin, Comoros, Côte d'Ivoire, Djibouti, Eswatini, Ethiopia, Gabon, Gambia, Lesotho, Liberia, Madagascar, Malawi, Mauritania, Mozambique, Republic of Congo, Sierra Leone, Togo, Tunisia, Uganda, Zimbabwe |
| Opportunity | Defined by predictability, not perfection. Rule of law consistent; contracts enforceable; corruption relatively low. Best entry points for scalable investment. | High (3-5) | Moderate (2-3) | Botswana, Cabo Verde, Cape Verde, Egypt, Ghana, Kenya, Morocco, Namibia, Rwanda, Senegal, South Africa |
| Resilience | Defined by endurance, not excellence. Institutions hold together; diversity present but not destabilizing; governments imperfect but predictable. Platform-building environments. | High (3-5) | High (3-5) | Mauritius, Seychelles, São Tomé & Príncipe, Tanzania, Zambia |
| Edge Case | Countries that do not fit neatly into one quadrant due to island isolation, micro-economy size, post-conflict anomaly, or rapidly shifting conditions. | Varies | Varies | |

## Examples from Matrix

I have put together a detailed spreadsheet covering all countries in Africa, and I've included a few extracts below so you can see their rationale and some of the investment implications.

| AFRICA INVESTMENT ZONE CLASSIFICATION · Trust & Diversity Framework | | | | | | | | |
|---|---|---|---|---|---|---|---|---|
| Country | Region | Investment Zone | Trust Score (1-5) | Diversity Score (1-5) | Trust Profile | Diversity Profile | Investment Implication | Suggested Approach |
| Algeria | North Africa | Transition | 3 | 2 | Moderate state trust; institutional opacity; improving business climate | Relatively homogeneous (Arab-Berber); Berber (Amazigh) tension simmering | Region-specific entry; monitor political reform trajectory | Monitor inflection points; Region-specific entry; Patient capital |
| Egypt | North Africa | Opportunity | 3 | 2 | Functional institutions; rule-of-law improving; currency pressure remains | Predominantly Arab; Coptic Christian minority significant but stable | Entry-point for North Africa; strong fintech and agri-tech ecosystem | Primary entry market; Scalable ventures; Institution-ready |
| Libya | North Africa | Friction | 1 | 3 | Collapsed state trust; two rival governments; contract enforceability near zero | Arab tribal factionalism; significant regional militias | Avoid at system level; relational-only engagement; humanitarian lens | Relational entry only; Faith network first; Avoid systemic exposure |
| Morocco | North Africa | Opportunity | 4 | 2 | Among Africa's most stable; consistent rule of law; strong FDI track record | Arab-Berber; relatively integrated; low ethnic tension | Premium entry market; hub for West Africa access; real estate, logistics, fintech | Primary entry market; Scalable ventures; Institution-ready |
| Tunisia | North Africa | Transition | 3 | 2 | Post-Arab Spring reversal to authoritarianism; institutions weakening | Predominantly Arab; low diversity fragmentation | Watch for democratic inflection; educated workforce; cautious entry | Monitor inflection points; Region-specific entry; Patient capital |
| Sudan | North Africa | Friction | 1 | 4 | Near-total institutional collapse since 2023 civil war; humanitarian crisis | High ethnic-tribal fragmentation; Arab/African fault lines | No-go for conventional investment; faith-based humanitarian only | Relational entry only; Faith network first; Avoid systemic exposure |
| Burundi | Central Africa | Friction | 1 | 3 | Post-2015 crisis; repressive government; Hutu-Tutsi legacy still live | Hutu-Tutsi-Twa; post-genocide tension | Avoid; political persecution ongoing; faith community under pressure | Relational entry only; Faith network first; Avoid systemic exposure |
| Ethiopia | East Africa | Transition | 2 | 5 | Post-Tigray war; Abiy government rebuilding; institutions under stress | 80+ ethnic groups; Oromo, Amhara, Tigray; ongoing tension | High upside; massive market (120M+); volatile; region-specific only | Monitor inflection points; Region-specific entry; Patient capital |
| Kenya | East Africa | Opportunity | 4 | 3 | East Africa's commercial hub; M-Pesa ecosystem; strong private sector | Kikuyu, Luhya, Luo, Kalenjin; managed; English-Swahili bridge | Leading entry point; fintech, agri-tech, logistics; innovation hub | Primary entry market; Scalable ventures; Institution-ready |
| Tanzania | East Africa | Resilience | 4 | 4 | Gold standard of East African stability; Swahili national identity strong | 130+ ethnic groups; unified by Swahili and national identity | Platform investments; replicable models; lower friction than peers | Platform investment; Replicable models; Lower friction |
| Uganda | East Africa | Transition | 2 | 3 | Museveni long-rule; institutions politicized; improving investment climate | Baganda, Banyankole, Basoga; strong identities; uneven cohesion | Regional-specific; Kampala commercial activity; governance risk | Monitor inflection points; Region-specific entry; Patient capital |
| Rwanda | East Africa | Opportunity | 5 | 1 | Africa's governance benchmark; Kagame-led institutional excellence; Kigali hub | Hutu-Tutsi-Twa; post-genocide; unity enforced; national ID abolished | Premium entry; fintech, health, tech hub; governance confidence highest | Primary entry market; Scalable ventures; Institution-ready |

## Countries That Require Special Attention (Edge Cases)

These do not fit neatly, and as such, they are nations where applied insight becomes essential. The Friction zone being the largest category at 17 countries is sobering but accurate — and reinforces the need for faith-based trust networks compellingly. Rwanda at Trust Score 5, Diversity Score 1 is the strongest Opportunity Zone outlier, which matches what we discussed in the book.

| Country | | | Tension |
|---|---|---|---|
| Kenya | | | Strong economy, periodic ethnic tension |
| Ethiopia | | | Huge upside, high fracture risk |
| Rwanda | | | Centralized (trust is vertical, not broad) |
| South Africa | | | Mature systems + Friction-zone inequality underneath |
| Nigeria | | | Nationally high friction, but Opportunity in micro-clusters (Lagos, etc.) |

MOROCCO
TUNISIA
ALGERIA
LIBYA
EGYPT
MAURITANIA
REPUBLIC OF CABO VERDE
MALI
NIGER
CHAD
SUDAN
ERITREA
DJIBOUTI
SENEGAL
THE GAMBIA
GUINEA-BISSAU
GUINEA
BURKINA FASO
BENIN
NIGERIA
ETHIOPIA
SOMALILAND
CÔTE D'IVOIRE
GHANA
LIBERIA
CENTRAL AFRICAN REPUBLIC
SOUTH SUDAN
CAMEROON
SOMALIA
EQUATORIAL GUINEA
SÃO TOMÉ AND PRINCIPE
UGANDA
KENYA
GABON
REPUBLIC OF THE CONGO
RWANDA
DEMOCRATIC REPUBLIC OF THE CONGO
BURUNDI
TANZANIA
COMOROS
ANGOLA
ZAMBIA
MOZAMBIQUE
MADAGASCAR
ZIMBABWE
NAMIBIA
BOTSWANA
SOUTH AFRICA
KINGDOM OF ESWATINI

# Appendix: More detailed Zone Analysis

For those interested in a less prosaic and more analytical view of the friction zones, this appendix gives you a more bullet point version of the analysis.

## • FRICTION ZONES

High Diversity + Low Trust Architecture→Systemic Friction
(*Operate relationally, not systemically*)

Friction Zones are where trust has collapsed at the system level—but often survives at the relational level.

Characteristics:

- Low institutional trust, pervasive corruption and unreliable contract environment.
- Fragmented identity structures: Strong ethnic regional or tribal division.
- Infrastructure constrains basic economic activity: Roads, power, banking.

Why these matter:

- Informal relationship-driven economies.
- People function, but systems do not
- Risk is not occasional; it is structural.

## • TRANSITION ZONES

**Moderate–High Diversity + Uneven Trust Architecture**
(*Watch for inflection points—can move either direction*)

Transition Zones are where systems are being built—but not yet trusted.

Characteristics:

- Identity still contested – inconsistent Trust
- Institutions uneven but present – can be politicized
- Unity is situational, not structural

Why these matter:

- Often one election or reform away from major shift.
- Rules can change quickly, and leadership shifts matter significantly
- High upside backbones to shocks: political, security, currency.

- **OPPORTUNITY ZONES**

**Moderate Diversity + Functional Trust Layers**
(*Best entry points for scalable investment*)

Opportunity Zones are not defined by perfection, but by predictability—the ability to act, invest, and scale without constant friction.

Characteristics:

- Rule of law is consistent, Contracts are enforceable, Corruption is relatively low
- Bureaucracy is efficient and predictable
- Social cohesion supports economic activity
- Fewer currency restrictions and functional banking systems.

Why these matter:

- Stronger institutions
- Business-friendly environments
- Language bridges (English/French/Swahili)
- Might bridge Africa to the world.

- **RESILIENCE ZONES**

High or Moderate Diversity + Strong Unifying Layer
(*Platform-building environments*)

Resilience Zones are not defined by excellence, but by endurance—the quiet ability of a system to hold together long enough for trust to compound.

Characteristics:

- Institutions generally work; Contracts are usually honored

- Diversity is present, but it is not destabilizing
- Governments are imperfect but predictable
- Infrastructure is good enough; this enables real economic activity, not just survival.

Why these matter:

- Less volatility than Transition and Friction zones
- Stability is cultural, not just enforced
- Markets are compounding, not boom-bust

## ● SPECIAL / EDGE CASES

(Require nuanced, sub-national strategies)

- **Ethiopia** → Ethiopia is one of the most fascinating and difficult-to-classify economies in Africa. It genuinely straddles the transition and friction zones, depending on which lens you apply. It is a paradox economy in that it's one of the fastest-growing economies and the second most populous country in Africa, but with deep internal fragmentation and periodic conflict. So the high potential plus high fracture gives rise to an edge case.
- **Kenya** → This is marked as an edge case or hybrid because, while it has a strong economy, there are periodic ethnic tensions. It is known for having a well-educated entrepreneurial sector.
- **Rwanda** → Rwanda is one of the most deceptive economies in Africa—not because it's unclear, but because it looks like a clean Opportunity Zone… while carrying deeper structural tensions underneath. It is a high-functioning system built on a fragile historical foundation. Since the 1994 genocide, Rwanda has pursued centralized governance, vigorous anti-corruption measures, a clearly defined national vision (Vision 2050) and a technology-forward positioning. For investors, this can feel like Mauritius-lite, or as they position themselves, Singapore-in-Africa. They are aiming to be a regional hot player.

- **South Africa** → Advanced economy but with deep internal divides. Theoretically, this makes South Africa a more difficult place to invest, but in reality, it is often the gateway to investing in Africa. When dealing with larger scale investments, however, one must factor in the black economic empowerment requirements of the government. A recent case in point has been Elon Musk's attempt to get Starlink into South Africa and Namibia. (The Namibian government turned down his request since there isn't the requisite percentage of local ownership. This might seem empowering and equitable and inclusive of locals, but it could also be robbing the people of a transformative technology with the hopes of lining the pockets of government officials.)
- **Nigeria** → With its massive market and a slice of the workforce being highly educated and entrepreneurial, it is a special opportunity zone. A high percentage of Africa's entrepreneurs are located in Nigeria. While many businesses operate in the informal sector, those that operate in the formal sector have real potential.

## Ethiopia: Unpacking one example of an Edge Case

Ethiopia demonstrates that growth does not eliminate fracture—it can actually amplify it if trust does not keep pace. I've included a case study for Ethiopia and why it can sit in two different zones. This is on the website. You can view a summary, then download a PDF from there.

## The Hope Estate: Tackling the Global Giant of Urban Slums

The thesis of this book is illustrated in a project anchored in real estate but that touches many spheres of a society. It is wonderful to speak about Africa's demographic dividend, but for millions of people, this comes at a price. They moved to cities and cannot afford to purchase a home, particularly in markets where there is an inadequate mortgage market. Countless millions of young adults are on their way to a slum outside a city.

**The Hope Estate and Global Giants**

As part of the Global Giants initiative to identify and capitalize opportunities that tackle the world's greatest challenges, urbanization and the rise of the Slum Economy have been identified as a priority Global Giant.

The Hope Estate represents a live, investable platform designed to directly address this challenge through scalable, master-planned urban development. This is not a theoretical model. It is a real project, in motion, positioned to demonstrate how this Global Giant can be tackled at scale.

### On the website

The full Hope Estate story is on the website at https://investingwithafrica.com/#case-studies You can see more details and download a PDF there.

### Conclusion

The Slum Economy is one of the most significant Global Giants of our time. The Hope Estate represents a **practical, investable response**:

- Turning crisis into structured opportunity
- Converting informal growth into planned development
- Aligning capital with transformation

- Creating a working case study that can be emulated in other nations.

We recently asked the mayor of Bulawayo, Mr. David Coltart, what his dream was for the city.

> *I want to restore the former glory of the city.*

This is not just a development. It is a platform to tackle a Global Giant and build the cities of the future that restore glory. Remember the well-known promise that was given to those who "seek the peace of the city where I have caused you to be ... and pray to the Lord for it."

> *For I know the plans I have for you, says the Lord, plans for welfare and not for evil, to give you a future and a hope. Jeremiah 29:7+11*

# McKinsey Global Institute opportunity areas

Ten practical ways that African businesses and governments can improve productivity and restore economic vitality:

- **Pivot from growth for growth's sake to a focus on productivity:** Leaders should set targets and track productivity by sector to implement concrete plans for broad-based, productivity-led growth.
- **Fully embrace digital technologies and systems:** Rapidly deploying digital innovations at scale across all sectors, particularly services, can close the competitiveness gap, improve citizen experience, and help identify growth opportunities through data analytics.
- **Develop African talent to serve the continent and the world:** Creating relevant educational curricula and training programs will enhance the workforce and produce next-generation leaders who can meet both local needs and global talent shortages.
- **Reimagine manufacturing for domestic consumption and export:** Focusing on promising growth areas like agro-processing and vaccine manufacturing can improve self-sufficiency, while boosting global manufacturing exports will enhance industrial resilience.
- **Increase regional connectedness:** Strengthening intra-African trade through the African Continental Free Trade Area (AfCFTA), lowering transportation costs, and coordinating regulations can drive accelerated growth and build regional resilience.
- **Invest to enhance resource productivity and tap new opportunities:** Improving productivity in extractive industries through automation and digital technologies, while positioning the continent as a key supplier of metals and minerals needed for the global energy transition, can spread prosperity more broadly.

- **Benefit from the global net-zero agenda:** Capturing opportunities in green hydrogen, carbon credits, and green manufacturing can deliver benefits such as expanded energy access and improved urban mobility.
- **Spur the agricultural transition by improving farming productivity:** Improving sector productivity is vital for food security and can be achieved through rationalizing crop production, developing better trading systems, and utilizing smart financial solutions.
- **Increase and improve urban infrastructure in primary and second cities:** Closing gaps in transportation, power, water, and sanitation through coherent planning and digital technologies will increase the productivity of urban populations and businesses.
- **Grow and cultivate African business champions:** Supporting the growth of large corporations, which fuel supply chains and attract talent, can drive productivity across the entire corporate ecosystem of small and medium-sized enterprises.

**Strategies for African Economic Growth**

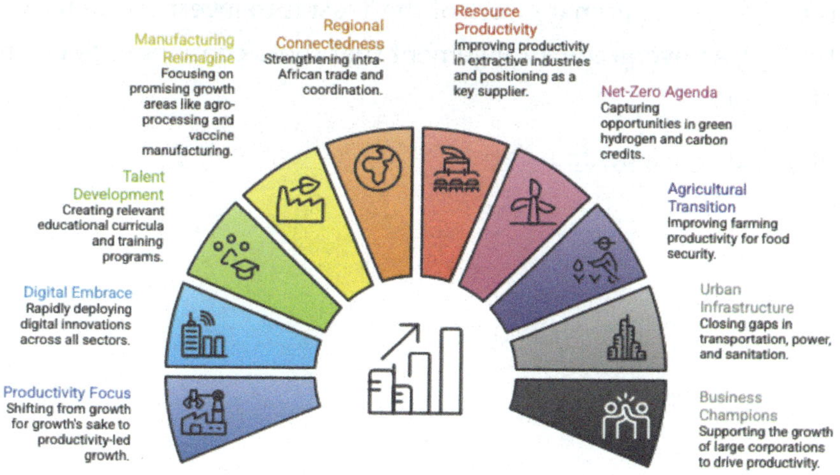

## About the Author

Brett Johnson is the co-founder of The Institute for Innovation, Integration & Impact, Inc. Passionate about the abolition of dichotomy-—eradicating the false barriers between facets of life, Brett is particularly interested in removing the barrier between the so-called secular and sacred. A Chartered Accountant, writer, father and social entrepreneur, Brett is dedicated to societal transformation through business, capital and leadership transformation. A South African native, Brett has lived in the USA with his family since 1986. He has authored numerous books and papers including Repurposing Capital, 50 Principles of Faith-based Finance and Kingdom Economics. http://brettjohnson.biz

Brett Johnson is also behind The Global Giants Trust based in the Isle of Man. The Trust and Global Giants Limited seek to comprehensively capitalize inspired innovations that address global issues. Practically speaking, it is a vehicle for receiving and deploying capital either as a charitable contribution (in Global Giants Trust) or an investment (via Global Giants Limited). The primary beneficiary of Global Giants Limited is the Trust; the primary work of the Trust is to invest via Global Giants Limited, an evergreen arrangement that seeks continuous deployment of capital.

http://globalgiants.foundation

## Other books

I have never explained in a list of books exactly why I wrote the book. Given the subject of this book and the discussion of giants, I thought it would be helpful to point out the giant I was tackling with each of the books I wrote.

| Title | Why I wrote the book |
|---|---|
| Convergence—Integrating your Career, Community, Creativity & Calling | The secular-sacred dichotomy is the giant that robs the Church of resources and relegates 95% to being second-class citizens. In the world of Work-Faith Integration, this is the big gorilla from which many others are spawned. |
| Convergence Study Guide | Video testimonies from real people and practical worksheets help frame life as one integrationed whole, overcoming dichotomy. |
| I-Operations—How the Internet can transform your Operating Model | In my view, the world adapts its operating model or wins 50 to 100 times quicker than the church. Failure to deploy God-given technologies to operating models is a giant. This is as true with Web 3 as it was with Web 2 and Web 1. |
| LEMON Leadership—Radically fresh leadership | Hierarchical leadership is a giant, and Western organizations are smitten by it. The Biblical model is plural leadership, and this is reflected in the five types of the Leman Leadership Model. |
| Repurposing Capital—Rediscovering Faith-based Financing | Christians abdicated the world of capital for centuries. We lost sight of the natural laws of capital, the |

| Title | Why I wrote the book |
|---|---|
| | foundation principles of faith-based financing. The vacuum has been filled by other philosophies. |
| 50 Principles of faith-based financing | Continuing from Repurposing Capital, if the head of a central bank or the president of a country asked, “How can I base my nation on biblical principles?” we must be able to answer in ways that go beyond personal finances. |
| Transforming Society—A framework for fixing a broken world | Christians have talked about discipling nations for decades, but most of the language has been verbal fog. I wrote "Transforming the Society" so we could get beyond religiosity and get to practicalities. |
| CYCLES—A journey to Purpose (a novel) | Often, people outside the Christian faith have a clearer philosophy of business than followers of Jesus. This short model illustrates the differences and what it means to evaluate a business through the lens of heavenly due diligence. |
| X-Ordinary—The amazing stories of ordinary people in business with God | 64% of the first 100 companies we worked with in Cape Town experienced a significant miracle during or shortly after our consultation. The marketplace is God's primary space for doing the miraculous. Our problem is we have low expectations or short memories. This book captures many stories of God doing extraordinary things through everyday people in business. I |

| Title | Why I wrote the book |
|---|---|
| | wrote it so that we will expect and remember. |
| The Initiative Index—What women wish men knew about the signals men send | In the early 2000s, we noticed an epidemic of singleness among Christian young people. For many reasons, men were failing to take initiative. This book gives me practical pointers.<br><br>What is the giant? If the next generation of believers do not get made, they will not have children. What is the impact on the future of the Church? |
| The Availability Index—What men wish women knew about the signals women send | Still on the topic of singleness as a potential giant in the Church —where is the next generation if the current generation does not know you have children — This short book encourages approachability. As a side note, I have a Google sheet recording 180 singles in our community who have married. Still, this is a topic that vexes me, and we have a long way to go. |
| LEMON for Lovers | As we worked with leadership teams and companies, we noticed that the principles of LEMON Leadership had a positive impact on marriage. There are many assaults on marriage, and LEMON Leadership helps people understand each other. |
| This land is your land, this land is my land—the | Land expropriation without compensation is not just a problem in South Africa, but that is where it has |

| Title | Why I wrote the book |
|---|---|
| looming prospect of the next land grab in South Africa | been signed into law. This is a giant that undermines capitalism and a free society. Economies do not flourish without property rights. There is a rising giant of Marxism and socialism, and land expropriation is one outworking of this flawed philosophy. To be clear, I am not a land expert, but when I saw Christians respond to the South African government's call for comment, they quoted one scripture. At the back of this book, I have included an appendix with 1,500 scriptures dealing with land, property rights, ownership, restoration, and more. |
| rēStart: How to reset your foundations for a fresh future | During the coronavirus pandemic, many were worried about the future. Worse than long COVID is the lingering hopelessness that plagues many people. But God is no stranger to restarts, and in this book I include 50 principles that help set the frame for a fresh future. |
| 10 Steps to Restoration | This book is not written for people who live behind a white picket fence. It is for those who have believed God for great things, hoped for meaningful progress, and faced the difficulties of delay. Drawing from the book of Isaiah, I share a sequence of steps in restoration so that we keep believing God for a better future and collaborate with him as he takes us there. |

| Title | Why I wrote the book |
|---|---|
| Work like God in 31 Ways | Since discipleship is teaching people to work the way that God designed them to work (our first commission), I must understand how God works. Yet work itself is under attack, and a lack of understanding of the biblical value of work is a giant. |
| LEMONpreneur—A Fresh Generation on the Entrepreneurial Journey | Billions of young people are hoping to enter a job market that is not there. They have to become entrepreneurial, yet only 15% are wired as entrepreneurs. This book addresses the single biggest reason for entrepreneurial failure: the leadership team. LEMONpreneur proposes how this giant can be overcome. |
| Kingdom Economics | Kingdom economics is a term thrown around loosely by Christians, but few understand the difference between the economies of Babylon or Egypt, the Desert, and the Promised Land. If we don't understand God's economy, we will live in someone else's economy while still using faith-oriented language to talk about money, finance, capital, investing, etc.<br><br>Mammon—greed deified—is still a giant and not absent from our lives as Christ-followers. |
| Repurposing People—Finding work on purpose in a post-pandemic era | How do you know that the person you are hiring is a Kingdom person? How do you know that the company you are planning to join is a Kingdom company? Never before have people |

| Title | Why I wrote the book |
| --- | --- |
| | entering the workplace had such high aspirations yet low preparation for true biblical work.<br><br>Being a Christian employer/employee is challenging. This book provides practical tools for both, with a focus on personal and corporate purpose.<br><br>Remember, underemployment is a giant; under-deployment of talented people is the giants cousin. |
| The Power of Households: Impacting your real sphere of influence | The Household is the primary organizing principle for God's family, our families, and other organizations. In Scripture, God made covenants with whole families, and entire households got saved at once. I have found that when CEOs recognize who is in their household and take heart level responsibility for them, it changes their game entirely. Without this, the giant of mass orphanization still stands. |
| Bizcipleship—Recovering the Lost Purpose of Business | We have relegated discipleship to church programs and marketplace ministries. Nothing could be further from the truth. When we integrate disciple making into core business processes, then every day at work is a day of making disciples. Business rediscovers its purpose with practical tools that are deployed not as a separate program but as an integral part of the business. |

| Title | Why I wrote the book |
| --- | --- |
| Inspired Innovation—From Toil to Transformation | God is still in the business of creating. He gives new products and ideas that solve problems he cares about, to us, his junior partners. The giant is this: the majority of inspired innovations never come to market.<br><br>At a personal level, many Christ-followers are wrestling at work, toiling at tasks assuming this is a consequence of the Fall rather than collaborating with God and working from a place of rest. |
| Investing with Africa: Flyover | This is an invitation to investors to participate with God by investing with Africa, not just for the sake of Africa, but for the advancement of the Kingdom. |
| Investing with Africa: Context, Considerations, Call to Action (published July 4, 2026) | For too long, the purposes of God have been starved of the resources that same God has entrusted to his people. This is a call to apostolic, household to household, nation to nation, investing so that Giants can be humbled and God exalted. |

Link to Amazon author page

Contact info, Blogs, Podcasts

https://investingwithafrica.com

## Tell us your stories

Each of us has stories of investing, innovation and deploying business to advance human flourishing and the discipling of nations. No doubt your own stories have come to mind as you read this book. Why not share your stories with others?

https://www.brettjohnson.biz/tell-us-your-story

## Africa Investing Survey

If you have not yet completed the survey, I invite you to do so now. It helps build a clearer picture of who is actually doing this work — where they are, what they are investing in, and what is needed to go further.

Made in United States
Orlando, FL
04 November 2026

90201162R00148